# Caamaño in London

## The Exile of a Latin American Revolutionary

Edited by

Fred Halliday

INSTITUTE FOR THE STUDY OF THE

# AMERICAS

UNIVERSITY OF LONDON · SCHOOL OF ADVANCED STUDY

**British Library Cataloguing-in-Publication Data**
A catalogue record for this book is available from the British Library

ISBN 978 1 900039 96 3

INSTITUTE FOR THE STUDY OF THE
**A M E R I C A S**
UNIVERSITY OF LONDON · SCHOOL OF ADVANCED STUDY

Institute for the Study of the Americas
School of Advanced Study
University of London
Senate House
London WC1E 7HU

Telephone: 020 7862 8870
Fax: 020 7862 8886

Email: americas@sas.ac.uk
Web: www.americas.sas.ac.uk

# CONTENTS

# ACKNOWLEDGEMENTS

In November of 2009 Fred Halliday submitted the manuscript of this book to ISA, and once the book was approved, he worked with the editorial team on his last revisions. In January 2010 he fell gravely ill and spent four months in hospital before he died in April 2010. The publication of this book meant a great deal to him and it was the last of his books that he saw through to the final stages prior to publication. We thank Jon Halliday for tracking down missing sources and references, and Hamlet Hermann for permitting the inclusion of the translation of a chapter of his book *Francis Caamaño, Coronel de Abril, Comandante de Caracoles* (2000). We are also grateful to Román Caamaño for supplying us with, and granting us permission to use the image on the front cover.

Every effort has been made to obtain permission to use other copyright material quoted in this book. Should there be any omissions in this respect, we apologise and will be pleased to make the appropriate acknowledgements in any future edition of the book.

Series Editor
Maxine Molyneux
Director, Institute for the Study of the Americas

# FOREWORD
# CAAMAÑO AND HIS CIRCUMSTANCES:
## A PERSONAL AND POLITICAL PORTRAIT IN PARTS

*James Dunkerley*

'Yo soy yo y mi circunstancia', José Ortega y Gasset

In November 2009, some six months before he died, Fred Halliday wrote
to me from Barcelona asking for my views on a draft of the text that is now
before you. 'My big concern,' he said, 'is whether "it works" ... the material
is very, as they used to say, heteroclite'. In particular, Fred was worried about
the amount of space he had devoted to 'some of the rather weird ... Oxford
left history of the time which Caamaño's visit intersected'. Although I was
working in New York when he sent the email, I sensed that Fred was looking
for a 'British take' not only on the substantively British material in this book
but also on the unusual format in which it is presented.

This volume is in the style of what were — in the days when 'heteroclite'
was a quite regular term for irregularity — sometimes denoted 'detached
recollections'. Perhaps Fred was subliminally retrieving a 19th-century
tradition of memorialisation and critique that was particularly vigorous in his
native Ireland? One thinks of Simón Bolívar's chief of staff General O'Leary,
of that great progressive cosmopolitan Richard Madden, 'the Superintendent
of Liberated Africans' in the Havana of the 1830s and historian of the United
Irishmen, and Francis Meagher, Waterford *quarante-huitard* firebrand, US
Unionist general and Governor of Montana Territory (Humphreys, 1969;
Madden, 1858, Cavanagh, 1892).

Perhaps the subject matter of the text encouraged him to retrieve something
of the Oxford examination tradition of 'gobbets' — unseen primary documents,
the exegesis of which students were required to undertake in order to test
their recognition of esoteric material and hone their capacity for placing it in
familiar context? In either case, the combination of conclusive analytical essay
with punctilious consideration of primary documentation is of a piece with
Fred Halliday's intellectual method from a young age — well before he, an

uncommonly learned radical, was accepted onto the faculty of the LSE. Yet it is also typical that the research presented here was primarily undertaken to provide the people of the Dominican Republic with a historical resource rather than to promote a metropolitan academic career.

For those who followed Fred's pieces on the *openDemocracy* website in recent years, the present tapestry of personal memoir, reprinted speeches, biographical excerpts, and publication of official papers will come as no surprise. Indeed, the principal elements of his editorial approach here are prefigured in an article of April 2009, 'The Dominican Republic: a time of ghosts', where literature, memory, structural conditions and personal endeavour are all employed to girder a strategic portrait of characteristic cogency, spatial range and temporal depth. Typical of Fred Halliday's *modus operandi*, that essay was based upon a personal visit to the Republic, animated by an hour-long television discussion with one of the two survivors of Caamaño's abortive guerrilla action of early 1973, and — despite Fred's very fragile state of health — informed by an intensive series of interviews. Few scholars could match his document-based knowledge, if only by dint of his formidable command of languages, but fewer still deign to venture beyond their metropolitan comforts and the quasi-factual universe of the internet, entering the 'global backlands' in order to conduct first-hand forensic investigation.

Although the heart of this project is deeply personal, at no stage does it entertain the delusion that the actors involved are constantly at the centre of anything other than their own lives. Fred's 2005 obituary of Maxime Rodinson had celebrated his 'unceasing belief in universal values ... and an enduring, unyielding scepticism towards the values and myths of one's own country', but it also attributed much of Rodinson's politico-intellectual contribution precisely to his independence and marginality from the mainstream left.[1] Likewise, the portrait here of Caamaño does not simply restore to the historical record (and translate into English) a largely ignored and unknown story of intrinsic human and political worth; it also throws considerable tangential light on the Cold War headlines from the equivalent of, as A.O. Westad puts it, a global footnote. Even the apparently inconsequential hiatus of Caamaño's semi-exile in London yields much richer information than one might legitimately expect. The documentary sources provide within and between the lines an eloquent depiction of an historical 'conjuncture' that is now two generations old and best heard in its own voice, even if it has also to be understood from the living vantage-point of the 21st century.

The mixture of varied voices — from Halliday's wry but poignant reflections on his university days, through Caamaño's stirring rhetoric and the heroic register of Hamlet Hermann's biographical chapter, to the coolly clipped

1    'Maxime Rodinson: in praise of a "marginal man"', *openDemocracy*, 9 August 2005.

diplomatic memoranda of the Foreign Office and State Department — encourages a variegated strategy of reading. We are candidly told in the preface that this is no effort at a standard biography, but the sum of the parts enables the reader to 'get to know' Colonel Caamaño and his circumstances in just as rewarding a manner as Graham Greene's encounter a decade later with General Omar Torrijos, another progressive soldier who became head of a Caribbean state only to fall victim to Cold War conspiracy (Greene, 1984).

In a strategic survey of the Caribbean written for New Left Review (NLR) in 1983, Fred Halliday noted that the 'integration of the Caribbean into world politics after 1959 seemed to undergo a further halt after 1965', not least because of the pre-emptive US invasion of the Dominican Republic (Halliday, 1983a). Within the wider, global appraisal of *The Making of the Second Cold War*, published in the same year, he links the 1965 invasion to the deployment of US combat troops to Vietnam, the complementary repression of the Indonesian revolutionary movement, and the later overthrow of Allende's *Unidad Popular* constitutional government in Chile (September 1973) (Halliday, 1983b, pp. 6, 84). Whether taken within a narrower regional context or a fully international frame, the Dominican experience is the least well-known of these struggles, and, despite recent renewal of scholarly attention to the country, it remains thinly studied, even by Latin Americans (Moya Pons, 1998; Martínez-Veregne, 2005; Roorda, 1998; Collado, 1992; Hartlyn, 1998; González et al. (eds.), 1999; Klein, 1991; Brennan, 2004; Levy, 2005; Gregory, 2007). Its trajectory, like that of Indonesia, was assuredly overshadowed by that of an earlier and more extensive local conflict (Cuba and Vietnam, respectively). Moreover, the fact that the US had occupied and governed the country between 1916 and 1924, and that the prolonged, 'exotic' dictatorship of Trujillo had already been overthrown (1961) with marked ambivalence on the part of Washington, complicated the picture and arguably diminished the international drama of subsequent developments.[2] Yet as the preface makes abundantly clear, this was a key Cold War event, the 40,000 US troops deployed far exceeding the 7,000 engaged in the invasion of Grenada in October 1983 and the 26,000 used in the invasion of Panama in December 1989.[3]

---

2    For a wonderful, revisionist account of the Trujillo regime, see Derby, 2009. For a detailed denunciatory account of the regime by one of its foremost victims, see Galíndez, 1973.

3    This was a comparison on which Fred Halliday was working late in the development of the present book. He once remarked to me that people sympathetic to his treatment of revolutions tended to dislike his analysis of invasions, even though the same concern with social processes underlay his treatments of these distinct events. This fair point is brought home with pungency in his appraisal of the Falklands/Malvinas War of 1982:

> The temptation to see the Malvinas war as an isolated, exceptional event should ... be resisted. In particular, the covert United States-British collaboration which was central to eventual British victory helped to consolidate a far more momentous (and far less publicised) military project then being implemented, one whose destructive impacts are still reverberating across the region and

Within the Americas the invasion formed part of a distinct pattern of political polarisation. Although the right-wing coups in Brazil and Bolivia had been staged in March and November 1964, those regimes only implemented fully repressive measures after the invasion (Barrientos's attack on the tin mines in May 1965, and Castelo Branco's Institutional Act no. 2, which in November withdrew all constitutional guarantees for up to a decade from named individuals and groups). In Argentina an embattled conservative civilian government banned all trade union activity in October, and a state of siege was imposed in Uruguay. Such was the signal from Santo Domingo that Fidel Castro announced that Che Guevara had decided to renew his international guerrilla campaign, which would take him to Bolivia the following year.

On the other side of the now-figurative barricades, on 20 September the US House of Representatives passed by 312 votes to 52 a laconic resolution that 'acts possessing characteristics of aggression and intervention carried out in one or more member states of the Organisation of American States (OAS) may be responded to in either individual or collective form, which could go as far as resort to armed force'.

In effect, the military intervention that been practised in an almost extemporaneous fashion in the Dominican Republic was now formally endorsed as general policy. The era of 'Dirty Wars' and disappearances was just over the horizon.

The experience of defeat that ensued seemed remorseless. It is, of course, the case that Caamaño returned to his profession of arms in the first weeks of 1973 — before the collapse of the Chilean government headed by Allende — but, even allowing for the contrary advice issued by Castro, that decision should not greatly surprise us, given the local balance of forces and political atmosphere of the time. In Cuba, where Caamaño was living, the failure of the '10 million ton harvest' in 1970 cast the disorganised legacy of Guevara's 'moral economy' in even more sober light; demonstrating students in Mexico City had been shot down by the score in 1968, seriously undermining the ideological compact that had held that country together for decades; an uncertain transition to civilian government in Guatemala (scene of Washington's last major political intromission before the Cuban Revolution) had been brought to a bloody halt; in Nicaragua the Somoza dynasty had hugely enlarged its larceny on the back of the 1972 earthquake; polarisation was deepening in Argentina and Uruguay, with the clear likelihood of reactionary dictatorships in both states; Paraguay

the world: the *jihad* against the then Soviet occupation of Afghanistan ... The real legacy of the 1982 war is, then, one of profound strategic and ideological irresponsibility, whose consequences were to be seen in the local wars and pitiless massacres perpetrated in many poor countries in the 1980s — El Salvador and Nicaragua, East Timor and Angola — by the friends of Margaret Thatcher. 'The Malvinas and Afghanistan: unburied ghosts', *openDemocracy*, 5 March 2007.

remained firmly under the Stroessner-Colorado dictatorship; a short-lived radical regime in Bolivia had been snuffed out by Banzer's coup in 1971; social democratic electoral advances in El Salvador had been halted by paramilitary violence.

Where were the prospects for democratic progress? Arguably in Venezuela, but there the Communist Party that had been an integral element of the anti-dictatorial alliance was firmly excluded from public politics; in Colombia the vestiges of rural violence and the oligarchic stranglehold on power had yet to be loosened. In Peru, it was the military which had taken power in 1968, introduced agrarian reform and nationalised key industries. In Honduras, it was also the military that had forced through agrarian reform. In Chile, the socialist Allende certainly presided over a constitutional government, but it was embattled by the legislature and judiciary, and in his conversations with that arch-*foquista* Régis Debray, the president was more eloquent in defending Chile as an exception than as a model (Debray, 1971). Before 1973 was out, he would be dead, Pinochet's dictatorship installed with such ferocity that it would last another 17 years.

That, of course, was rather shorter than the authoritarian regime over which Balaguer presided in the Dominican Republic until 1996. (Balaguer, who died in 2002 aged 95, served as president three times: 1960–62, 1966–78 and 1978–96). Balaguer did not just extend the Trujillo era deep into and well beyond the Second Cold War; he provided a recalibrated *caudillismo* consistent with the post-invasion balance of forces whereby no open opposition that pursued genuine social change could prosper for long. By the early 1970s that had become a widely recognised *fait accompli*. But Caamaño, whatever the advice and whatever the odds, rejected acquiescence and acted — as the speeches reprinted here express so vividly — according to the deepest and most dangerous of his convictions. As a result, he lost his life within a matter of weeks.

For Latin American radicalism, we might talk of a 'long 1960s', arching from the Cuban Revolution of January 1959 through to the Chilean coup of September 1973, from astounding triumph to desperate defeat.[4] This was the era in which Fred Halliday's political and intellectual skills were tested and developed. Of course, they were subsequently consolidated and applied much more expansively to the Middle East and international relations in general.

---

4    Halliday visited Cuba three times — in 1968, 1981 and 2000 — witnessing quite distinct
     phases of national life. His general attitude may be gleaned from a late appreciation of
     Fidel Castro: 'a man of vision, courage, honesty and charisma, but also of demagogy,
     inconsistency, episodic vindictiveness and cruelty, grotesque verbal self-indulgence,
     intolerance, contempt for intellectuals and homosexuals, and plain administrative ineptness'.
     'Fidel Castro's legacy: Cuban conversations', *openDemocracy*, 19 February 2008.

However, reading Fred's own essay and the texts that follow, one gains a sharp sense of the early Latin American influence on his outlook.[5]

# References

Brennan, D. (2004) *What's Love Got to Do with It? Transnational Desires and Sex Tourism in the Dominican Republic* (Durham N.C.: Duke University Press).

Cavanagh, Michael (1892) *Memoirs of Gen. Thomas Francis Meagher, comprising The Leading Events of His Career* (Worcester, Mass.: The Messenger Press).

Collado, L. (1992) *El tíguere dominicano* (Santo Domingo: Editora Collado).

Debray, Régis (1971) *Conversations with Allende. Socialism in Chile* (London: New Left Books).

Derby, Lauren (2009) *The Dictator's Seduction. Politics and Popular Imagination in the Era of Trujillo* (Durham N.C.: Duke University Press).

Galíndez, Jesús (1973) *The Era of Trujillo. Dominican Dictator* (Tucson: University of Arizona Press).

González, R., R. Cassá, P. San Miguel and M. Baud (eds.) (1999) *Política, identidad y pensamiento social en la República Dominicana (Siglos XIX y XX)* (Madrid: Ediciones Doce Calles).

Greene, Graham (1984) *Getting to Know the General. The Story of an Involvement* (London: The Bodley Head).

Gregory, S. (2007) *The Devil behind the Mirror: Globalization and Politics in the Dominican Republic* (Berkeley: University of California Press).

Halliday, Fred (1983a) 'Cold War in the Caribbean', *New Left Review* 141, Sept.-Oct.

5   On a personal note, I saw quite a bit of Fred in 2005–8 because he was living in an apartment in London's Tavistock Square, where I had an office. He liked to read the morning papers in the beautiful garden centred on the statue of Gandhi and dedicated to the cause of peace. Always jovial, even when palpably suffering, he would regale me in his burnished baritone with the latest news from Bishkek, ask about the balance of forces in Quito, and deconstruct conspiracies in Sanaa. But the most vivid memory I have of him is from 1984, after he was appointed to the LSE. Although he had left the editorial board of NLR, relations with it were such that he was able to attend a party organised by the NLR/Verso publicity officer, Misha Glenny, who blew what must have been an entire annual budget with a very big party at the Groucho Club in Soho. Amidst jollity quite unusual for the comrades, Fred accepted congratulations upon his new post with the challenging observation that he now had '26 years to make a difference'.

Halliday, Fred (1983b) *The Making of the Second Cold War* (London: Verso).

Hartlyn, J. (1998) *The Struggle for Democratic Politics in the Dominican Republic* (Chapel Hill: University of North Carolina Press).

Humphreys, R.A. (ed.) (1969) *The 'Detached Recollections' of General D.F. O'Leary* (London: Institute of Latin American Studies, University of London).

Klein, A. (1991) *Sugarball: The American Game, the Dominican Dream* (New Haven: Yale University Press).

Levy, S. (2005) *The Last Playboy: The High Life of Porfirio Rubirosa* (New York: Harper Collins).

Madden, Richard R. (1858) *The United Irishmen, their Lives and Times. With several additional memoirs, and authentic documents, heretofore unpublished; the whole matter newly arranged and revised* (Dublin: James Duffy).

Martínez-Veregne, T. (2005) *Nation and Citizen in the Dominican Republic, 1880–1916* (Chapel Hill: University of North Carolina Press).

Moya Pons, F. (1998) *The Dominican Republic: A National History* (Princeton: Marcus Wiener).

Roorda, E.P. (1998) *The Dictator Next Door: The Good Neighbor Policy and the Trujillo Regime in the Dominican Republic, 1930–1945* (Durham N.C.: Duke University Press).

# PREFACE

*Fred Halliday*

The events which took place in the Dominican Republic in 1965 constituted one of the most dramatic and important chapters in the modern history of the Caribbean and Latin America, and formed a significant, now too easily overlooked, chapter in the history of the Cold War. On the one side, the uprising on 24 April by a group of 'Constitutionalist' officers, seeking to restore the elected President Juan Bosch, previously overthrown in the coup of September 1963, and the widespread popular support this unleashed in the Dominican Republic, strikingly demonstrated the strength of nationalist and social movements in the region. On the other, the United States of America's intervention on 28 April, officially justified on the grounds of 'protecting American lives' and deploying over 40,000 troops on land and sea, was the largest it had ever made in Latin America, not just during the Cold War, but in the whole of Latin American history. Responding to the success of the Cuban Revolution six years earlier, and as a precursor to the despatch of combat forces to Vietnam that began two months later, the Dominican crisis was highly significant both regionally and internationally.

The subject of this book, Colonel Francisco Caamaño Deñó, was a central figure in these events. A career officer in the armed forces of the Trujillo dictatorship that ended in 1961, Caamaño became involved in the movement formed by 'Constitutionalist' officers after the September 1963 coup. In April 1965, Caamaño, then aged 32, emerged as a leader of the nationalist movement during its confrontations with the Dominican military seeking to crush the uprising, and during its resistance to United States (US) forces after 28 April. He was elected President of the Dominican Republic on 3 May 1965. His image, decked out in a Stetson hat and with a rifle in one hand, addressing crowds of enthusiastic supporters in central Santo Domingo, became familiar around the world. After months of standoff and clashes with the American forces and their Dominican allies, Caamaño agreed to resign as President under a compromise agreement and handed power to a new transitional President, Héctor García-Godoy, on 3 September 1965. In January 1966, against a background of continuing clashes and uncertainty within the country, Caamaño and over 30 officers from both sides of the conflict agreed to go into exile. He flew to London via Puerto Rico and New York with five members of his family on 23 January 1966 to take up the post of military attaché at the Dominican Embassy.

The book that follows is an inevitably incomplete account of the 20-month period that Caamaño spent in London. This chapter of his life, of Dominican politics, and of the history of Latin American exiles in London, is too little known: the chapter from Hamlet Hermann's biography reproduced below is virtually the only account published of this London sojourn. In one sense, he was playing a waiting game, his frustration growing as the situation in the Dominican Republic deteriorated and the opponents of the 24 April uprising, Dominican and American, gained the upper hand. Caamaño's impatience is evident from the Uruguayan journalist Carlos Nuñez's graphic description of him pacing restlessly in his South Kensington rented flat during the interview reproduced below. Published in late March 1966, this is an almost verbatim record of a speech he had given in Oxford some three weeks before. As Hamlet Hermann relates, this impatience was also revealed to friends and former comrades in Santo Domingo through correspondence and extensive phone conversations. This was also, however, a time of reflection and political radicalisation for the exiled former President: as the hopes of a rapid return to the Dominican Republic faded, especially after the victory of the right-wing and US-supported Joaquín Balaguer in the June 1966 elections, Caamaño began to develop links with various parts of the ever-fractious Dominican left and, through them, with Cuba. While maintaining relations with the British government and the US embassy in London, as shown in the documents in Chapter 4, Caamaño began to prepare for a visit to Cuba. In October 1967, shocked by Che Guevara's death in Bolivia, he departed from London secretly, travelling via Holland and proceeding in disguise to Prague, where he took a plane to Havana. There, he got to know Fidel Castro and other Cuban leaders: he never wavered in his determination to return to the Dominican Republic, and, as repression there intensified under Balaguer with an average of 1,000 political killings per year, he formed a small guerrilla group. With the moral support of the Cuban leadership, but against their advice, he returned to the Dominican Republic in February 1973 and was captured and killed.

The chapters and documents collected in this book are not intended to be a full biography of Francisco Caamaño, or to form the basis of an overall evaluation of his career and political development. They constitute one of the — perhaps four — main chapters of that career: as an officer of the Dominican armed forces; as a national and revolutionary leader in 1965; his time in London; and finally, his later period in Cuba and return to the Dominican Republic in early 1973. These materials focus specifically on the period Caamaño spent in London and cannot therefore provide an in-depth evaluation of his entire life and political record. They include, in addition to the translation of the Hamlet Hermann chapter, recently-released documents

on Caamaño's time in London — many hitherto unpublished — from British
Foreign Office, US State Department and Central Intelligence Agency (CIA)
archives. It is particularly significant that some of the most informative US
documents can only be found in the British archives. Archival material from
1965 itself is also included: in addition to material on Caamaño's London
period and subsequent disappearance, Part II contains the text of 1965 press
cuttings found in the archives as they reveal how Western governments viewed
events in Santo Domingo and their understanding of Colonel Caamaño's role,
past and future, during his time in London.

The book also includes a number of statements by Caamaño himself, the
better to understand his thinking and personality, and the calculations he
was making at different stages of his sudden emergence into public life. My
own chapter is an account of a visit Caamaño made on 4 March 1966, upon
my invitation as president of the Labour Club, to speak at the University of
Oxford. So far as can be ascertained, this was the only occasion on which he
spoke in public in Britain, other than at his press conference upon arrival in
January 1966, but was also the last time in his life he made a public speech. We
do not have a record of what he said in the Oxford speech, but on the basis of
what I, Professor Laurence Whitehead and others who attended can recall, its
content, reflecting Caamaño's hopes prior to the scheduled elections in June,
was similar to that covered in his interview with Carlos Nuñez, which took
place around the same time and which is printed below.

There is, inevitably, much that remains to be told about this period of
exile.[1] It was perhaps the most important stay in the British capital by any
Latin American revolutionary since the six-month sojourn of Simón Bolivar
in 1810 and the 16-year extended exile of the Venezuelan nationalist leader,
Francisco de Miranda, in the last decades of the previous century. In one sense,
Caamaño's time in London was an interlude: he engaged little with British
life, official or unofficial, and remained preoccupied with events in his own
country and region. Yet, as Hamlet Hermann's chapter shows and as we have
ascertained from others in the Dominican opposition who knew him at this
time, this was for him a period of much political rethinking, forming a decisive
link between his earlier role as the unexpectedly emergent leader and elected
President of the Constitutionalist movement in Santo Domingo and his later
option for an alliance with Cuba. Caamaño's London exile therefore forms

1    In particular, material from two sources. First, the extensive correspondence Caamaño sent
     from London and the diary he kept during his six years in Cuba remain unpublished and
     contain much relevant material. Secondly, whatever material the British and American
     intelligence services collected from surveillance and interception of communications during
     his time in London also remains unavailable. Caamaño and his colleagues suspected that
     they were objects of covert surveillance, but there is no evidence of what this entailed or
     what information was gathered.

part of the modern history of the Dominican Republic, and of the nationalist and revolutionary movements of the Caribbean and Latin America as a whole.[2] In addition, the London months were not entirely devoted to politics. Distant though he kept himself from Whitehall and, it seems, from the Latin American academic and journalistic communities, Caamaño enjoyed his time in the city, where he lived in Prince's Gate, SW7, and later Richmond. He vindicated his reputation back home as a sharpshooter by winning a shooting competition at the rifle ranges in Bisley, Surrey. Other pastimes included: flying a model airplane in Hyde Park; visiting Marks & Spencers in High Street Kensington; discovering Portobello Road and the maze at Hampton Court; and eating with his family at *Dino's* on Kensington Church Street.[3] Neglecting his responsibilities as military attaché, he never ceased to remind his family that he was not a professional diplomat, but was in London as a 'political exile'. Talking to me in Santo Domingo 43 years later, his wife and his cousin, Rafaela, recalled their annoyance when he refused to accept an invitation from the Queen to a diplomatic garden party at Buckingham Palace. The one major social event they organised in their Kensington flat was a celebration of Dominican National Day on 27 February. The unifying theme to emerge from these pages is Caamaño's political exile and the events to which it led. Incomplete as they inevitably are, I hope they contribute a new chapter to our knowledge of modern Dominican and Latin American history, and to over two centuries of interaction between London and the nationalist and radical movements of Latin America (Decho & Diamond, 1996).[4]

Many people have helped in the preparation of this book, pursuing material on a subject that remained almost completely unknown in both the Dominican Republic and Britain. Over a meal in 2006, the Dominican journalist, Kenny Cabrera, was the first to encourage me — 40 years on — to write about the visit Caamaño paid to Oxford and to publish the first version of my chapter here in the journal of FUNGLODE, President Leonel Fernández Reyna's foundation (Halliday, 2007). Gudie Lawaetz, translator of Caamaño's Oxford speech, gave generously of her time in relating subsequent conversations with the Dominican leader in London. Renata Albuquerque and Olivia Sheringham in London, Alex Woolfson in Washington and Silvia Forno in Barcelona, were indefatigable in pursuit and preparation of the documentary material. Olivia

---

2   According to Caamaño's wife, it was President García-Godoy who chose London for them as he had recently served as a diplomat there. He told Caamaño he was sending him to his favourite city, somewhere he would find the tranquillity he needed after the events of the preceding months.

3   Interview with Caamaño's wife, Maria Claudia Acevedo, and cousin, Rafaela Caamaño, Santo Domingo, 30 Jan. 2009.

4   Significantly, this otherwise informative book, while mentioning many other Latin American political, musical and literary figures, does not mention Caamaño and the low profile he kept in London.

Sheringham, Daniel Abreu and Julie Wark were invaluable as translators. Daniel also acted as adviser on all matters of Dominican history and society. As ever, Andrew Sherwood, my assistant at the London School of Economics (LSE), was indispensable in resolving problems of organising material. Thanks to the LSE Staff Research Fund and to IBEI (the Barcelona Institute of International Studies) for financial support in preparation of this book. Above all, my thanks to Hamlet Hermann, Francisco Caamaño's close comrade and biographer, an invaluable source of information, guidance and contacts in Santo Domingo, and above all an enthusiastic collaborator on the English and Spanish editions of this book.

# INTRODUCTION: THE UNITED STATES, THE DOMINICAN INTERVENTION AND THE COLD WAR

*O.A. Westad*

The US intervention in the Dominican Republic in April 1965 was a watershed in the Cold War, not so much because of what the intervention achieved as for the implications it had for the global view of the US as an interventionist power. Coming at a time when Washington was getting engaged in the Vietnam War through the use of its own ground forces, a year after the US-supported coup in Brazil and right before the US-supported coup in Indonesia (in October 1965), the Dominican intervention became a symbol of US attempts to roll back a period of left-wing change in the Third World, a kind of counter-revolutionary offensive that radicalised youth in Western Europe and North America and made many revolutionary Third World movements progress towards a closer alliance with the Soviet Union. It was the Dominican intervention that caused some Third World radicals to support the 1968 Soviet-led invasion of Czechoslovakia, on the (totally erroneous) assumption that it was necessary in order to protect world socialism against an American onslaught. The invasion of the Dominican Republic was, of course, one in a series of US interventions in the region, which began in the mid 19th century and continue to the present day. But the timing made it significant for a much wider contest on a global scale.[1]

The Dominican Republic had a long and difficult birth as an independent country in the 19th century, which saw a number of bloody wars with neighbouring Haiti. It was the only part of Latin America to be recolonised by Spain in the latter part of the century and it came under US dominance from the 1870s on, when US president Ulysses Grant tried, unsuccessfully, to annex the country to the US. In many ways the contemporary history of the Dominican Republic began with the US military occupation of 1916–24,

---

1   For some of these issues, see Westad, 2005.
    Series Editor's note: Three further sources on Caamaño can be instanced: Feltrinelli (2001) includes Fidel Castro's views on Caamaño, and on Juan Bosch at the time [10 May, 1965]. Also see Mao's 12 May 1965 'Statement in Support of the Dominican People's Opposition to U.S. Armed Aggression' in Zedong, 1998, pp. 432–3. The context of Mao's engagement with the Dominican Republic is discussed in Chapter 43 of Chang and Halliday, 2005.

when Woodrow Wilson attempted to impose US-style institutions and US-led economic modernisation on a reluctant country. During the guerrilla war that followed the occupation, thousands of Dominicans were shot, jailed or tortured by US forces and the atrocities reached such levels that after Wilson left power, a Republican-led US Senate considered it necessary to conduct a series of public hearings in which the incompetence and harshness of the occupation was revealed. For Dominican nationalists the conflict with the US became the defining part of their creed; Washington symbolised the kind of control and overlordship that most Dominicans strived to resist (even if local politics were chaotic, the economy a shambles, and a large part of the population aimed to emigrate to the US).[2]

Much the same as in Cuba and Nicaragua, two other countries which suffered US occupations at the beginning of the 20th century, Washington's attempts at setting up a 'new' military — in all three countries called the National Guard — produced a long-lasting dictatorship in the Dominican Republic. The one-time commander of the Dominican National Guard, Rafael Leonidas Trujillo Molina (nicknamed 'El Jefe') ruled the country from 1930 to his assassination in 1961, murdering opponents and paralysing the economy through his personal greed. The Trujillo era was a disaster for the country, making it an outcast even among other Latin American dictatorships and, increasingly, an embarrassment for the US, whose leaders had supported the staunchly anti-Communist Trujillo until the latter stages of his rule. The 1961 overthrow and killing of Trujillo had at least tacit support from the Kennedy Administration, even though the US president himself had hesitated in giving the CIA the go-ahead to help initiate a coup until a clear non-Leftist alternative to the dictator was available. Kennedy saw the benefit of being associated with the removal of an unpopular right-wing tyrant just a month after the unsuccessful attempt at invading Cuba at the Bay of Pigs. But JFK hesitated as to which direction the US wished to take in finding a successor to the dictator, saying, according to the historian Arthur Schlesinger, one of his advisors, 'There are three possibilities in descending order of preference: a decent democratic regime, a continuation of the Trujillo regime or a Castro regime. We ought to aim at the first, but we really can't renounce the second until we are sure that we can avoid the third' (Schlesinger, 1965, p. 660).[3]

The US intervention in 1965 was therefore built on a massive historical precedent of previous US meddlesomeness and attempts at controlling Caribbean and Latin American politics. It was also linked to a policy for Latin American countries of forced modernisation and improvement along US lines that had developed from Wilson to Kennedy. In themselves neither of

2   For a discussion of the complexities of Latin American attitudes towards the US, see Grandin, 2006.
3   For a good discussion of US policymaking see Rabe, 1999, especially pp. 34–48.

these trends were in their origins linked to the Cold War; they may well have developed and produced an intervention even if there were not an international confrontation between US political and developmental ideals and left-wing or Communist trends after World War II. But the particular stage that the US encounter with global socialist radicalism had reached by the mid 1960s framed the intervention and produced much of the urgency that went into it in Washington. Both the Kennedy Administration and that of his successor, Lyndon B. Johnson, believed that they were losing the confrontation with Communism and radicalism (and therefore also with the Soviet Union) in the Third World. By the mid 1960s, Washington was intent on reversing this trend by military means and through supporting enemies of radical leaders wherever they could be found. Johnson's decision to use US ground troops in Vietnam came out of this approach, as did the support for military coups in 1964–6 in Brazil, Indonesia, Algeria and Ghana. The ferocity of the US response to the attempts at reintroducing constitutional rule in the Dominican Republic must be understood within this larger Cold War defined framework.

From the US side, President Johnson himself stood at the centre of the Dominican operation: according to George Ball, an important Johnson foreign policy advisor, 'The President became the desk officer on the thing. He ran everything himself'.[4] Cyrus Vance, later US Secretary of State and a key Johnson staffer during the crisis, saw the president's attempts to win over Colonel Francisco Caamaño Deñó — perhaps the most influential commander within the Dominican military — to the US view of what was going on as a central part of the US plan for the Dominican Republic.[5] When Caamaño sided with the Constitutionalists, a direct US intervention was unavoidable. As President Johnson himself put it on 30 April 1965:

> I am not willing to let this island go to Castro. OAS is a phantom—they
> are taking a siesta while this is on fire. How can we send troops 10,000
> miles away and let Castro take over right under our nose. Let's just
> analyze—we have resisted Communists all over the world: Vietnam,
> Lebanon, Greece. What are we doing under our doorstep. We know the
> rebel leaders are Communist, and we are sitting here waiting on the OAS.
> We know Castro will hate us. We got rid of the dictator and we will now
> get a real dictator.[6]

Fred Halliday's text provides a rich portrait of Colonel Caamaño and a good overview of the circumstances around the US intervention. From an international history perspective, it is about time that the events in the

4  George Ball oral history interview II, p. 22, Oral History Collection, Lyndon B. Johnson Presidential Library, Austin, TX (hereafter LBJL).
5  Cyrus R. Vance oral history interview I, p. 17, LBJL.
6  Jack Valenti's notes of meeting in White House Cabinet Room, 30 April 1965, *FRUS, 1964–1968*, vol. 32, *Dominican Republic; Cuba; Haiti; Guyana*, pp. 100–2.

Dominican Republic were developed as something more than a mere footnote to the Cold War. As Halliday and the documents that accompany his text show, the real significance of the Dominican revolution and its suppression was not in the Cold War framework that Washington tried to impose on the Caribbean, but in the conflict between Third World nationalism and superpower intervention that Colonel Caamaño stood at the centre of. In this sense the book continues the engagement with analysing Third World resistance to foreign domination that has motivated so much of Halliday's scholarly work since he met Caamaño in Oxford in 1966.

## References

Chang, Jung and Jon Halliday (2005) *Mao: The Untold Story* (London: Cape).

Feltrinelli, Carlo (2001) *Senior Service* (London: Granta Books).

Grandin, Greg (2006) 'Your Americanism and Mine: Americanism and Anti-Americanism in the Americas', *The American Historical Review* 111, no. 4 (October).

Mao Zedong (1998) *On Diplomacy* (Beijing: Foreign Languages Press).

Rabe, Stephen G. (1999) *The Most Dangerous Area in the World: John F. Kennedy Confronts Communist Revolution in Latin America* (Chapel Hill: University of North Carolina Press).

Schlesinger Jr, Arthur M. (1965) *A Thousand Days: John F. Kennedy in the White House* (London: Andre Deutsch).

Westad, Odd Arne (2005) *The Global Cold War. Third World Interventions and the Making of Our Times* (Cambridge: Cambridge University Press).

# PART I

# CHAPTER 1

# A LATIN AMERICAN REVOLUTIONARY IN OXFORD

## The Dominican Republic Crisis of 1965

In his autobiography, published in English in 2007, based on interviews with Ignacio Ramonet, editor of *Le Monde Diplomatique,* Fidel Castro is asked his opinion about the president of Venezuela, Hugo Chávez. Before answering in detail, Castro points out that throughout the history of Latin America in the 20th century, Chávez is one of several military leaders who have also distinguished themselves as nationalist and revolutionary leaders: he cites Jacobo Arbenz in Guatemala, ousted in a CIA-backed coup in 1954; the Argentinian leader Juán Domingo Perón; and Liber Seregni in Uruguay. He then mentions another revolutionary leader: the exiled Constitutionalist President of the Dominican Republic, Colonel Francisco Caamaño Deñó. In Castro's words:

> Nor must we forget Francisco Caamaño, the young Dominican military officer, who for many months heroically fought against 40,000 US soldiers that President Johnson had sent into the Dominican Republic in 1965 to prevent the return of constitutional president Juan Bosch. His tenacious opposition to the invaders with only a handful of soldiers and civilians — an opposition that lasted for months and months — is one of the most glorious revolutionary episodes ever written in this hemisphere. After a truce that he won from the Empire, Caamaño returned to his homeland and gave his life fighting for the liberation of his people.[1]

Even after the passage of more than three decades, Castro's account of his relationship with Caamaño, whom he had come to know in Cuba, remains circumspect. He does not mention that the Dominican leader spent over five years on the island from late 1967 to 1973 secretly preparing to return and launch a guerrilla war in his own country, nor that he tried hard to persuade Caamaño not to do so. But his admiration for him is not new: on other occasions he compared him to Che Guevara, in terms of his heroism and self-

---

1   Castro with Ignacio Ramonet, 2007, pp. 532–3. On Caamaño himself, see Hermann, 2000. There is no biographical study of Caamaño in English.

sacrifice, and as leader of revolutionary Cuba he could never forget the dramatic events of 1965 when, in what was evidently a warning to Cuba itself, US forces overran the democratic revolution that had just begun in the neighbouring island of Hispaniola.

In the mid 1960s, there was perhaps more awareness of the Dominican Republic among the European public, particularly those of us who were on the left, than there is now. We had all read, in articles sometimes serious and sometimes more trivial, about the 31-year dictatorship of General Trujillo, which ended with his death in 1961. His cruelty, vanity and corruption, the fact that he erected 2,000 statues dedicated to himself across his country and even named the capital, Ciudad Trujillo, after himself, were known to many of us, not to mention the follies of his son Ramfis and of his son-in-law Porfirio Rubirosa. In retrospect, Trujillo seems to have combined the worst excesses of the Latin American *caudillo* with the more grotesque forms of personality cult seen in the European dictators of the 1930s and 1940s. Mario Vargas Llosa's novel, *The Feast of the Goat,* published in 2001 and later made into a film, evokes this period. More immediately, we had all followed with concern and anger the events of 1965: the uprising led by Constitutionalist military elements in April 1965, demanding a return to the democratic order abolished in 1963 with the removal of President Juan Bosch; the subsequent and entirely illegitimate invasion of the Dominican Republic by up to 40,000 US troops under the pretext of 'protecting' US citizens, who were in no real danger at all; and the long standoff which followed until Colonel Caamaño, elected legitimate President of the country by the Congress on 3 May, was forced into exile in January 1966 and to his posting as military attaché in London.

However, Castro's praise for the Dominican President may find little resonance among Castro's readers today:[2] compared to other countries in Latin America and the Caribbean, the Dominican Republic receives relatively little attention in the international press. This neglect is compounded by the way in which the 1965 invasion of the Dominican Republic — although a major event in the post-war history of the Caribbean and of Latin America; indeed, the largest ever military operation conducted by the USA against a Latin American country — is relatively marginalised in later histories of that region and of the Cold War. In the substantial body of literature published since the end of the Cold War, based on documents and interviews conducted after it ended, we have acquired much new information on some events, such as the October Missile Crisis of 1962 in Cuba, the Chilean coup of 1973 and the outbreak of the Korean War in 1950. However, little new has been said about the 1965 events in Santo Domingo. In one of the main retrospective studies about the Cold War, Arne Westad briefly mentions the 1965 events (Westad

2    Mention of Caamaño was indeed absent from the first Spanish language edition of the book.

2005, pp. 151–2)[3] but in John Lewis Gaddis' major study published in 1997, *We Now Know. Rethinking the Cold War*, there are no references to them. In most tourist guidebooks to the country, the events of 1965 are simply omitted.

We already knew much of the background at the time to the events in the Dominican Republic and, in the broader logic of the Cold War, the USSR made comparatively little protest about the US intervention, in part because — wanting to legitimate its own intervention in Hungary in 1956, or its later one in Afghanistan in 1979 — it implicitly conceded that the Dominican Republic was in Washington's 'back yard'.[4] Thus did the Monroe Doctrine serve to reinforce the Soviet equivalent, the Brezhnev Doctrine of 'limited sovereignty', enunciated in 1968 to justify the Soviet invasion of Czechoslovakia in August of that year. This was brought home to me when I happened to spend the evening of the US invasion of Grenada in October 1983 with Georgi Arbatov, the Soviet foreign affairs expert and head of its Institute for US and Canadian Studies, who was in London to promote a book I was due to review for the *New Statesman*. By chance, he was staying in the Royal Garden Hotel, the very hotel where Caamaño had given his January 1966 press conference. Having met for a stroll along the south side of Hyde Park, and passing the flat in Prince's Gate where Caamaño and his family first lived when they came to London, Arbatov emphasised that there was little or nothing Moscow could, or would, do or say in response to the US action that day. As with the use of Organization of American States troops in Santo Domingo in 1965, so, in 1968, the Soviet forces entering Prague had been accompanied by token forces from the Warsaw pact.

## 1966: The Oxford University Labour Club

In the early part of 1966 these dramatic events on the world stage found a curious echo in the internecine quarrels of the student left in Oxford. I was 19 at the time and president of the Oxford University Labour Club (OULC), the student group affiliated to the party then in office under Harold Wilson. We had just suffered what is termed a 'split': a group of self-styled 'Social Democrats', an

3 Westad, using subsequently released tapes of President Johnson's telephone conversations, reports that the invasion was decided on 'only after much soul-searching'. Johnson at one point stated that he was 'in a hell of a shape either way. If I take over, I can't live in the world. If I let them take over, I can't live here' (note 101), source telephone conversation with Senator Mike Mansfield, 30 April 1965, p. 437.

4 Discussing the Soviet invasion of Afghanistan in December 1979, Raymond Garthoff writes: 'The situation was, in the Soviet view, comparable to that involving American interests in the Dominican Republic where the United States had intervened directly in 1965 without an invitation from a previously recognised government' (Garthoff, 1994). The precedent of Hungary 1956 was not lost on the resistance in Santo Domingo. As Tad Szulc reports in his entry for 9 May: 'The word "Budapest" began to be used with increasing frequency by the rebels as they expressed their fears that the United States would use its own troops to liquidate the Constitutionalist movement in much the same way as the Russians brought their tanks into the Hungarian capital in 1956 to do away with the freedom fighters there.' (Szulc, 1965, p. 184).

early variant of the group that broke from Labour in 1983 under David Owen and Shirley Williams, had broken away with the majority of the executive committee (the breach lasted until the late 1970s). One of their first acts was to invite Roy Jenkins as a speaker, a minister who had declined a similar offer made by the OULC some months before. Among those prominent in the split, were Iain Maclean, later professor of politics at Oxford University, and Douglas MacIldoon, a prominent Labour organiser in Northern Ireland. Also part of this group, as he gently reminded me when we met recently at a conference in the medieval Llotja de Barcelona trading hall, was Martin Wolf, a *Financial Times* correspondent whose incisive writing I admire. As things turned out, I, as the sole remaining elected officer, had control of the OULC funds and of the official name as well as the indulgence of the 'senior member' Gerry Fowler, then an Oxford city councillor and don, later an MP and minister of state for education and science in the Wilson cabinet (1969–70), and subsequently Rector of the Polytechnic of East London (1982–92).[5]

To gauge the impact and significance of Colonel Caamaño's visit, a brief recall of the political atmosphere, at once remote and episodically engaged, of the university at that time may be useful. The Oxford of the mid 1960s was

5   The 'split' was a vivid index of the state of the British Labour left at that time and provoked some conflict with the university authorities. On one occasion, when I wrote to the MP, Tam Dalyell, informing him that he had agreed to speak to a breakaway grouping, he protested to the university authorities claiming I had written him 'the rudest letter I have ever received in my life', and I was duly compelled to appear, dressed in academic regalia ('sub-fusc'), before a disciplinary hearing of the university 'proctors'. Luckily, I had kept a carbon copy of my original letter to Dalyell (years later I was to meet him at the LSE and he was the soul of courtesy). After the departure of the 'Social Democrats' group, a few staunch souls remained to support me. They included: Tariq Ali; Mary Kaldor; Steven Marks, who became a militant in the Socialist Workers Party; Bob Liebenthal, subsequently a leading World Bank economist; the late Alan Clinton, later a leading Labour councillor in Islington; the future social policy professors David Piachaud and Michael Harloe; and the veteran CND campaigner, Rip Bulkeley. My closest ally during my term as OULC secretary was George Myers, a good-humoured and capable organiser, who, with Alan Clinton, was later to throw himself into the SLL, which became the Workers' Revolutionary Party. He subsequently lost his life in a motorcycle accident while commuting between Hull and Darlington in his role as the main Workers' Revolutionary Party organiser for both cities. The world of university political clubs at that time was self-enclosed and intense, with many of those involved aiming to get a guaranteed or 'safe' seat in Parliament after graduation. I was soon marked out as a trouble-maker; initially for making a timid speech in support of recognising the German Democratic Republic, an issue in which I was interested after spending my 'gap year' studying in Munich. When China exploded its first nuclear weapon in October 1964 (on a famous day of coincidences which also saw the election victory of Harold Wilson in the UK and the ousting of Khrushchev in the USSR), it triggered a fierce argument within the Labour Club and I remember speaking in favour of this development in the good company of Tariq Ali. I have never forgotten the moment when a Labour loyalist from Liverpool, who reported direct to Labour Party headquarters, interjected: 'Wait till Transport House hears about this, Halliday. You'll never get a safe seat now!' and so, indeed, it turned out. Much time and effort, as I recall, went into college and other elections and the bartering of block votes with representatives of other parties: my most reliable collaborator in this endeavour was the Liberal Party representative, Helen Rushworth (better known as Professor, also as Lady Helen Wallace) and later a leading international expert on the European Union.

in many ways a milieu in the doldrums: the excitements of the early 1960s, Campaign for Nuclear Disarmament (CND), existentialism and *la nouvelle vague* had faded, while 1968 was yet to come. Among the prominent speakers who came to the Union were: Mark Lane, the US lawyer who challenged the conventional account of the Kennedy assassination and who took us on his revisionist tour of the Book Depository and the Grassy Knoll; Bobby Kennedy, then expected to be the next Democratic President; and, with a fiery and unforgettable, if also misleading, speech in December 1964, the Black Muslim leader Malcolm X, just weeks before his assassination. Towards the end of 1964, I helped found a Vietnam solidarity committee with two colleagues, Peter Waterman and Michael Adler, one of the first in the UK, and during its last year, 1966–7, the first 'Teach-in' — a new US practice — took place on Vietnam. Caamaño's visit coincided with the second year of the Harold Wilson government and criticism was rising over a range of issues such as Rhodesia and Vietnam. In those months we hosted Richard Gott on *The Appeasers*, the book he had just co-authored with Martin Gilbert, *New Left Review* editor, Robin Blackburn and the trades unionist Clive Jenkins among others.

## The Visit of President Caamaño

So it was that, in the best internationalist spirit, we invited the exiled Colonel Caamaño, military attaché to the embassy of his country in London, to speak to us in March 1966. Caamaño had arrived in England on 23 January 1966, following an agreement made on 6 January under which 34 Dominican officers, including the leaders of both the regular armed forces and the nationalist militia, had been assigned to posts outside the country. His arrival in London, accompanied by his wife, two children and an uncle, was reported in the British press, as was a press conference three days later, in which he declared his lack of interest in diplomatic activity, or indeed political life, and stated his wish to return to the Dominican Republic as soon as possible. The correspondent of *The Times* saw fit, in the report published next day, to draw attention to the human side of the colonel's statement:

> Throughout the conference Colonel Caamaño remained calm and good
> humoured; his audience were agreeably surprised by his frankness and
> lucidity. The Army, he said, was too big. To a British audience, accustomed
> to hearing their own colonels saying only that their Army was too small,
> his remarks had a pleasantly heretical flavour.[6]

In the letter I wrote to him on behalf of the OULC, I expressed our support

6   'Col. Caamaño did not want post. Desire to return from London', from a staff reporter, *The Times*, 27 Jan. 1966. So far as I have been able to ascertain, this was the only general public appearance Caamaño made in his 19 months in the UK. I have not been able to find any other press reports of his time in London, apart from speculation in late 1967 on his disappearance (see pp. 199 below) and have not found any correspondents, or Latin American specialists, other than Gudie Lawaetz, who recall meeting him.

for the Constitutionalist and nationalist cause in the Dominican Republic and attached, with the letter, a copy of an article I had published a year earlier in May 1965 on the occasion of the US invasion. This had appeared in the Oxford student weekly, *Isis*, where I was political editor under the editorship of Mary Kaldor, then a student of PPE (Philosophy, Politics and Economics), and Angus Hone, an economist at Nuffield College. In the article, I had shown how the reasons given for the US invasion of the Dominican Republic were unfounded:

> Why did the Americans invade? As in the Congo they had "humanitarian reasons" — to rescue US citizens. In itself this is no justification and anyway it was merely an excuse as after the evacuation the invasion went on. They also claim that they are neutral and merely want to preserve order. This again is a lie. They have encircled the rebel areas, backed up the forces of their puppet general and declared their intention of suppressing the revolt … The real reason for the US decision to invade was far simpler and nastier. A thoroughly rotten pro-American regime was crumbling. The Americans had to back it up. Mouthing idiotic clichés about "ideological balance" and "spheres of influence" they have tried to justify what was quite simply an act of aggression. The guff about Castroites and Communists is completely irrelevant as a defence of the US action. The arguments advanced by the US are depressingly similar to those used by Khrushchev in 1956 over Hungary. (Halliday, 1966)[7]

To my great surprise and pleasure, Colonel Caamaño accepted our invitation and we met him at Oxford railway station on the afternoon of 4 March 1966, accompanied by Captain Pedro Julio Guerra, a junior colleague from the London embassy and a graduate of the French military academy at St Cyr. As was conventional with other visiting speakers, we took him and Captain Guerra to supper at the Oxford Union building and then walked to the OULC meeting venue. The Latin American specialist, Laurence Whitehead, now a professor at Nuffield, then a student and OULC member, recalls walking with Caamaño down Oxford High Street and the latter observing that the rooftops and crenellations of the colleges there would afford excellent cover for snipers — this being a radical redefinition of what, in indulgent accounts of Oxbridge, are often referred to as the 'dreaming spires'. Later in the Newman Rooms at Oriel College, our normal meeting place for guest speakers, he gave his speech

---

7    On re-reading the article 42 years later, I note two stumbles — a confusion between the Dominican Republic and the island of 'Domenica' (not that injurious insofar as people from the former often refer to it in Spanish as *la dominicana*) and, sign of the times, a flourish of a last sentence in which, anticipating wide hostility to the USA in Latin America as a result of the invasion, I invoke the famous words of Mao Tse-tung: 'A single spark can light a prairie fire'. There cannot, however, have been too much in this quotation, as I had published an article in the same journal Denóuncing the Cultural Revolution, which went against much current left-wing thinking.

to an attentive audience of around 50 people.[8] As OULC president, it was my honour and pleasure to chair the meeting.

Colonel Caamaño spoke for about an hour and then answered questions. His speech was ably interpreted by Ms Gudrun ('Gudie') Lawaetz, a Danish journalist, whose father had been born in Christiansted in the former Danish Virgin Islands of the Caribbean. Ms Lawaetz, then working for *The Observer* newspaper's Observer Foreign News Service, was accompanied by her husband, the distinguished Spanish historian, Professor Joaquín Romero Maura, later to become the first head of the Centre for Iberian Studies at the University of Oxford. There was a certain affinity, of theme and destiny, between the Dominican President and the Spanish historian: both were in exile from authoritarian regimes in their own countries, both were committed to the reconciliation of armed forces with democratic constitutions, both were, despite aspirations, unable to re-engage with new opportunities within their country.[9] Professor Maura was to devote part of his life to promoting and researching the life of his grandfather, Miguel Maura, the Conservative Spanish politician whose father was prime minister several times during the 1920s and who is today a hero of the Spanish right. Miguel Maura served as a minister and adviser during the reign of Alfonso XIII and played, as minister of the interior, an important role in ensuring a stable and democratic transition to the Spanish republic of 1931. But the rise of an authoritarian right, and the radicalism of parts of the left, had in the end overtaken his commitment to constitutional politics (Maura, 1962).[10]

Through a twist of fate, Gudie Lawaetz was already familiar with recent events in the Dominican Republic: she had worked in Paris in the late 1950s, where she had met some of the exiled radicals from the Dominican Republic, among them Hugo Tolentino, who later became foreign minister of his country. Others whom she knew, such as José Cordero Michel, had returned to the Dominican Republic in June 1959 to launch a guerrilla war on the Cuban model and lost their lives in that endeavour. Landings from Cuba and Venezuela took place at Constanza, Maimón and Estero Hondo. This political tendency came to be known in Dominican politics of the 1960s as *catorcista*, literally 'the 14thists', after the date when they launched their armed struggle (14 June 1959: the official name was *Movimiento Revolucionario 14 de Junio* or *MR14J*). Along with the Communist Party, they played a significant, though not leading role in the events of 1965. It was to be *catorcista* survivors who introduced Caamaño to the Cubans in London.[11]

8   The rooms were named after the famous 19th-century Roman Catholic thinker, Cardinal Newman, a former fellow of Oriel College.

9   A British historian who knew both well records arranging the first meeting between Professor Maura and the then leader of the Spanish socialist opposition and later prime minister, Felipe Gonzalez. It did not go well.

10  See the article on Joaquín Romero Maura and his grandfather in *El País*, 15 April 2007.

11  See the account of Caamaño's contacts with the Dominican left and with Cuba, Chapter 3 below, pp. 43–9.

After the meeting, I and the other OULC organisers were unsure what to do, so we invited Colonel Caamaño and his colleague, Captain Guerra, to a student 'fancy dress party' that was being held at the Oxford College of All Souls,[12] an occasion made possible because the father of one of the organisers was bursar of the college. In what was, in retrospect, a surreal display of Oxford eccentricity, although one perhaps not totally alien to the spirit of the Dominican festivities for Carnival, the three hosts of the party included a future senior correspondent of *The Economist,* dressed as a Regency dandy, and a future best-selling biographer, disguised as a gorilla. Although senior All Souls faculty members had been alerted to this festivity, the evening was marked by some friction, including a testy encounter between the warden, John Sparrow, and a small child, something never known to have happened on college premises before. The historian Robert Rhodes James, a fellow of the college trying to get an early night in anticipation of travelling the next day, also voiced his complaints.[13] Happily unaware of these intra-Oxonian tensions and their arcane all-male culture, Colonel Caamaño was delighted to accept and stayed for some time, dignified though somewhat reserved in his formal suit, among the mass of student revellers in various forms of extravagant attire. After a glass of wine, and with a train to catch back to London, he bid us farewell. I never saw him again.

Gudie Lawaetz and her husband did meet Colonel Caamaño again a few weeks later in London, and had dinner with him, Captain Guerra and Caamaño's uncle, Alejandro Deñó, also a former officer in the Dominican army, who was to stay on in London for a while before moving to Spain. In subsequent weeks, Ms Lawaetz had further discussions with Colonel Caamaño about his earlier life, his training at military colleges in the USA, his role in the Dominican army, and his subsequent engagement with the Constitutionalist movement. Ms Lawaetz describes how Colonel Caamaño, based at the military attachés' office in London, had arranged for a special, low-cost telephone link to be established with the other Constitutionalist leaders exiled in 1965. They would talk for hours on the phone including conversations with the exiled leader, Juan Bosch, urging him to return to the country to lead the Constitutionalist movement. Dominicans said at the time that, after the despatch into exile of over 30 Constitutionalist officers in January 1966, the Dominican Republic had the highest per capita number of military attachés in the world.

In his OULC speech, delivered in calm, clear Spanish, Colonel Caamaño analysed the events of 1965, his role as leader of the constitutional movement, the illegality and deceits of the US intervention and occupation, and the

12  Although All Souls has a reputation for the most remote scholarship and eccentricity, having long been a college without even graduate students, its origins would have been of more interest to Colonel Caamaño, since it was established to commemorate the English victory, under King Henry V, at the Battle of Agincourt in 1415.

13  My thanks to Edward Mortimer, later a distinguished *Financial Times* correspondent and a speech writer for United Nations Secretary-General Kofi Annan, for this information.

need for genuine, free, elections and the restoration of other freedoms in his country. His speech in March 1966, given as new presidential elections were being prepared in the Dominican Republic for the following June, reflected his hope that a constitutional order could be restored and the interference of the US in his country terminated. As we know from other declarations he made at the time, notably the work of Hamlet Hermann and an interview with the Uruguayan journalist Carlos Nuñéz in the same month, Caamaño thought at the time that elections would be held, despite the many difficulties, and that Bosch and the Constitutionalist cause would prevail. It would be difficult, he said, 'but the Dominican people cannot be fooled'.[14] For all of us present, it was a moving and unforgettable occasion.

## April 1965: The US Invasion in International Context

As already indicated, contemporary amnesia and some diplomatic convenience have served to obscure what was one of the most dramatic events in modern Latin American and Cold War history.[15] The American invasion of the Dominican Republic was a major event not only in the history of that country, but in the evolution of US foreign policy and of the Cold War in the third world as a whole. These events provoked a wave of protest across Latin America and more widely: among those moved to sympathise with the Dominican people and their new leader, were the French President, de Gaulle, who conveyed his disapproval of the US action in the most direct of terms, and Pope Paul VI, who was later to grant Colonel Caamaño and his wife an audience in Rome.[16] The invasion appeared at the time, and still appears today, as part of the broader pattern of intervention and counter-revolution which characterised US policy towards Latin America and East Asia in the 1960s. In broad terms, the second half of the 1950s and the first part of the 1960s had seen a rash of revolutionary and radical developments in the Third World: in East Asia, the rise of the guerrilla movement in Vietnam; in the Middle East the revolutions of Iraq, Algeria and Yemen; in Africa, the emergence of Lumumba and the independence of the Congo and outbreak of guerrilla war against Portugal in Angola, Mozambique and Guinea-Bissau; in Latin America, the Cuban Revolution and the increasing militancy over oil of Venezuela.

The tide then began to turn the other way: for the USA, as for its opponents, the events in Santo Domingo were linked to those in Africa and Indochina: President Lyndon Johnson, for one, saw a direct connection between the need

14 Interview with Carlos Nuñéz, *Marcha*, Montevideo, 25 March 1966, translated and reproduced below, pp. 25–32.

15 For a dramatic account, see Szulc, 1965. Tad Szulc later visited Caamaño in London, but I have not been able to trace any press record of that meeting.

16 According to Caamaño's widow, the Pope refused to permit Caamaño to perform the conventional form of obeisance, by kissing his ring: 'I will not allow a man such as you to kiss my ring!' declared the Holy Father (author's interview with Maria Teresa Acevedo, Santo Domingo, Jan. 2009).

for the US to act in the Dominican Republic and in Vietnam. The American invasion also served as a model, not least in its manipulation of the issue of 'protecting' US citizens, for later invasions: that of Grenada in 1983 and of Panama in 1989. For those of us following developments in the third world at that time, it appeared to be part of a series of right-wing military coups and US interventions that included: the 1964 coup against President Goulart in Brazil; the overthrow of President Sukarno and the subsequent massacre of the left in Indonesia in late 1965; the coup against President Nkrumah in Ghana in 1966; the Greek fascist coup of April 1967; and the Israeli attack on its Arab neighbours in June of that year.

We did not know for sure, but certainly suspected, that the USA had also been involved in the 1963 coup in the Dominican Republic that had precipitated the crisis in that country. It had also been involved — via the CIA, lest it be forgotten — in helping the Ba'th Party of Iraq in February 1963, at that time ferociously anti-communist, to seize power in Baghdad for the first time. In this sense, while the 1965 invasion marks one important moment in the history of Latin America and the Cold War, that of 1963 should also be recalled, since it was part of a pattern of military coups against democratically elected leaders that had already included Jacobo Arbenz in Guatemala in 1954 and João Goulart in Brazil in 1964, not to mention Mohammad Mossadeq in Iran in 1953. The culmination of this policy was, however, to come eight years later with the September 1973 coup in Chile.

It was easy for the left to claim that *in all these cases* the prime or sole source of the coup was the CIA, but this was to obscure a more complex, and multi-layered, situation in each. In the cases of Guatemala and Iran, a direct, CIA, instigatory role was later proven, in the others not, but in all cases a combination of a local military initiative with some broad approval from Washington was evident. Washington had made public its disapproval of Bosch and had cut aid to Santo Domingo, and some in the US embassy were active against him: but this is not to say that the coup did not have internal roots as well like the one in Chile in 1973. The Dominican Republic's history is uniquely tragic as within a few years in the early 1960s it experienced both the fate of Chile, a military coup against a democratically elected government (1963) and the fate of Vietnam, mass invasion by the USA (1965).

In the case of the Dominican Republic, Washington could not use conventional means: a military coup along the lines of the Brazilian or Guatemalan model was not possible as a significant part of the Dominican armed forces supported the Constitutionalist movement. A landing by exiles, such as was tried at the Bay of Pigs in 1961 and throughout the 1980s with the *contra* in Nicaragua, was also not viable as the overwhelming mass of the Dominican people, especially in the rural areas, was on the side of the forces that rose up in April 1965. Washington, alarmed at the international repercussions of the Cuban revolution throughout Latin America and conscious of the weakness of its military and civilian clients inside the Dominican Republic, therefore decided on a full-scale invasion.

Santo Domingo was the first case of what later came to be known as the 'Johnson Doctrine', after Lyndon Johnson, the then president: Johnson's was one of a long line of such 'Doctrines', all related to managing intervention and control in the third world, which US Presidents, from Truman in the 1940s, through to Eisenhower, Kennedy, Nixon, Carter, Reagan and even Clinton, were to elaborate on. Johnson's was the most extreme, illegal and crass of all these post-1945 US policies, a return in effect to the imperialist model of the 19th and early 20th centuries, even as it adumbrated, though few could have guessed it at the time, the invasion of Iraq half a century later, where the pretext for war, 'Weapons of Mass Destruction', was as bogus as that of 'protecting' US citizens in Santo Domingo in 1965. Born in the crisis of Santo Domingo in April 1965, the Johnson Doctrine was to receive its full and most violent and momentous realisation, and later rebuttal, in Vietnam. Two months after the invasion of the Dominican Republic, apparently encouraged by his 'victory' there, Johnson ordered US combat troops to land in Vietnam, their number totalling around half a million at the height of the conflict. Up to 57,000 American soldiers were killed and perhaps two million Vietnamese before, exactly a decade after the Marines landed in Santo Domingo, US forces and their advisers fled ignominiously from Saigon in April 1975.

However, the Dominican Republic is not and was not Vietnam. In 1965, it was a small country of around 18,750 square miles with a population of 3.7 million people. Close to the USA, it was exhausted by decades of exploitation and humiliation by Trujillo and his associates, while the left and revolutionary forces, inconsistently led by Juan Bosch of the Revolutionary Party, were divided over how to react. There were revolutionary 'Castroite' (*catorcista*) and communist elements in the 1965 movement, but they were not dominant. The Dominican constitutional forces were unable to resist the USA outright or to hold Washington to the promises it made when, in September 1965, the leaders of the constitutional movement, among them Colonel Caamaño Deñó, agreed to a truce and consented to go into what they understood to be temporary exile. They left in January 1966 on the assumption that new and free elections would shortly be held and the constitutional order of 1963, the cause for which the military had rebelled in April 1965, would be restored. However, when the next presidential election was held in June 1966, the process was accompanied by a mass of irregularities and illegal manipulations, with the result that the clear favourite, Juan Bosch, the Constitutionalist President of 1963, was defeated and Joaquin Balaguer, the conservative and former Trujillist, was elected. It was not until the late 1970s that legitimate elections were held.

## President Caamaño: His Place in History

As anyone can testify who heard his speech in Oxford that night in 1966, or who reads his statements (reproduced in this book), Caamaño was a committed and courageous man, determined to restore the independence of his country and the constitutional order that had been abrogated by the military and the US forces. He was not a natural adventurer, innate rebel or dreamer, but a practical, dedicated and organised person, representing the best in Latin America's progressive military traditions. The directness, modesty and good humour which impressed the *Times* correspondent at his initial London press conference in January were also much in evidence at Oxford. If we compare him to Fidel Castro and Hugo Chávez, the difference, to which I can personally testify, is striking: he had neither the logorrhea, vanity or intellectual confusion of the first, nor the rhetoric, swaggering and self-aggrandisement of the second.[17] Caamaño was, as documented by those who knew him, very moved by the example of Che Guevara and his call for heroism and self-sacrifice, but he had none of the coldness or the arbitrary and, at times cruel, arrogance of his Argentinian hero.[18] At Oxford he talked admiringly of the USA. And this is the impression he made on Tad Szulc, the American journalist and subsequently biographer of Fidel Castro, when they met in his Santo Domingo military headquarters in 1965:

> On the whole, Caamaño gave the impression of being a sincere and
> dedicated fighter for an idea in which he happened to believe. But, at least
> at this point, it was difficult to discern in "Francis" Caamaño mesmeric or
> charismatic leadership qualities. He was tough, all right, but he was not a
> Fidel Castro. He sounded like an idealist for democracy, but he was not a
> Rómulo Betancourt. He did not have the political sophistication of either
> the Cuban demagogue or the Venezuelan statesman. He was a figure whom
> fate had hurled to the center of the world's attention in this tragic hour of
> his country. (Szulc, 1965, pp. 147–8)

However, Caamaño was frustrated by his exile in London. His biographer, Hamlet Hermann, the Dominican left-wing writer and Caamaño's former

---

17  I heard Castro speak live on two occasions during a visit to Cuba with a group of European sympathisers in 1968 and I met Chávez at an official lunch in Lancaster House, London, in late 2001. The latter occasion was enlivened by much friendly banter between Chávez and his host, the then Deputy Labour Leader, John Prescott. In his welcome speech, Prescott pointed out that this was the second time he had offered lunch to a President of Venezuela, since, as a steward on a Cunard liner docked in Maracaibo in 1960, he had waited on the then President Betancourt. The general air of bonhomie at this lunch nonetheless failed to impress one crusty British foreign policy veteran who, on leaving, remarked to me that President Chávez's relation to Fidel Castro was not unlike that of Tony Blair to George Bush.

18  The words of Guevara that reportedly most affected him and which, taken from Che's message to the 1966 conference of the Organisation for Solidarity of the Peoples of Asia, Africa and Latin America (OSPAAAL), contained a tragic premonition of his own death in 1973 were: 'It is not a question of living heroically, but of choosing the moment to die heroically'.

comrade, describes his restlessness as military attaché and how he saw his future as lying increasingly with the revolutionary left in Latin America and his own country.[19] Radicalising factors were the rigging of the June 1966 presidential elections he had based his hopes on and his reading during that time of revolutionary works by the Vietnamese General Giap and Che Guevara among others. Caamaño could not be inactive while his country's situation deteriorated. According to Marcel Niedergang, Colonel Caamaño 'stagnated' in London until October 1967, then resigned his position as military attaché and disappeared from view (as *Le Monde's* Latin American correspondent, Niedergang's reports on the Santo Domingo conflict in April and May 1965 had impressed Carlos Nuñez) (Niedergang, 1968). Niedergang surmised: 'In the spring of 1968 some of his friends thought it possible that Caamaño might be somewhere in the Caribbean — probably Cuba — preparing to make a triumphant comeback' (Niedergang, 1968, vol. 2 p. 282). Significantly, Caamaño left London and travelled in secret to Cuba to prepare for a guerrilla war in the Dominican Republic the same month as Che Guevara was captured and killed in Bolivia on 9 October.

At the time one could only speculate as to whether these events were connected, but it later emerged that Caamaño had been in touch with Havana for some time via Dominican left members associated with two major internationalist conferences held there in 1966 and 1967.[20] Following the events of 1965, the Dominican left had split into several factions, some oriented to China, some to Cuba, and Caamaño had, it would seem, little patience with their internal disputes. But when the situation in the Dominican Republic deteriorated after the rigged elections of June 1966, Caamaño envisaged himself increasingly tied to Cuba and planned a visit there to co-ordinate opposition efforts. The news of Che Guevara's death in October 1967 acted as the final spur. A few weeks later, while apparently visiting Captain Hector Lachapelle Diaz, a fellow Constitutionalist officer posted to The Hague, he vanished and, having been met in Holland by Cuban intelligence operatives, travelled (with bald pate disguised) by land to Prague and by plane to Havana.[21] What was originally intended to be a short visit to Cuba turned into a stay of over five years.

Marcel Niedergang's surmise was therefore correct. Remaining quietly in Cuba for a number of years, Caamaño decided, against the advice of the Cubans, who by that time had grown sceptical of the 'foco'[22] theory of guerrilla

19   See p. 26 below.
20   The Organisation for Solidarity of the Peoples of Asia, Africa and Latin America (OSPAAAL) in January 1966; and the Organisation of Latin American Solidarity (OLAS) in August 1967.
21   Hermann p. 48 below.
22   The word *foco*, Spanish for 'focus' or 'nucleus', was the term given to the theory of guerrilla warfare developed by the Cuban revolution and applied by Che in Latin America. Contrasted to the more traditional idea of establishing 'liberated areas', it emphasised the importance of a mobile group of revolutionaries, whose actions would have wider,

war, to return secretly to the Dominican Republic in early 1973.[23] Landing at
Playa Caracoles on the north of the island with a group of nine supporters,
he went into the mountains of the Cordillera Central and began to mobilise
peasant support against the Balaguer regime. But he was not able to provoke an
immediate popular uprising and was captured by government forces after two
weeks. As had happened with Che Guevara in Bolivia six years earlier, Colonel
Caamaño was then executed; his body was thrown from an aeroplane into the
Caribbean Sea.[24]

For me personally, the meeting with Colonel Caamaño Deñó was one of the
most moving occasions of my political life and one I shall always recall with
emotion and pride. He ranks with the finest political leaders it has been my
privilege to meet, closely comparable in his dignity, calm and directness with
the leader of the opposition to Portuguese rule in Africa, Amílcar Cabral, whom
I interviewed in London in 1971, with the former German prime minister
and anti-Nazi hero, Willy Brandt, whom I invited to speak at LSE, and with
the Chilean foreign minister, Orlando Letelier, with whom I worked until his
assassination by Pinochet's DINA [Dirección de Inteligencia Nacional, the
Chilean secret police] in 1976. As it happened, Colonel Caamaño's speech
in Oxford in 1966 was also the first time in my life that I had heard someone
deliver a speech in the Spanish language. On that occasion I tried, to the best
of my ability, to follow his words through my knowledge of Latin and Italian:
I have often attributed my growing competence in Spanish in later life to
Colonel Caamaño's clarity of thought and diction; in effect, he was my first
teacher in that language.

There is much else that has been said, and could be said, about this truly
remarkable man, and about the many misinterpretations which have come to
attach themselves to the 1965 events in Santo Domingo in subsequent years.
Others, above all writers from the Dominican Republic and those who shared
his career, political activity and final guerrilla campaign, have written with
far greater authority about his life as a whole and the relationship between
his period in London and his later guerrilla actions. Apart from eye-witness

---

radicalising, impact. The classic formulation of this theory, later repudiated by its author,
was Debray, 1967.

23  At the time, Cuba said nothing about the guerrilla landing and their support of it, in
contrast to their open support of the 1959 expedition. In a speech at the end of July 1973
alluding to Caamaño's death, Castro referred to him only as a former president of the
Dominican Republic (*Granma*, July 28 1973, p.4). Apart from an aside to some visiting
American journalists (Mankiewicz & Jones, 1974, p. 38), it was to be another decade and
a half before Castro was to speak further on this matter. This was in an informal meeting
with Dominican journalists after his first, and by then amicable, encounter with President
Balaguer at a Latin American summit in Caracas. By that time, beginning in 1987, even the
Balaguer government was treating Caamaño as a 'national hero'.

24  For more on these events see in particular Hermann, 2000 and 2008. The latter contains
the fullest and most accurate account yet given of the preparations for, and execution of, the
Caracoles landing.

accounts at the time, several books have been published on Caamaño's life and on the background to, and course of events in, his country between 1965 and 1973 (see references below) Only in recent years has the government of the Dominican Republic, headed by President Leonel Fernández Reyna, a follower of the late Juan Bosch, officially confirmed Colonel Caamaño's status as a President of the Republic and named a thoroughfare in Santo Domingo, on the western shore of the Ozama river near the harbour, *Avenida Presidente Caamaño*. Colonel Caamaño Deñó is thus today a hero in his country, on a par with other great Latin American radical leaders of modern times such as Che Guevara, Emiliano Zapata, Augusto César Sandino and Salvador Allende. His reputation and his honour as a patriot and soldier are restored as is his status as a legitimate President of his country.

For all of us who met and heard him on that night in Oxford in 1966 he remains an outstanding personality, clear, modest and determined, without any of the demagogy, vanity or anti-democratic inclinations that affect so many other radical leaders in Latin America or elsewhere. He was, as his resignation speech of September 1966 demonstrates, committed above all to the independence of his country and to the constitutional role of the military. He dedicated himself and ultimately gave his life for that independence and for a just social and political order in the Caribbean and Latin America.

## References

Blein, Hugo Ríus and Ricardo Sáenz Pedrón (2000) *Caamaño* (Havana: Tricontinental).

Castro, Fidel with Ignacio Ramonet (2007) *My Life* (London).

Debray, Régis (1967) *Revolution in the Revolution?* (New York: Monthly Review Press).

Decho, Pam and Claire Diamond (1996) *Latin Americans in London: A select list of prominent Latin Americans in London 1800–1996* (London: Institute of Latin American Studies).

Garthoff, Raymond (1994) *Détente and Confrontation. American-Soviet Relations from Nixon to Reagan*, 2nd ed. (Washington: Brookings Institution Press).

Gleijeses, Piero (1978) *The Dominican Crisis: the 1965 Constitutionalist Revolt and American Intervention* (Baltimore: Johns Hopkins University Press).

Halliday, Fred (1966) 'American Treachery', *Isis*, 5 May.

Halliday, Fred (1983) 'Cold War in the Caribbean', *New Left Review* 141

(September–October).

Halliday, Fred (1999) *Revolution and World Politics. The Rise and Fall of the Sixth Great Power* (Basingstoke: Palgrave Macmillan).

Halliday, Fred (2007) 'Caamaño: un revolucionario latinoamericano en la universidad de Oxford', *Global,* no. 18, Santo Domingo: Fundación Global Democracia y Desarrollo (September–October).

Hermann, Edward S. and Frank Brodhead (1984) *Demonstration Elections. U.S. Staged Elections in the Dominican Republic, Vietnam, and El Salvador* (Boston: South End Press).

Hermann, Hamlet (1993) *Caracoles, La Guerrilla de Caamaño,* 3rd ed. (Santo Domingo: Tele 3).

Hermann, Hamlet (2000) *Francis Caamaño, Coronel de Abril, Comandante de Caracoles* (2nd ed. Santo Domingo: Amigo del Hogar).

Hermann, Hamlet (2008) *El Fiero; Eberto Lalane José* (Santo Domingo: Buhó).

Mankiewicz, Frank and Kirby Jones (1974) *With Fidel: A Portrait of Castro and Cuba* (New York: Random House/Ballantine).

Maura, Miguel (1962) *Así cayó Alfonso XIII,* originally published in 1962, re-issued in 2007 with an introduction by Joaquín Romero Maura (Madrid: Marcial Pons).

Moya Pons, Frank (2008) *Manual de Historia Dominicana,* 14th ed. (Santiago: Caribbean Publishers).

Niedergang, Marcel (1968) *The Twenty Latin Americas* (London: Penguin).

Schlesinger Jr, Arthur M. (1965) *A Thousand Days: John F. Kennedy in the White House* (London: Andre Deutsch).

Szulc, Tad (1965) *Dominican Diary* (New York: Dell).

Westad, Odd Arne (2005) *The Global Cold War. Third World Interventions and the Making of Our Times* (Cambridge: Cambridge University Press).

# CHAPTER 2

# STATEMENTS MADE BY PRESIDENT CAAMAÑO: SANTO DOMINGO AND LONDON

**1. 'We could not win, but nor could we be defeated': Speech of Resignation as President of the Dominican Republic, Independence Square, Santo Domingo, 3 September 1965**

Members of the National Congress and people of the Dominican Republic:

It is the people that gave me power and I have therefore come to return to the people what is rightfully theirs. No power is legitimate unless it is bestowed by the people whose sovereign will is the source of every public office. On 3 May 1965, the National Congress honoured me in electing me as Constitutional President of the Dominican Republic. Only thus could I accept this high office since I have always believed that the right to govern can be granted by no one other than the people themselves.

This was a highly legitimate right forged by the majority of our great nation, in the purest elections of all our history, and entrusted to me at a time when the Dominican people were giving their all in the struggle to regain their democratic institutions. These institutions, arising from the elections of 20 December 1962, were crushed by the infamy and ambition of a minority that has always despised the people's will.

The Dominican people fought back with all their might when this minority stripped them of their freedoms on 25 September 1963.[1] This is the same minority that has always robbed, imprisoned, deported and murdered our people. It is the minority that, represented by the Triumvirate presided over by Donald Reid, came to believe that the country belonged to them and that its people were their slaves.

All of these vices and errors brought the greatest suffering and pain upon our people. Life became unbearable. Not a single hope was left alive in the

---

1   On this date, after only seven months in office, during which time President Juan Bosch embarked on restructuring the country and promulgated a new liberal constitution granting the Dominican people freedoms they had never previously known, he was overthrown in a coup and replaced by a three-man military junta, headed by Donald Reid Cabral.

hearts of the Dominican people while these usurpers were in power. In order to revive this hope it was necessary to return to a freely elected government, which is to say the democracy that is upheld in the Constitution of 1963. Everything suggested that the members of the ruling minority, which thought and acted as if they were the owners of the nation, would cling to power even in the face of the most emphatic demands of the masses clamouring for the deliverance of the democratic regime.

Armed rebellion against this illegitimate government became, then, an imperative social necessity. Fruit of this need and of the determination of the Dominican people to be free, whatever the price, was the glorious 24 April Movement.

This Movement, inspired by the noblest democratic spirit, was not just another putsch. Professor Juan Bosch was right when he said from his enforced exile in Puerto Rico that the people of the Dominican Republic were waging a social revolution. This was so because the democratic sectors among our people, after immense suffering and great frustration, reflected deeply on their historic role and, joining forces with those soldiers who were true to their oath to defend the law in all its majesty, came out to fight for their lost liberty.

Heroically, with more faith than arms and a great wealth of dignity, the Dominican people opened wide the doors of History in order to build their future. The roots of this struggle went deep, very deep. Ever since Independence, ever since the Restoration of the Second Republic,[2] our people have been fighting and dying for their right to be free. This day, 24 April, represents a giant step towards the establishment of this right and towards the democracy that would fully enshrine it.

The enemies of the people who have placed their own interests above those of our country in their vain attempt to remain in power have caused our people's generous blood to run in rivers. Yet we shall always arise, evermore powerful, over the bodies of our dead. The Revolution advances triumphant. All the countries of Latin America have gazed in admiration on our land, anxiously hoping for our victory, seeing in it the triumph of democracy over the oppressor minorities that, like a plague, are the scourge of the entire continent of South America.

---

2    In 1861, after only 17 years of independence, General Pedro Santana asked Spain to re-
     colonise the country. After a series of revolts and guerrilla actions, the insurgents set up a
     provisional government in Santiago on 14 September 1863. Their proclamation of an Act
     of Independence launched the War of Restoration (1863–5). On 3 March 1865, Queen
     Isabel II of Spain approved a decree repealing the annexation of Santo Domingo and, on
     16 August, independence was restored and the Second Republic proclaimed. Thereafter
     the country was subjected to a long power struggle between those who wished to remain
     independent (the Blues) and those who were in favour of the annexation of the country to
     France, Spain or the US (the Reds).

Unfortunately, on 28 April four days after the Revolution began, when freedom was in the process of being reborn victorious, when an entire people fervently rushed to embrace democracy, the Government of the United States of America, violating the sovereignty of our independent State and making a mockery of the basic principles underpinning international coexistence, invaded our soil in a military occupation.

What right could the ruling circles of the United States invoke in order to trample over the freedom of a sovereign people? Not a single one! They were guilty of a serious crime, of an attack on our nation. It was an attack on Latin America and on the rest of the world. The principle of non-intervention, the cornerstone of relations among civilised peoples, was thus brutally ignored, even while the echoes of our people's most steadfast rejection of the invaders were still being heard throughout all the vastness of the planet.

In this continent of brothers and sisters, alongside the outcry of the governments of Chile, Uruguay, Mexico, Peru and Ecuador, which came together in their international response thereby doing honour to the sentiment of fraternity among the different peoples of this continent, one could hear the vibrant protest of millions of indignant people from all over Latin America in solidarity with our cause and in defence of the principle of non-intervention and of the sovereignty of our country.

The humiliation to which the government of the United States of America subjected the Dominican Republic with its military invasion is also a painful humiliation for all of Latin America. To what rules, what principles can the nations of Latin America turn in order to support their desire for, and their right to, independence when the ruling circles of the United States decide, with empty excuses and backed by cannon fire, to take charge of their political destiny? Where can they go to claim recognition of the right of a people to be independent and master of its own existence? What organisms, what institutions can defend these rights and encourage the different peoples to exercise them without fear of intrusion by others who have appointed themselves the arbiters of distant decision making?

It is the misfortune of the Dominican Republic and of all Latin America, that the Organisation of American States, instead of coming to the defence of our sovereignty, instead of harshly sanctioning the military intervention and thereby honouring the principles it claims to uphold, not only turned its back on its own founding Charter[3] but thrust in still deeper the dagger that is now plunged into the heart of our country.

Four days after the military intervention of the United States of America, the Organisation of American States decided to do 'everything possible to obtain the

3    See http://avalon.law.yale.edu/20th_century/decad062.asp.

re-establishment of peace and normal conditions'[4] in the Dominican Republic."
In the text of the Resolution that expresses this intention nothing at all is said
about the violation of our sovereignty. Nothing! There is not a single word that
refers to the monstrous crime of 28 April 1965 which, for years to come, will
shake the fragile foundations of the inter-American juridical order. On the
contrary. The Organisation of American States set about ignoring and twisting
principles by justifying and endorsing the military intervention of the United
States of America. It believed it could do so by creating the Inter-American
Force. The Resolution that enshrines this pernicious measure, registered as
*Document of Recommendation 2 of the Tenth Meeting of Consultation of Ministers
of Foreign Affairs*,[5] clearly reveals the stance of the regional organisation in this
regard. In it one reads, "The formation of an inter-American force will signify
*ipso facto* the transformation of the forces presently in Dominican territory into
another force that would not be that of one state or of a group of states but
that of the Organisation of American States, an inter-statal organization (…)"[6]

Transformation! This is the word that betrays the connivance of the
Organisation of American States with the invaders. The marines were
transformed into an inter-American force. That was the institutionalisation of
political crime as the norm in our continent's international relations.

The intervention of the United States of America waylaid the triumph of
Dominican democracy while also shoring up the minority that denies and
contests the rights of our people. With the so-called Government of National
Reconstruction, work of the servants of foreign intervention, our people were
treated with contempt, corruption set in and crime spread throughout the
country.

Despite the momentary setback of the Revolution in those tragic days, the
Constitutional Government decided to defend its rights. Naturally, in the face
of the violence and might of the United States of America, represented by more
than 40,000 soldiers, the Dominican democratic movement could no longer
seek victory through armed struggle. We had to negotiate with the invaders in
order to conserve part of the treasure of democracy we had begun to create.

During the month of negotiations we always upheld our principles. If we
abandoned some of the conquests for which the Dominican people had fought,
it was not because the Organisation of American States brought forth proposals
of greater democratic content than what we had sought with our initial goals.
We were only yielding to the reality imposed on us by the intervention of the
United States of America. The corridor arbitrarily and unjustifiably established
by the foreign troops, dividing Santo Domingo in two, was solely to prevent
our struggle spreading from this glorious city to the rest of the country.

4   See www.oas.org/consejo/MEETINGS%20OF%20CONSULTATION/Actas/Acta%2010.
    pdf, p. 337.
5   *Ibid.*, pp. 338–40.
6   *Ibid.*, p. 339.

The whole Republic had vibrated with its yearning for democracy. The cause that the people of Santo Domingo defended with weapons in their hands was the cause of the nation. This city, four centuries old, was home to the vanguard of the struggle and from here we launched our attack against our Creole oppressors. The victory of our democratic arms was already in sight and, just as we were about to claim it completely, the United States of America intervened, invading us in order to protect the worst interests and the most despicable ambitions.

It was then that we had to yield in some of our objectives, because we could not win the battle with arms. However, despite all the power and all the violence of the military might of the United States of America, we did not acquiesce out of fear or because we were afraid of defeat. The world is our witness, of the struggle we undertook and of the courage and valour of our people, both in the terrain of honour and on the battlefield.

At this point it is fitting that I render homage to those heroes who gave their lives fighting for democracy and our national sovereignty. The Unknown Soldier who is laid to rest in the Plaza de la Constitución symbolises the sacrifice and love of freedom of the Dominican people. Like him, thousands of others died. From this fertile soil of heroes the future of our country will vigorously grow. Those who gave their lives trying to prevent the establishment of the international corridor that halted our victorious march are heroes. Those who, with stones in their hands, stopped the steel-armoured tanks on Duarte Bridge are heroes. Those who defended the Northern Zone of the city to their dying breath are heroes. Those who dauntlessly withstood the aerial attacks on the National Palace are heroes. Those who, on 15 and 16 June, so bravely received foreign shrapnel in their bodies are heroes. Those of 29 August are heroes. And heroes, too, are those who have died on all our fronts, in the fields and in the cities and towns, fighting for our national integrity.

Never before in their existence, perhaps, have the Dominican people fought with such tenacity against an enemy that was so superior in numbers and arms. We fought, and we fought with legendary courage because, with right on our side, we were clearing the way of History.

We could not win but neither could we be defeated. Bolstered by our cause, truth was our greatest strength and our greatest source of encouragement to resist. And resist we did! This is our triumph because, without having resisted so steadfastly, we could not take pride in what we have achieved today.

We yielded, it is true, but they, the invaders who came to thwart our revolution, to destroy our cause, also had to yield before the revolutionary spirit of our people.

Thus we have them, speaking for themselves, the victories won and that are now on record, ennobled by the blood of the fallen, in the Institutional Act[7] and the Act of Dominican Reconciliation.[8] We have attained recognition of many social and economic rights. We have achieved a commitment to free elections in the near future. We have won freedoms in the public sphere, respect for human rights, the return of our political exiles and the right of every Dominican citizen to live in the country without fear of deportation. However, more than anything else, we have made one conquest that is beyond any expressible value, one of fertile future prospects: democratic consciousness! It is a consciousness that is against the coup d'état mentality, against corruption in the administrative sphere, against nepotism, against exploitation and against interventionism. We have won the consciousness of our own historic destiny. In brief, it is the people's consciousness of their strength. If this strength was mustered on 24 April in order to overthrow the civilian and military oligarchies, today, nourished by this marvellous experience and astonishing struggle, it will enable them to forge, in peace or in war, their freedom and their independence. The people were roused because their consciousness was aroused!

These are the achievements of this revolution. Not only our achievements but Latin America's as well. The principles we have fought for here are the same ones that are stirring the peoples of all of its nations today. When the peoples to the south of the Rio Bravo expressed their solidarity with our struggle, their own dearest and most intimate aspirations were deeply united with their fraternal encouragement. From Mexico to Argentina, democracy is the dream of millions of men who wish to make it a reality. It is a dream of creative peace, of peace that goes with dignified freedom. Yet this beautiful dream is marred, to the point of becoming a nightmare, by the greed and exploitation of minorities whose aims are far from those of the noble ideal of human coexistence.

If I can claim any credit for having prominently participated in this democratic revolution, thanks to the presidential mandate bestowed on me by the Honourable National Congress, it is none other than having understood the painful reality of our people and having ardently fought in an attempt to transform it into a future laden with hope.

I firmly believe that the Dominican people will finally achieve their happiness, and that 24 April will always be a symbol that urges them towards its definitive attainment. It is our obligation, as defenders of democracy, to nourish the seeds that were so generously sown on that immortal date. We must cultivate them with growing enthusiasm, with all our hearts, tirelessly and without hesitation. The best way to do so is in the unity of us all, in the

7   *Acta Institucional*, 3 Sept. 1965, the country's provisional constitution.
8   *Acta de Reconciliación Dominicana*, 31 Aug. 1965, setting the bases for democratic institutions and adoption of the *Acta Institucional*.

vigilance of us all, prepared tomorrow, as we have been today, to face every risk in our defence of Dominican democracy and our honour as a nation.

Before the people of the Dominican Republic, before its distinguished representatives who embody the Honourable National Congress, I resign as the Constitutional President of the Republic. God willing — and may our people ensure it is the case — let this be the last time in our history that a legitimate government is forced to step down under pressure of national or foreign armed forces. I trust it will be so.

Finally, I invite every one of our people assembled here to take the following oath:

In the name of the ideals of *los Trinitarios*[9] and the restorationist patriots[10] who forged the Dominican Republic;

Inspired by the selfless sacrifice of our military and civilian brothers who have fallen in the Constitutionalist struggle;

Interpreting the sentiments of the Dominican people;

*We swear* to fight for the withdrawal of foreign troops that are presently in our country's territory.

*We swear* to fight to ensure that democratic freedoms and human rights are respected, and that we shall not countenance any attempt whatsoever to bring back tyranny.

*We swear* to fight for the unity of all democratic sectors in order to ensure that our nation is wholly free, wholly sovereign and wholly democratic.


Francisco Caamaño

---

9   In February 1884, Juan Pablo Duarte, Francisco del Rosario Sanchez and Ramon Matias Mella founded the clandestine political organization *los Trinitarios* (the Trinitarians), which consisted of thousands of cells, each composed of three individuals. Their aim was to free the country of foreign influence (mainly Haiti, Spain, France, and England) and obtain its independence. *Los Trinitarios* are generally credited with the creation of the Dominican flag and the founding of the Dominican Republic.

10   See footnote 1.

**2. 'Col. Caamaño Did Not Want Post: Desire to Return from London', *The Times*, 27 January 1966.[11] Press Conference in London, 26 January 1966**
From A Staff Reporter

Colonel Francisco Caamaño, former leader of left-wing elements in the Dominican Republic, now military attaché in London, spoke with military frankness at a press conference in London yesterday about the circumstances of his appointment.

He had taken the post against his will, he said, speaking through an interpreter. It had been an order from the President of the republic which he had obeyed as a matter of principle.

He wanted to return as soon as possible. He was an Army man, and not interested in diplomatic life, or for that matter in politics.

Señor Garcia Godoy, the provisional President, said on January 6 that he was sending 34 officers, including the chief of both the contending forces in the republic, to posts abroad.

Colonel Caamaño said he hoped for their sake that the leaders of the opposing party would also accept the President's order, otherwise the people of the republic might take the matter into their own hands.

He said the United States forces were not wanted in the Dominican Republic. They did not come there to save people but to kill them.

Throughout the conference Colonel Caamaño remained calm and good humoured; his audience were agreeably surprised by his frankness and lucidity. The Army, he said, was too big. To a British audience, accustomed to hearing their own colonels saying only that their Army was too small, his remarks had a pleasantly heretical flavour.

---

11   *The Times* of 24 January had also carried a short report about Caamaño's arrival in the British capital: 'Colonel Francisco Caamaño Deñó, former leader of left-wing elements in the Dominican Republic, flew into London yesterday to take up his post as military attaché at his country's embassy … Colonel Caamaño, aged 33, who led the "Constitutionalists", as the supporters of the former President Juan Bosch became known, is the most important of the officers so far to have taken up his appointment abroad. He was accompanied to London by his wife, their two children, and an uncle, who will also be an attaché at the Embassy.

### 3. 'Whatever happens, I shall return': interview with Uruguayan journalist Carlos Nuñez, *La Marcha*, March 1966

*He has lost — at least, at least for the time being — his Stetson and a few kilos; but essentially the photographs seem to have done him justice: the beginnings of a bald patch are visible through his greying hair, a frown extending across his forehead lends an air of sternness to his face, the strong curl of his lips can be seen beneath his thin moustache. For more than two hours throughout the interview, one that inevitably evokes harsh memories of violence, he will try, albeit unsuccessfully in the end, to maintain an air of calmness.*

*Francisco (Francis) Caamaño, aged 33, professional soldier, leader of the Dominican Republic's popular revolt, current military attaché for his country's embassy in London, paces uneasily between the paintings on the wall and the curtains. He seems out of place in the context of this elegant, wallpapered, drawing room, smoking filtered cigarettes in the unnatural calm of a British apartment. The memory of violence beats in his head, in his hands, empty without their gun, in the booming voice through which he recreates faces, acts of courage, deaths.*

*Caamaño embarked on his military career in 1949, having completed his studies in a semi-military academy in the US ('they teach you to do one thing, and then they do the opposite themselves'). He became a Colonel in 1963. Until the uprising of April 1965 he had no involvement in politics: 'None at all. I believe that no member of the military should. In my case, I was forced to by circumstances, it was an obligation that I couldn't, and wouldn't, have avoided, participating in the patriotic struggle of the Dominican people against the foreign invasion'.*

*Why did you agree to leave the Dominican Republic?*

There were three main reasons. Firstly, one of the fundamental principles of our struggle was precisely that of obedience to civilian authority and, although in the end we were forced to compromise — we signed, to our shame, — and I repeat, even though it was an imposition — the *Institutional Act* that now governs our country.[12] Secondly, I thought that, in compliance with that which had been laid out by President García Godoy, members of the military from the extreme right would be forced to leave the country; and once those on the extreme right lose their leaders, it's hard for them to acquire new ones. It's different with popular leaders, because when there's a popular movement, any one of its participants could become a leader. Had the extreme right members of the military left, it would have facilitated the country's transition to electoral democracy. Thirdly, and most importantly: the young, the masses, the Dominican people, in order to defend their sovereignty, their desire for

---

12  On 28 August 1965 the two main Dominican parties to the conflict, the Constitutionalist government, headed by President Caamaño, and the 'Government of National Reconstruction', backed by the USA, signed two agreements, the *Institutional Act* and the *Constitutional Act*, in which both agreed to step aside in favour of President García Godoy as provisional president.

freedom and for social reform, could have risen up again to struggle. I had to avoid this happening, because I was absolutely sure it would be no more than a futile sacrifice, another sterile bloodbath that would lead to nothing except the loss of the best of our nation — its youth. At the moment, we cannot drive the Americans out by force, it's completely impossible. But the electoral process is already underway, so anyone who tries to stop it should beware.

*Do you plan to return to Santo Domingo?*

I'm returning very soon.

*Do you think that will be possible?*

According to the terms the government gave me, I can return when I feel it's appropriate. This was what was agreed when I left the country, and President García Godoy confirmed it again recently through a personal emissary. I can go back when I feel it's appropriate, unless they deport me, but I don't think that's in the government's plans since it would be illegal — the government would be undermining the bases of its own legitimacy.

*But do you think that legal reasons would stop them? When I ask if you think that going back to the country would be possible I'm thinking of real concrete obstacles. Even here, right now you're being watched...*

Of course, I wouldn't be at all surprised to find that somewhere around here there was one of those machines recording me. But when I need to return to my country, even if I do it secretly, I will do it. There's no doubt about it; I will go back.

*What event could lead you to decide to do that?*

If the electoral process were violated, I would go immediately to Santo Domingo. While I am here, I am kept completely up to date on what is happening in my country. If there were a coup d'état, I would go back. In either of these cases a civil war would break out immediately, which would be, as it has been, a patriotic war, and a war against the American invaders. And note that I am not talking about the Inter-American Peace Force; that is a smokescreen. I am talking about the Americans.

*Will the elections solve the problem of intervention? Indeed, will the elections be possible with American troops in the country?*

In my opinion it will be very difficult to establish the appropriate atmosphere for elections. But I also firmly believe that the elections will be won by the Dominican people. Because Dominicans will not be fooled by anyone anymore, Dominicans now know who represents their desires and aspirations. In a clean electoral process, the extreme right will have no chance at all. And even in a dirty electoral process; supposing that they manage to steal, let's say, 25 per cent of the vote, the unity of the Dominican people is so strong that the right would still have no chance.

*But American troops are still in Santo Domingo…*

Elections are the only way to resolve that. I have no doubt that the government that emerges from these elections will be a government that genuinely represents the interests of the people; and a government of this type would have to demand the immediate withdrawal of the invaders. After the elections, there will be no justification for their presence.

*Do you think the Americans would accept such a situation?*

Indeed, the big unknown that I don't dare answer is what the Americans will do after the elections. If you take into account how, with a government that represents popular interests, the 'inter-American' system — the OAS [Organisation of American States] — will deteriorate even more — what will the Americans do? I don't know.[13]

*For now though, even taking into account the elections, it seems that what they will try to do is break that unity that you refer to.*

For sure. Fragment, confuse, they're already doing that. They've already launched a new fake 'third force', with one Bonel as a candidate. It's the same thing, of course. Bonel is none other than a pure representation of the Dominican oligarchy… Oh no! And here I am talking about politics, with all its serious consequences. But these kinds of manoeuvres will lead nowhere; they won't be able to achieve anything. Despite them, the elections will be decided by the people and that means that there will be 95 per cent against 5 per cent. And I'm not exaggerating. The unity among popular forces is total, and not only in the capital, but across the whole country. The very experience of struggle, as a patriotic struggle, a struggle against the invaders, and the awareness of this struggle and of its objectives, has touched the entire population, even the peasantry.

And one more thing, since I have started talking about politics: another reason why I temporarily abandoned my country is precisely that, the development of the political struggle would have led me to renounce my position in the army had I stayed in Santo Domingo. And the problem of the armed forces is the first that has to be solved. The Armed Forces in the Dominican Republic need to be shown, in one way or another, that their mission is to defend the interests of the people, to support a legal government and not, incited by the North Americans, to overturn constitutional governments. The people now have sufficient social and political conscience with regard to this, and they will not be fooled again. But for this reason it is my duty to go to Santo Domingo when I need to. During a period of elections, or if there's a struggle, a

---

13   *Some days later, after I had left London, I imagined Caamaño hearing on the radio at the same time as I did, the first answer to his question: the State Department had launched — through their usual channel — an editorial in the* Herald Tribune *or* The Times *— a trial balloon: proposing the postponement of the elections for one year, with an interim coalition of Bosch and Balaguer. So far, it doesn't appear to have been accepted.*

well-organised struggle against the foreigners, like the resistance in France during the Nazi occupation. If there are elections, or if there's a struggle…

*Juan Bosch recently stated: 'For a people that has fought with guns in their hand, as the Dominican people have done, you cannot give them only democracy'. A minute ago, you talked about the Dominican peoples' 'desires for freedom and for social reforms'. Are there any concrete objectives with regard to this?*

OK, well, I'm going to answer you as a Dominican citizen. Right now, every Dominican wants to do something for his country so that it can achieve peace, tranquillity and freedom. Agricultural reform is an essential part of these social reforms. Although I know that's something that everyone says, it is indeed for us essential because we need to drive forward the agricultural boom so as to prevent the exodus of rural peasants to the cities.

The majority of Dominicans are living in poverty and starvation, in a situation where an elite minority exploit the vast majority. Agricultural reform is crucial; all as part of major constitutional reform. In terms of social and economic reforms, everything that will prevent the widespread administrative corruption must be included. For a long time smuggling, theft and crime were the order of the day in the Dominican Republic. What's needed is the creation of sources of employment, to establish an institution that will protect Dominican sources of revenue, which are primarily from the land; and above all, I repeat, it is fundamental that we prevent by all possible means the continuing corruption within the government and the armed forces. Let me tell you something that is related to these problems of corruption and land. In my country, the state owns 60 per cent of the land that can be exploited. Or rather, Trujillo owned it. On his downfall, this land remained in the hands of the government, who managed it so badly that the land passed, through bribes of course, into the hands of new private exploiters. These were bribes that even involved the President who was misgoverning the country. And today there still remains land that has not been exploited as a result of the government's neglect; both irrigation works and good planning are needed in order to stimulate agricultural production.

*You have emphasised that these reforms must be carried out 'within the constitution'. What constitution?*

This is what the Congress would need to establish, through a meeting involving many men who represent the majority in a regime that is genuinely democratic.

*The constitution of 1963 for example? Bosch was unable to do very much …*

During the seven months of Bosch's Presidency, those reforms did begin to take shape and there were signs of agricultural growth. But it was only seven months. This is my personal opinion. We have not struggled for men, but for principles, we have struggled to maintain institutional order. Our country suffers from another serious problem: the armed forces receive 50 per cent of the national budget, while the country sinks deeper into poverty. We do not need such a large army. We need to reduce the size of the armed forces: this must be one of the immediate tasks of the new government that is formed after these elections. They must reduce the size of the armed forces within a fairly short time scale, although not so drastically as to create a serious problem of unemployment. But as well as reducing the armed forces, we must train them professionally and, above all, show them what their duty is to the Dominican people.

*At the moment, Balaguer seems to be the only real candidate for the elections, apart from the 'third force' of Bonel that you mentioned. Who will be the candidate for the popular forces, or let's say the PRD [Partido Revolucionario Dominicano, Party of the Democratic Revolution]? Bosch has said that he won't run for election, would you?*

No, definitely not. I am not a politician.

*You say that the agrarian problem in Santo Domingo will only be resolved through the exploitation of state-owned land. Is there also any foreign — North American — investment in this land? During Trujillo's leadership the Dominican economy was linked to American corporations. Am I right in thinking that this situation hasn't changed?*

Of course you're right. We must nationalise ... Look, I know that they will call me, not once but a thousand times, a communist, but if you want I'll explain to you why the United States invaded Santo Domingo. There's a political reason: there are currently a large number of military dictatorships across the continent, Brazil — which has sent troops to participate in the charade of the Inter American Peace Force, Paraguay, Honduras, Nicaragua, even Costa Rica which has managed to send ... five politicians to Santo Domingo. The Organisation of American States is, in various ways, under the direct control of the United States. And the United States wanted to prevent a popular uprising breaking out as it did in Santo Domingo because if the popular forces triumphed in my country, then the situation will also explode in other countries, such as Brazil, which is under a horrific military dictatorship. And there is also an economic reason: although they don't currently have large investments in the Dominican Republic, apart from the La Reforma sugar refinery, they do have big investments in other countries in the region and their economic interests would be seriously damaged if these exploiters could not continue controlling Santo Domingo. Indeed, the system is well-known: the United States buys raw materials from developing countries at the prices of the global market, imposed by the US, they manufacture these raw materials, and then sell the manufactured products back to the developing countries. It's what is happening in Venezuela, for example, with oil, and the Americans make a profit of 195 per cent. The Dominican Republic has been forced to sell sugar to the US at a loss of 15 million dollars. At the moment we depend on the share that the US decides to give us for our sugar trade. If we were to trade with the Russians, we would be labelled communists, and there would be an invasion. They won't invade Cuba now because they would have to fight against many thousands of Cubans. In our case, it's different.

*Well, it was not necessary for you to start negotiating with the Russians — the invasion happened anyway.*

Yes, that's right. The problem now is what the Americans will do. If there are elections, they will have to leave. What can they do? In the meantime, they will try to break up the opposition forces. They may force a coup d'état, and even try to assassinate the provisional President; that is a real possibility. In the resulting chaos, they may even assassinate other left wing leaders or rather, popular leaders — well, it's the same thing. I don't want to go into these issues, but I consider myself left wing, meaning the democratic left. Then parties would be formed from principles based on nothing and a dictatorship will emerge and there will no longer be peace. Of course, there isn't peace at the moment, but if this happened there wouldn't be peace ever again. What would they achieve by this? No more than to offer an opening to communism. Dominican youth, without any other options, would very probably become more extreme in their views, even anarchic. It is no longer possible to impose governments who are against the majority.

*The North Americans continually used the excuse of the threat of communists to invade Santo Domingo. What role did the Communist Party play in the insurrection in April?*

The Dominican Revolution was not led by any party: it's the first time that Dominican people have been completely united, without parties, without classes.

*In any case, now we need to go further back. If in April Dominicans were calling for institutional reform as a means to achieve social justice, an obstacle has been put in their path: first they need to get rid of the invaders. The rebellion seems to have caused a historical regression.*

I disagree. In my view, the onward march of history may stop, but it never goes back. The invasion has created a widespread awareness in Dominican society of the warlike and reactionary policies of the United States. Besides, I believe that we have advanced 20 years in terms of enhancing public awareness of what the United States represents. When in the past would Dominicans, for example, have dared to confront the US? They themselves have shown us who they are. What did I know before about the OAS? Before the revolution, the OAS was for me on a kind of pedestal, an apolitical, legalistic, organisation; now I know full well that it is an instrument used by the United States to impose its power on smaller countries. In the Dominican Republic today, even the most ignorant peasant knows what the OAS is. They know because they've experienced it. And as well as knowing this, they also know *exactly* who its true representatives are. The OAS broke its founding charter of non-intervention, obeying the instructions of the North American government so as to legalise the invasion. This is a lesson, not only for me, but for two hundred million Latin Americans. The governments who voted against the Inter American Peace Force acted responsibly and with dignity on behalf of the people they represent. The others are pure rubbish. Let's tell it as it is, without ambiguity: those who voted for it did so thinking only of their own benefit within those governments.

*Colonel Caamaño, how did you end up leading the uprising in April and the Constitutional Government?*

Because of circumstances that were beyond my control. I was the head of operations during the uprising, and I assumed the role as head of the government according to the will of the Dominican Congress. The provisional government was led initially by Doctor Rafael Molina Urena as we awaited the arrival of Professor Bosch. Since Bosch was unable to leave Costa Rica, he sent a recommendation stating that I should take over the role of President. That was how the Congress agreed, unanimously, to name me as provisional president. Professor Bosch was my spiritual father. I only knew how to fire shots. I knew nothing about politics.

*And now?*

I have seen what actual experience can teach you. The Dominican Republic needs to go through a socio-economic evolution. I don't think that communism could be successful in the Dominican Republic today. The population still believes in democracy, in the electoral process. But if there are no elections, who will be able to cheat again the three million and a bit Dominican people who believe in democratic elections? The North Americans arrived in Santo Domingo when the victory of the popular forces was only a question of hours; Wessin's troops were nearly destroyed and in disarray. The North Americans entered and, alongside Wessin's force, they attacked the Dominican people. The North Americans have, step by step, shown Dominicans who they are. But this is new; with Kennedy it was different. I followed closely Kennedy's policies and you could see that he had different intentions, he clashed with the big corporations, for example in April 1962 when he strongly criticised the steel industry for increasing the price of steel by $6 per ton. Now, look at the case of Vietnam, they have spent US$4,800 million; as someone said, you could build four new Vietnams with that kind of money. In Latin America we have the problem of hunger; that is something real and dramatic. And in Santo Domingo, the more they try to impose their policies, the stronger the popular resistance will be. Dominicans aren't frightened any more. They aren't afraid of dying. This is a serious situation.

*'Santo Domingo, the Lyrical Illusion'. Again and again the title of the series in 'Le Monde' by their correspondent Marcel Niedergang comes to my mind, as Caamaño talks to me about the elections, about Kennedy, about corruption and constitutionalism.[14] Again and again, however, my gaze fixes on his restless hands and I recall the raised arm with its closed fist in the photographs, I imagine the gun that must soon return to those hands. In that instant, the luxurious London flat becomes haunted by the spectres of dust and blood, of the bodies doubled over on the moving ground, of blind fury or heroism, of cries and horror.*

Wessin's tanks were trying to enter Santo Domingo across the Duarte Bridge. They had to be stopped before entering the city. If a tank managed to enter, the troops would enter behind it, protected by it, and then we would be lost. People paid no attention to the machine guns, they ran towards the tanks, opened the hatches and brought the soldiers out by the scruff of their necks. They were French tanks, which have two 75 machine guns, and one 50 and they're like this. The projectiles of the 75 were like this, about half a forearm's length, and highly explosive. Each time one was fired, it killed 50 men. On our side, at first people only had sticks and stones until I decided to open the arsenal and give them weapons. But even with only their hands they stopped 17 tanks. I had to tell people who were under my control to wear civilian clothes because people would see a military uniform and not think twice about firing. That afternoon one man grabbed me by my shirt and said to me: 'Colonel, don't go out, they could kill you with a machine gun. Stay here and watch how a man dies.' That's what he said: 'Watch how a man dies.' A tank came over the bridge and the man had a Molotov cocktail. I had never seen one before. He pulled the cocktail's fuse and ran towards the tank. The man was so driven that he didn't let go of the explosive: he got as far as the tank and hit the bottle against the steal, setting himself on fire. He stopped that tank.

*Caamaño stubs out his cigarette in the ashtray, and looks at me without seeing me, with eyes that have lost their spark and repeats:*

'Watch how a man dies', that's what he said to me.

In some ways yes, a lyrical illusion. But in some ways also something more, something more intimate and real than some smooth revolutionary dialectical process. Because Francisco Caamaño, who at 32 years old 'only knew how to fire a gun', now knows a lot more: for one thing, he has learnt through his own experience, he knows who the enemy is. And, for sure, neither he nor those he is with are afraid of them.

*So, will you go back to Santo Domingo?*

Very soon, for sure. For sure.

---

14   Niedergang was later to write a book about his experiences in the Dominican Republic. See also his account in *The Twenty Latin Americas*.

# CHAPTER 3

# CAAMAÑO IN EXILE

## 1. Hamlet Hermann

### Francisco Caamaño in London 1966–7. Diplomatic Exile and Political Radicalisation[1]

The Francisco Caamaño Deñó that arrived in the British capital in January 1966 was a very different political person from the one that interrupted his lunch for a military revolt on 25 April 1965. Many novel experiences had taken place in the course of the preceding nine months, during which the course of events in his country, the role played in them by the Dominican people and the changes in his own personal circumstances had combined to make of him a popular hero and a national leader. London press reports spoke of his arrival as that of a mythical character from Atlantis or out of some legend. Comparisons with other historical figures were made in journalistic efforts to cast Colonel Caamaño as the symbol of the patriotic struggle of an entire continent. Nevertheless, everything that had contributed to make him a fervent Constitutionalist, the essential qualities that had led him to become President of the Republic in arms, remained unchanged. It was in the defence of the constitutional order that he had chosen to demonstrate that his attitude towards life had not been mistaken. Unlike so many other political and military leaders, he was neither a thief, nor an oppressor, nor an assassin. Many of his companions from the San Isidro Naval Academy base could not claim the same: they had preferred to sell themselves to the highest bidder of the moment, whether that was Trujillo, or the Triumvirate who made the coup of September 1963, or the American invaders of 1965. When he arrived in London, Colonel Francisco Caamaño Deñó remained what he had chosen to be since 1949: a military man. His respect for the Armed Forces had taken him to rebel first, in 1963, against the police chief, Belisario Peguero, in suppressing popular unrest, and afterwards against the Triumvirate. Later, he had opposed

---

1 This chapter was first published as chapter 17 of Hamlet Hermann (2000) *Francis Caamaño, Coronel de Abril, Comandante de Caracoles* (2nd ed. Santo Domingo: Amigo del Hogar).

the military invasion of the US, deploying the weapons in his hands to defend Dominican sovereignty, in compliance with the duties of the Armed Forces.

In his press conference upon arrival in London, he stated:

> The issue of the armed forces is the first one to be solved. It has to be
> made clear to the Dominican Armed Forces, in one way or the other,
> that their mission is to defend the interests of the people and to support
> the legal government, not to be pushed by the Americans into ousting
> constitutional governments.

This was the same message that he had enunciated before the civil war and during the patriotic war in 1965 and which he continued to state during his time as military attaché in Great Britain. Caamaño's behaviour had been entirely consistent throughout his 32 years. However, with or without the consent of Caamaño, the reality was that he had now become a political actor. He was no longer a military man involved in politics; rather, he was now a politician in a military uniform. While, as a serving military and police officer in the early 1960s, he had been an instrument of repression under the Council of State of 1961 and the Triumvirate of 1963, his politics had been imposed on him from the residences of the rich and by business interests, or, through intermediaries in the National Palace, from the US Embassy. After April Caamaño took orders from no-one: as he told his nephew Claudio Caamaño during the night of 27 April, after the Duarte Bridge battle, he now saw himself as reflecting the will of the people. It was evident that the word 'people' had now entered his speech, never to leave it.

Caamaño agreed to leave the Dominican Republic in January 1966 because, being a professional military man, he wanted to demonstrate his obedience to civilian authority. Even though he had been forced to negotiate due to the US invasion, he had signed an agreement to step down as President, the Institutional Act of August 1965, and was willing to abide honourably by what was agreed. Caamaño trusted the word of the provisional President Héctor García Godoy. He also trusted that, in order to contribute to fostering stability in the country, the officers who had allied with the invaders would also leave the Dominican Republic. However, the Constitutionalist leader was to be deceived by the very person whom he assumed was playing the role of arbiter, García Godoy himself: Caamaño did not realise that he was becoming the victim of a conspiracy organised in Washington, and in which the President had a key role. Caamaño agreed to accept a diplomatic position in London, because he believed that his continued presence in the Dominican Republic would have been an invitation to the youth of his country to rebel again and to take to the streets. He was completely sure that at that moment a resumption of armed struggle would have been 'a futile sacrifice, another sterile bloodbath that would lead to nothing except the loss of the best of our nation — its youth'.[2]

2   See above, p. 26.

While Caamaño had great political ability, a facility easily to perceive and to understand events, he still lacked political formation. He needed time to reflect in tranquility and with personal calmness in order to gain full understanding of the events he had just lived through. In exile, Caamaño required a great deal of time to get to grips with the new situation, in the country and in the world: the months of struggle against the foreign invader the Dominican nation had, in a way, condensed years of its history even as it moved towards its future. It had been the rifles of the US Marines and of the parachutists of the US 82nd and 101st Divisions, that had taught him what 'imperialism' really meant: but only in London would he begin to get acquainted with other dimensions of the imperial power, which came out in more subtle ways, including harassment and surveillance. Despite all of this, Colonel Caamaño was confident that the elections to be held in a short time in the Dominican Republic were going to be transparent and that he would be authorised to return once the situation was normalised. He expressed this view in an interview:

> In my opinion it will be very difficult to establish the appropriate
> atmosphere for elections. But I also firmly believe that the elections will
> be won by the Dominican people. Because Dominicans will not be fooled
> by anyone anymore, Dominicans now know who represents their desires
> and aspirations. In a clean electoral process, the extreme right will have
> no chance at all. And even in a dirty electoral process; supposing that
> they manage to steal, let's say, 25 per cent of the vote, the unity of the
> Dominican people is so strong that the right would still have no chance.[3]

For Caamaño the victory of Juan Bosch in the elections of June 1966 was assured. He recognised in Bosch the political leader of the Dominican people and assumed that the unity of the people around his candidacy was almost total. Even though he maintained this conviction, he declined the offer that Bosch made to him to run together on the electoral ballot of the PRD. In a letter from London dated the 21 April 1966, he tried to explain to Juan Bosch '… the reasons for my decision to pursue a military career'. In this letter Caamaño stated:

> … believe me that I will never forget all the generosity demonstrated by
> you when making me this proposition. This confirms that you are only
> motivated by the interest of helping our people. This has also been the only
> interest that moved me to fight yesterday, that moves me today to maintain
> with more firmness than ever the principles sustained in that fight and
> which strengthens me in order to keep serving my Motherland until the
> last breath of my life.

Removed from the Dominican situation, Caamaño was not in a condition to comprehend fully the machinations of the representatives of the US in the Dominican Republic. The invaders and their Dominican clients had as their

3   See above, p. 26.

main task to influence the electoral process before it took place. This would avoid any need for them to intervene later if the results were not in accord with their interests. Among other things, the electoral strategists sent by the Americans to Santo Domingo achieved in portraying the Bosch candidacy as one that would lead to another war. Although few Dominicans were able to appreciate this political manoeuvre to its fullest extent, there were some who, well before the start of the electoral campaign, anticipated this form of coercion. One such person was Rodrigo Jácome, the Ecuadorian ambassador to the OAS (Organization of American States), who had stated in an address to the Consultative Meeting of American Foreign Ministers on 3 May 1965:

> My sensibilities are offended at noticing that this (the creation of an
> Inter-American Force) could be interpreted in the sense that this foreign
> or internationalised force could remain in the Dominican Republic as
> the gendarme of the Dominican Republic, until the day, sooner or later,
> when following the realisation of all its political processes, its electoral
> campaigns, its electoral laws, its voter registrations, just then, if the
> constitutional government that has emerged from this process is to the
> pleasure of this foreign or internationalised force, it could then be possible
> to think of its withdrawal.

Naively, Caamaño lost sight of the USA's aggressive policy across the world. Because of this he persisted in his optimistic belief on the results of the elections. This led to his opinion as expressed in the March interview:

> But these kinds of manoeuvres will lead nowhere; they won't be able to
> achieve anything. Despite them, the elections will be decided by the people
> and that means that there will be 95 per cent against 5 per cent. And I'm
> not exaggerating. The unity among popular forces is total, and not only in
> the capital, but across the whole country.

With his continuing naive perspective, Caamaño believed that the Johnson Administration would not be able to carry on interfering in Dominican internal affairs. His excessive confidence in the Dominican people themselves made him lose sight of the broader political conditions the world was living through. Only those who had known Francisco Caamaño Deñó since his childhood could understand how it was possible he needed so much conclusive proof to be convinced of facts that for many were evident and irrefutable. The secretary general of the OAS, José A. Mora, had tried to bribe him in the midst of the war against the military invasion of the US. Then, after the frustrated attempts to eliminate him in the bombardment of the Copello building, there occurred the treacherous attack against the Hotel Matúm in Santiago.[4] Following that he was tricked by President García Godoy into leaving the country. What

---

4    On 15 December 1965 a group of right-wing military attacked the Hotel Matúm in
     Santiago, where Caamaño and other Constitutionalist officers were meeting.

else could be needed to convince a person that the Americans had the worst intentions against the natural leader of the Dominican people?

To understand what Caamaño was thinking in 1966 it is necessary to review the alternatives that he had at the time and later. Some might have expected Caamaño to remain in his post of attaché and wait for the promotions that he deserved, and which would be bestowed on him by successive governments. This would have been possible if those who headed subsequent Dominican governments had been respectful of the constitution and of the law. If those governments had tried to eradicate corruption among civilian and military officials, maybe then Caamaño would have agreed to remain outside the country for the benefit of preserving normality. However, if the government to be elected in June 1966 had been one that denied the very essence of Constitutionalist principles, it would, for a man like Caamaño, have been very difficult to renege on the oaths he made in his final speech as President, on the 3 September 1965, when he spoke to the Dominican people in Constitution Square (also known as Independence Square).[5] Furthermore, reneging in words alone from his recent just and glorious past would not have been enough for the foreign invaders. They would surely have also compelled him to collaborate with them and to betray his own partners, in effect to humiliate him. If he had given way, they might, after another 15 or 20 years, have granted him the rank of brigadier general, while the collaborators of the foreign intervention would have deported or annihilated those among the constitutionalist officers who remained firm.

Caamaño could have also taken advantage of his accumulated fame and thrown himself into a life of material pleasures. He could have renounced his military commission and cashed in the bill of his heroism, while at the same time becoming a museum piece to be utilised yearly every 24 April. He had many offers to appear all around Europe; however, he only accepted invitations to talk in front of audiences to which he could expound without censorship the objectives of the Dominican Constitutionalist cause. In March 1966 he agreed to talk at Oxford University, and gave some other speeches and interviews, yet without allowing himself to repeat the same ideas continuously. For him it was more important to try to create solutions for the benefit of his people. Moreover, there was always the risk that too much public exposure would turn into a sort of exhibitionism, by his becoming a cult figure or diluting his own moral standing.

The prestige and personal qualities of Caamaño also made him the centre of attraction for all the revolutionary parties of the Dominican Republic. Each of these parties wanted the 'Colonel of April' to join their ranks and to help them boost their membership. However all of them, without

---

5   See p. 17 above.

exception, underestimated Caamaño despite showering him with respect and compliments. All of them still saw in him the 'Sentinel', the 'Sharp Shooter', ignoring, consciously or unconsciously, the enormous human sensibility and the political potential still to be developed in him, but which could, even then, be appreciated. Those politicians and militants lost sight of the fact that leadership cannot be improvised, but can only be achieved with great effort when the indisputable arbiter, the people, recognises it as such. Caamaño had become the leader of the Dominicans and enjoyed their trust because since April 1965 he had represented their fundamental interests. He had become a leader because at all times he shared the same dangers that the Dominican people faced, even putting his own life at risk. In a moment of weakness he took refuge in the consulate of El Salvador, but he came out with more zeal and a clear decision to struggle while weaker spirits sought permanent diplomatic asylum.

From April 1965, Caamaño led the Dominican people and was, at the same time, led by them. This interrelationship was possible because he listened to his compatriots and made an effort to defend their interests. During the April armed conflict, he maintained communication with his followers with admirable consistency and his personal image expanded thanks to the untiring dialogue he sustained with the Constitutionalists. However, during his exile, some political leaders tried to take advantage of the 'Sentinel' Caamaño, using tricks and fake revolutionary policies. Some vain persons even tried to imagine themselves as being of the same leadership stature as Colonel Caamaño and took to calling themselves the 'representatives' of the Dominican working class.[6] Such people wanted Caamaño to work with them but on the condition of subordinating him: this was something they had never tried to do earlier on, when the risks were higher, when the demands of the struggle were incommensurable, when decisions had to be taken rapidly and efficaciously, and when, in a spirit of total dedication, actions had to be carried out for the benefit of the people. To take one example, in the Duarte Bridge battle nobody dared to dispute the leadership of Colonel Caamaño. However, when the prevailing state of affairs had become one of nervous expectation, a condition some people called peace, then 'leaders' appeared everywhere duplicitously trying to displace 'The Sentinel' from the leadership the Dominican people had given to him. The opportunists of that moment lost sight of the fact that an irreversible transformation was by then occurring within Caamaño. His human qualities reacted to the experience of the patriotic war as an impulse towards a better future where his dream of honesty and loyalty could find an echo in the Dominican Armed Forces. His character, behaviour and the sense he developed

6    A reference above all to one of the factions of the *14 June Movement* who, while proclaiming their supposed 'proletarian' character, criticised the 'petty bourgeois' politics of Caamaño and his associates.

of his own power, made him feel confident he could organise a different political mechanism from the ones in place, one that could overcome the sufferings that troubled the Dominican nation. The persecutions and murders of members of the constitutional military during the provisional government of García Godoy made him boil with rage. The impotence produced by the impossibility of counteracting such state terrorism infuriated him intensely. The only available comfort he found was to exhaust himself physically in long walks and daily exercises. He combined this activity with studying the experiences of other countries similar to the Dominican Republic, trying to get acquainted with the historical conjuncture that humanity was living through.

Following the 'election' of Dr Joaquín Balaguer as President of the Republic in June 1966, Caamaño understood that his chances of returning to the country had suddenly and permanently vanished. With the US's preferred candidate in the Dominican presidency,[7] Caamaño then understood that he was condemned to exile for life — unless, that is, he renounced his role in resisting the foreign invader, betrayed his comrades and ignored the thousands of Dominicans that had died defending their national sovereignty.

From that moment two figures came to have a special influence over the intellectual and political education of Colonel Caamaño. One was the Vietnamese General, Vo Nguyen Giap; the other, the Argentinian doctor and Cuban guerrilla commander, Ernesto Guevara de la Serna, the legendary Che. With regard to Giap, Caamaño admired his military genius demonstrated in the campaign that took the Vietnamese people to the victory of Dien Bien Phu in 1954 against French colonialism. In Che he saw the university professional coming from a wealthy family, but who sacrificed everything for the cause of a country not his own. For Caamaño, both Giap and Guevara embodied admirable human qualities, magnificent military ability and great dedication to their actions. Those men stimulated his political training and demonstrated to Caamaño, through their writings, that the will of the people and the spirit of sacrifice can defeat the greatest enemy in the world.

Enthralled by Giap's *People's War, People's Army*, Caamaño seemed to recognise episodes through which he had lived in the Dominican Republic. The victory of the Vietnamese people over French colonisation made him think of what the Dominicans had not been able to achieve in 1965. He learnt with interest of how France had spurned each of the agreements it had signed on Indochina and had convulsed the whole country, just as was happening in

7   In his memoirs, Ray Cline, CIA Deputy Director of Intelligence, described in detail the moment when he recommended that President Lyndon B. Johnson support Joaquín Balaguer to become President of the Dominican Republic. Balaguer was exiled in New York, while in the streets of Santo Domingo resistance was planned against the foreign invader. Cline includes in his memoirs President Johnson's blunt acceptance of his proposal: 'That's it! That's our policy. Get this guy in office down there!' (Cline, 1978, p. 212).

Santo Domingo. The rational and peaceful methods that had been attempted in order to solve the conflicts — as Caamaño discovered from reading Giap — had demonstrated their uselessness: it was necessary for the people to take up arms. At the same time, he noted how the Vietnamese sometimes had to give ground during the fight and how they had been forced to wait, fighting for many years until they achieved victory over the French colonisers.

Giap's conclusion to his book seems to have made a deep impression on Caamaño. It read:

> In the current international conjuncture, one nation, even if small and
> weak, that revolts like a single man under the direction of the working
> class to resolutely fight for its independence and its democracy, has
> the moral and material possibility of triumphing over the invaders, no
> matter who they are. In some specific historical conditions, this fight for
> national liberation can take the form of a protracted war and of prolonged
> resistance in order to reach victory.

General Giap's words were confirmed by the fact that, even though French colonialism had been defeated, imperialism in general was not willing to accept the defeat. As the French were leaving Indochinese territory in 1954,[8] the Americans came to replace them, even though they were only just able to control the southern part of the country. The fight against the external aggressors did not end at Dien Bien Phu: when Caamaño read Giap he was also following in the daily press the way in which the Americans had increased their participation in that war. Caamaño's experiences in 1965 had convinced him that the US was willing to intervene in the internal affairs of any Latin American country that intended to take its own and independent path. He also believed, however, that the people of the continent would confront and, in the long term, defeat them.

The political evolution of Caamaño can be appreciated from the letters he sent to his friends in the Dominican Republic. At the end of February 1966 he wrote to his friend Jottin Cury, minister of foreign relations in the Constitutionalist government, about the strafing to which students had been subjected in front of the doors of the National Palace on 9 February. In one emotional paragraph he said: '... the important thing is not to live with dignity, rather to choose the moment to die with dignity. This has been done by these young students who have not lived more than one third of their lives and are already national heroes ...' Caamaño felt pain every time the Dominicans suffered and was mortified by not being able to be there to join resistance to the state terrorism that took hold under García Godoy's provisional government. The election of Balaguer contributed to the institutionalisation of the persecution that had begun under the transitional government and the

---

8    French Indochina was composed of Vietnam, Laos and Cambodia.

main targets of that repression continued to be the Constitutionalist military. With the ascent to government of Balaguer's Reformist Party, the hatred of the collaborationists towards the Constitutionalists, 'far from diminishing, came to embody the frustrations of many of the failed plans of generals and colonels on the opposite side.' The *Gregorio Luperón* Mixed Brigade (Ayuso, 1967), created to group the Constitutionalist military and to isolate them from the rest of the armed forces, had been subjected to all kinds of abuses perpetrated by the government headed by Dr Balaguer. As long as one single soldier remained standing to defend constitutionality and the law, the contrast with those who supported the foreign invader would be the more evident. In consequence, the mission, first of the provisional government and later on of Dr Joaquín Balaguer, would be to crush or annihilate those that provided a 'bad example' to the other military who were dependent on the US.

President Balaguer dissolved the *Gregorio Luperón* Brigade by Decree on 8 November 1966, at the precise moment when one of its leaders was attending the Seventh Conference of American Armies in Buenos Aires, Argentina. On this occasion, all the collaborators' hatred of the foreign invasion was directed against the defenders of the sovereignty. And Colonel Osiris Perdomo,[9] commander of the Armoured Battalion that had clashed with the Constitutionalists in April 1965, described the Constitutionalist military as 'communists' and referred to Colonel Caamaño as a 'traitor'. After such a statement, the military patriots in exile would inevitably in future be perpetually condemned by the government that constitutionally they were supposed to respect and obey. Moreover, with these words General Perdomo eliminated any hint of doubt that might have persisted about the good will of Dr Balaguer's government towards the Constitutionalist military. What was, in effect, a 'declaration of war' closed off one of the alternatives originally considered by Caamaño and the other Constitutionalist leaders with positions outside the country.

Every incident of this kind affected Colonel Caamaño. His expectations had differed widely from what actually occurred and this served to push him in a more radical direction. The frustrations he suffered from time to time made him react aggressively to an enemy that was constantly causing him to be uneasy. This was possibly the objective of those who wanted to harass him, corner him and leave him without alternatives in order to neutralise him in the future. This situation was compounded by the fact that the men who had been closest to him during the months of confrontation in 1965 were now preoccupied with their own individual struggles for survival within the Dominican Republic in the face of an aggressive government. The Constitutionalists that at the

9   Osiris Perdomo, with the rank of colonel in 1965, was commander of the Armoured Battalion, who in deploying one of his tanks forced the Chief of the Air Force to bombard Santo Domingo city. The tanks defeated at Duarte Bridge, and those that massacred the population in the northern part of the capital, were part of this same battalion.

beginning of 1966 had sustained frequent contact with Colonel Caamaño did not, by the end of that year, have sufficient time to communicate with him. For someone who was in the country and engaged in such an individual war for survival, time rushed by. The constant danger and struggle for survival meant that on many occasions their attention was deflected to other comrades, near or far. Every man acted as his own Constitutionalist leadership. People were being killed at a rate greater than under any other government known in Dominican history and at a rate that competed with the death toll of the Patriotic War.

But for Caamaño the days in London passed slowly. He suffered from increasing anxiety about his enforced passivity. By the beginning of August 1966, he was already writing:

> My friend, I have to complain that you no longer write to me as we agreed
> prior to my departure. Since your last letter before the elections (June
> 1966), I have written to you twice and have not received any answer.
> When one is outside the homeland, but with one's thoughts constantly on
> it, as is my case, any information is desired and well received.

To his sense of being cornered by the enemy was added the frustration of lack of communication with his friends — something comprehensible enough but never justifiable for a figure like Caamaño, who embodied the spirit of rebellion and fight for freedom of the Dominican people.

At the beginning of 1966, the Tricontinental Conference was held in Havana,[10] and the majority of the representatives bombarded the Dominican delegation with questions about Caamaño. Fundamentally, they wanted to know about his prospects of becoming a revolutionary leader. Many people from Asia, Africa and the Americas inquired about the possibility of Caamaño catalysing the revolutionary forces in the Dominican Republic and perhaps in Latin America as a whole. Among those interested in knowing about Caamaño's situation were officials of the host country and, through one delegate who had been involved in the revolutionary Dominican 14 June Movement, the first links were established between Cuban political representatives and Caamaño in Europe.

The 14 June Movement was created in the aftermath of the Cuban revolution of January 1959. After the victory of the Cuban Rebel Army against the dictatorship of Batista, the oppressed peoples of the continent began to identify themselves with the Cuban example. Many Latin American revolutionaries only appreciated the romantic, diversionary, aspect of guerrilla war and craved to imitate it in their own countries. This then produced the illusion of 'instantaneous revolution', partially created by the mass media. After 1959, many of the Rebel Army combatants, both from Cuba and other nations,

10   *Organisation of the Peoples of Asia, Africa and Latin America*, celebrated in Havana, Cuba, 3–12 Jan. 1966.

were stimulated to begin a new phase of similar struggle in other countries of the continent. It was one of these groups that attempted, in June 1959, to overthrow the tyrannous regime of Trujillo in the Dominican Republic. Even though it did not have the anticipated success, the 14 June Movement planted the seeds for ousting tyranny.

All these Latin American guerrilla movements of the early 1960s were characterised by spontaneity. As a result, their combatants and leaders were killed and the political processes of the countries involved in guerilla activity were affected since they had lost their best men and had no time to replace them. The attempt to provide a minimum of coordination and coherency for these insurrectional movements was the main reason for holding the Tricontinental Conference in Havana in January 1966.[11] Once this international meeting had been concluded, it was possible to establish a working system of communication between Caamaño and the Cuban government. The Cuban representatives demonstrated their willingness to offer the Constitutionalist leader any support that he might need. Guevara was already preparing to depart to Bolivia on a mission that, if all went to plan, would have continental reach. With the purpose of enhancing Che's base support in Bolivia, the Conference of the peoples of Asia, Africa and Latin America also tried to coordinate all the forces seriously dedicated to following the revolutionary path. It seemed that popular insurrections in Latin America had reached their zenith at this time as there were also guerilla movements in Guatemala, Venezuela and Colombia. The incorporation of a figure like Caamaño into this political trend could have had an enormous impact on gaining support, or at least on securing the understanding of important political forces in Latin America.

Meanwhile in London, Caamaño was dedicating his time to organising a Patriotic Front with the participation of the Dominican Revolutionary Party (PRD), the 14 June Movement (1J4), and the Dominican Communist Party (PCD). However, at that time none of these organisations had sufficient cohesion, or the necessary capacity, to participate in the struggle. The PRD was involved in an internal struggle between those willing to cooperate with the government of Balaguer and those who were searching for solutions more congruent with the situation experienced in the war against the US invasion. The 14 June Movement was divided between, on the one hand, those who thought the organisation could become 'the vanguard of the working class', and those who, on the other hand, assigned the role of the 'proletarian vanguard' to the Dominican Popular Movement (MPD). In December 1966, the 14 June

11  Within the framework of the Tricontinental Conference, the Latin American delegates gathered at the request of the then Chilean Senator, Salvador Allende, trying to overcome the formal differences between them and to find the convergence points. This gathering initiated the formation of the Latin American Organisation of Solidarity (OLAS), see below p. 47.

Movement suffered a significant division when a large part of its membership transferred to the MPD. As for the PCD, it was barely visible in the arena of political struggle in its new incarnation separate from the Popular Socialist Party and was not enough of a force to sustain a national movement by itself. All of this meant that the politically most advanced parties in the Dominican Republic were creating confusion instead of clarifying the immediate goals of the struggle. They were unable to define a policy that distinguished allies from enemies, and this enabled Balaguer and the Dominican oligarchy to incorporate some of those who had been in the democratic camp into their ranks.

Caamaño was, unlike most of the party leaders in the Dominican Republic, not a person to waste time in internal quarrels or sterile discussions about an idealised future which few people were working to bring about. His thoughts were directed towards more general issues, those that mattered to the population as a whole, not just to a small group of intellectuals. He tried at the same time to overcome his own political deficiencies and contribute to practical solutions, and in so doing he had already begun to act like a statesman.

Caamaño had one advantage over those of his allies who remained in the Dominican Republic: he was not contaminated with the fevered controversies that affected the revolutionaries of that period. The so-called 'Cultural Revolution' in China provoked disagreements among revolutionaries all over the world with the result that it made dialogue and reconciliation almost impossible between those who claimed to share the same ideology. It was paradoxical that someone who could lead a population in arms was at the same time unable to organise dialogue and conciliation. Even though the enemy was mercilessly striking the opposition on a daily basis, other revolutionary leaders preferred to spend their time on talking only: discussing what form socialism should take without fighting first to achieve it. They were counting chickens before they were hatched.

The dialogue of the Dominican left was a dialogue of the deaf. The rulers of the US must have been laughing aloud as the 'revolutionary vanguard' concentrated its efforts on the internal 'ideological struggle' within its own ranks, and not on the ways in which imperial domination was being established in the Dominican Republic. The revolutionaries absented themselves from the fight against the invader and left the road open for the selective repression practised by Balaguer's government to achieve 'peace and order'. But this was the peace of the grave and the order of dungeons.

The conversations Caamaño had with the Dominican revolutionary groups did not get beyond the stage of subjective analyses. The isolation of the revolutionary groups within the country was becoming evident, something that signalled possible political extinction. It was then that Caamaño seriously started to consider the possibility of accepting the Cuban offer of collaboration as a way of realising the plans he was making. He still counted on the support of the main Constitutionalist leaders that had fought with him against the invader and he was confident they would support his plans. Caamaño absorbed the spirit of the times and followed the trajectory of Guevara with fascination. By that time Guevara had already disappeared from public view and the world could only conjecture as to his whereabouts.

Caamaño's admiration for Che grew when he saw the message he sent 'from somewhere' to the peoples of the world through the Tricontinental Conference. In reading those words, images came into Caamaño's mind of the Dominican people defending themselves against their eternal oppressors. Che asked:

> And for ourselves, exploited of the world, which is the role that
> corresponds to us? The peoples of three continents are observing the lesson
> of Vietnam. Since it is through the threat of war that the imperialists
> implement their blackmail over humanity, the right response is not to
> fear war. The general tactic of the peoples of the world should be to attack
> strongly and uninterruptedly at each point of confrontation.

Caamaño did not ignore the warnings of Guevara about the immense sacrifices that had to be made by the peoples to free themselves. However, could that suffering be greater than that the Dominican people already experienced daily in their fight against misery and oppression? Maybe the sacrifices sustained by an armed vanguard could make those of the nation less painful if this meant full combat was avoided and the ending of exploitation was left to the passage of time.

It was in this context that Caamaño began to elaborate a plan through which he would organise Constitutionalist military and revolutionary militants into a force that would become the vanguard of the fight for the definitive freedom of the Dominican nation. A small general staff, selected from among the most trusted of the Constitutionalist leaders, participated in the discussions and was updated about the evolution of events. Those who decided to participate would have to train themselves outside Dominican territory as it was impossible to do so within due to the repressive environment prevailing in the country. That training ground would obviously be Cuba which was offering the necessary support. According to these plans Caamaño did not initially plan to move directly to the Caribbean island; instead, another Constitutionalist leader would do so to prepare the vanguard group. Caamaño's role would be that of a politically unifying element, apart from the fact that his continued presence in public would be necessary to distract the attention of the US intelligence services. He then began preparations to travel to Cuba for a temporary visit to meet its main leaders. The chance to exchange experiences and opinions with the senior statesman, Fidel Castro, would be particularly valuable. That visit would have been for two to four weeks, during which time Caamaño would be able to see at first hand the progress of Cuban society and its economy in the few years since the revolution.

The task of setting up the armed force would be the responsibility of two of the main Constitutionalist leaders. Their mission would be to contact the most trusted fighters, and those who had the best combat experience in the April war, with the purpose of gathering them together in Europe and travelling with them to Cuba for training. To this end, the sum of US$55,000 was given to one and US$37,000 to the other to pay the fighters' travel expenses to Cuba and to help solve some of the immediate problems their families would face after they left. In the event, most of this money was wasted on party-going and personal expenditure while few of the men he had hoped to recruit joined Caamaño in Cuba.

In his message to the Tricontinental, Guevara had talked about the need for the armed forces of liberation to coordinate their actions in order to accelerate the final goal: 'This is the path of Vietnam; this is the path that should be followed by the peoples, this is the path that the Americas will follow, with the special characteristic that the armed groups would be able to constitute something like Coordination committees to make more difficult the repressive task of Yankee imperialism and to facilitate their own cause.' According to Régis Debray:

> The celebration in Havana, in August 1967, of the First Conference of
> the Latin American Solidarity Organisation (OLAS) marked the visible
> culmination of local revolutionary movements' efforts with regard to
> practical coordination and theoretical systematisation. This kind of event
> necessarily involved an element of theatre predominated by pomposity
> and phraseology. It is easy to cast doubt on such rhetoric and symbolic
> solemnity, but such embellishment had a simpler and more profoundly
> real value: to enhance the support base for Che. The convening of OLAS
> marked, in a public manner, a long period of unpublicised work. It was
> intended to revitalise or stimulate guerilla movements where they were
> already implanted (Guatemala, Venezuela, Colombia and Bolivia) and
> also to win support or at least the understanding of political forces in
> places where matters were not being decided through taking up arms.
> Nevertheless, its objective was immediate and pragmatic, although it could
> not be announced and was not perceived by all participants: to offer Che
> a support apparatus that was at once political, military and psychological;
> to break his political isolation by doing all that could be done to neutralise
> hostile parties; to ensure his rearguard in the borderline countries; and,
> by means of this indirect effort, to create everywhere that it was possible
> favourable conditions for the spreading of the armed struggle from the
> Bolivian *foco* (Debray, 1977, pp. 12–13).

The OLAS Conference coincided with the most critical moments of Che's guerrilla campaign in Bolivia and with the culmination of Caamaño's forward planning. Caamaño's contact with members of the 14 June Movement was reinforced after the split in that political organisation. The 'Transformers' were seriously preparing a guerrilla uprising for which they had already selected men and obtained supplies. Furthermore, two groups of combatants had gone out of the country to receive training in guerrilla warfare: one, headed by Amaury Germán, went to Cuba; the other, led by Homero Hernández, departed for China.

The 14 June Movement's plan envisaged an initial uprising without the participation of Caamaño 'on the grounds that he should join when the conditions to guarantee him security in the zone of operations were attained'.[12] In London, Caamaño's plans were evolving satisfactorily when news broke that caused consternation to all revolutionaries across the world: Commandante Guevera had been captured and assassinated in Bolivia. Accustomed to the sometimes misleading cables of the American news agencies, the revolutionaries did not want to believe this unpleasant news, but finally had to accept reality.

It is possible this news had more of an impact on Caamaño than on any other revolutionary. Che was his archetype, the one who served as an exemplar for the mission he was committed to accomplishing. Caamaño would have liked his name and actions to be remembered alongside Guevara's at some time in the future: leaders who contributed to the victory of the peoples of Latin America. When the death of Che was confirmed, Caamaño therefore took an immediate decision which responded to Guevara's last words expressed in his message to the Tricontinental:

> Anywhere that death surprises us, we will welcome it. Always that this, our
> war cry, had reached a receptive ear, and another hand extends to grasp our
> weapons, and other men prepare themselves to intone the sorrowful chants
> with the rattle of machine guns and new cries of war and victory.

Caamaño was indeed one of those 'receptive ears' and his hands would now grasp the weapons of Guevara.[13] He decided how to follow the path traced by Che, with the hope of introducing into the course of events a new and unexpected force, one that could bring fresh dynamism to the continental struggle. While taking a decision of this magnitude had modified his original plans, Che's death had introduced new conditions in regard to revolutionary struggle.

---

12  'El Desembarco de Playa Caracoles; Orígines y Consecuencias', Duvergé, Despradel and Pérez, *Renovación*, April 1973.

13  In an interview given to two American journalists a year later, Castro stated: 'Francisco Caamaño, leader of the Dominican Revolution of 1965, was very much like Che. Both were combatants of value, of great courage and with a large amount of energy. Caamaño returned to the Dominican Republic because he believed in his people, he had an immense trust in his people.' (Mankiewicz & Jones,1974, p.38).

Facing a blow as hard as the loss of Che Guevara, the belief that Caamaño had in the need for revolution increased his enthusiasm for the task. Since he felt he could make a valuable contribution to helping the popular forces achieve victory, he could not remain inactive. Since 27 April 1965, Caamaño had demonstrated the characteristics that enabled him to rally to the great call of his epoch and his country. He had become a national hero because, in a moment when many were vacillating, he appeared as an initiator, as a precursor, whose vision and will were revealed as stronger than others. It was not that in the battle on the Duarte Bridge he had altered what was already the natural course of the people in arms. However his actions, ideals and physical presence inspired the Dominican people to follow him. These events and personalities stand out as beacons of that stage of political and social development. Caamaño in the Dominican Republic in 1965, and Che in Bolivia in 1967, were symbols of movements that converged when the legendary internationalist combatant died.

The disappearance of Colonel Caamaño was first announced to the world in a statement by Juan Bosch:

> At around 11.30 on the night of 24 October 1967, Colonel Francisco
> Alberto Caamaño, on a visit to the home of Captain Héctor Lachapelle
> Díaz, left the house to take a walk in the neighbourhood. At that time
> it was drizzling and foggy in The Hague, the Dutch capital, where his
> Constitutionalist companion was also serving as Dominican military
> attaché. Captain Lachapelle and his wife wanted to go with him but he
> said he did not want company. He also said he needed to be alone because
> he wanted to think about some very serious problems. From that moment,
> the friends and companions of Caamaño living in Europe would never see
> him again.[14]

In those early days this was one of the most common explanations of how Caamaño had disappeared from view. However, the reality was that he was indeed accompanied by one of the Constitutionalist leaders that evening until he entered a restaurant, but had then disguised himself with make-up and a wig to cover his baldness. With the aid of a Cuban agent who was awaiting him, he went overland to Prague, Czechoslovakia, where he boarded a plane that took him to Havana.[15] The agreements he had made hitherto with Dominican

---

14  Statement by Juan Bosch, ¡Ahora!, 6 Dec. 1967.

15  One of the Cubans who participated in transferring Caamaño from The Hague to Havana was a double agent who also worked for the US Central Intelligence Agency (CIA). Some sources signal him as Hugo Castro and through him the US government knew about Caamaño's trip to Cuba before it happened. That they did not take the chance to assassinate or Denóunce him suggests that the espionage apparatus believed the trip would contribute to Caamaño's isolation and his separation from the political forces that followed him. They would also have been unwilling to reveal that they had an agent within the Cuban Security apparatus. This double agent, whose pseudonym was 'Antonio', was an official in the Cuban Embassy in Paris.

individuals and political organisations would now have to be adapted to take account of the new clandestine situation in which Caamaño would have to live in revolutionary Cuba.

# 2. Fidel Castro

## Cuba and Caamaño: Fidel Castro Press Conference, Caracas, Venezuela, 1989

*For many years, from the time of Colonel Caamaño's secret flight to Cuba in 1967, through his death in 1973, and well into the 1980s, the Cuban government made no comment on the Dominican leader's presence in Cuba, apart from Castro's brief mention of Caamaño's death and of his role in 1965 (but omitting Cuba's association with him) in his speech of 26 July 1973 ('Granma', 28 July 1973). Aside from informal remarks made in 1974 and reported by Frank Mankiewicz and Kirby Jones (see above p. 14, fn. 23), the following is, so far as can be ascertained, the first public statement by Fidel Castro on the matter. These comments were made during a meeting with Dominican journalists in February 1989 when Castro was on a visit to Caracas, Venezuela, on the occasion of the inauguration of Carlos Andrew Perez as President of Venezuela. The text, which is not an official one, is as published in the journal 'El Listin Diario,' and reproduced in the work of Melvin Mañón footnoted below. Mañón, whose controversial and in some respects tendentious work is based on personal experience but is critical of the Cuban role, stresses that the journalists questioning Castro at times misrepresent the argument of his book. This visit to Caracas was the first time the Cuban leader had met President Balaguer, who was also attending the ceremonies.*

*Nelson Encarnación (El Nacional)*: President, the last time we were in Cuba, you generously allowed us a very extensive interview. Yet I was left feeling troubled about a question I asked you about an issue which, although concerning events that are now quite long past, seems to have re-emerged with the recent publication of a book. It is with regard to what is said about how the Cuban government in some ways abandoned Colonel Caamaño at the time when he was planning to reproduce the Cuban revolutionary model.

*Fidel Castro*: Who wrote that?

*Nelson Encarnación (El Nacional)*: Melvin Mañón, a sociologist. He has children in Cuba.

*Fidel Castro*: What sociologist?

*Nelson Encarnación*: Melvin Mañón.

*Fidel Castro*: What does he say?

*Nelson Encarnación*: Well, that the Cuban government wanted to disassociate themselves from Caamaño and that when he embarked on his plan of coming to the Dominican Republic with a group of revolutionary fighters, the Cuban government saw this as an opportunity to get rid of Caamaño and thus didn't give him the support he deserved.

*Fidel Castro*: If history were written like that, future generations will learn nothing about what really happened. It is not an easy issue to discuss because Caamaño still has relatives, his wife and children, and they know about the contacts that existed the whole time. Our country welcomed him ... it was there that ...

I have to say that I don't know if I should be telling the whole story ... We had a very good relationship and we genuinely would not have wanted Caamaño to have gone back at that particular moment. We held him in very high esteem, we valued his qualities as a leader, and we did not want him to sacrifice himself. I'm not referring to national or political problems that involved Cuba; that didn't concern us. We merely wanted him to stay alive. He was determined to go back, he was determined to go back and we were prepared to pay the political price, and we certainly supported him in this, with exemplary friendship and loyalty. We didn't want him to go back, but we supported his return. It was his desire to return and he returned with admirable faith and optimism. I could not say whether with these words I am completely respecting the historical truth. I had lived through the experience that he was about to live through and maybe even in worse conditions, and with less experience than him. We began our struggle with very few men — a handful of men — in territory that was completely unfamiliar, so it would be unfair, dishonest even, if I were to tell you that he was naive and that he was aware of the great risks he was taking. I would have liked him to have stayed around for better opportunities, for the history of his country.

*Nelson Encarnación*: Was he driven to despair?

*Fidel Castro*: I don't think he was in despair because it had been years since he had been out of the country. In all frankness, I can name two great men who lost their lives and who I would have liked to have survived because of what these two great men could have achieved: Che and Caamaño. I can say that in all frankness. I would like them to have stayed alive, and wish that they hadn't had to fight in such difficult conditions at such a dangerous stage. But they were not victims and that's why I wouldn't use the word 'despair'. Perhaps in their situation I would have done the same. In a way I am not saying what he wanted to do, what Che wanted to do. It's still a sensitive subject, it's a sensitive subject. A long time has passed and our relations with the country, with Latin America, are different, but honesty must always prevail above any other consideration ...

*Máximo Diaz (Hoy)*: On the subject of the late Colonel Caamaño, the author of the book that Nelson Encarnación referred to, Melvin Mañón, who asserts in his work that he was an intelligence officer for the Cuban army and that he even participated in previous training sessions there with Caamaño, says that his daughters have been abducted in your country.

*Fidel Castro*: In Cuba?

*Máximo Diaz (Hoy)*: Yes, and that they are not allowed to leave.

*Fidel Castro*: It's most likely the mother of the girls who doesn't want to let them go. Could he be a traitor? I don't want to prejudge; he is probably a really fine person, a great liar, without doubt. There's no doubt that he's one of those, or at least that he has certain mistaken ideas, or that he has been badly informed, or that someone told him to write that. I can't judge this individual, and I don't want to judge him. But I will tell you that what he said is a lie. Were we going to send a Cuban army with Caamaño? Caamaño wouldn't have accepted. And Caamaño took with him a group that had been very carefully selected by him, a very selective group. And, well, I was in contact with Caamaño, I admired him, I sympathised with him. I regarded him as very honourable, very brave, and I admire brave people, I admire people who are decisive and hold strong convictions.

There were all sorts of people with him, and there could have been people he didn't take along with him. I haven't seen this book, I find it difficult to say. When we went to Cuba in the *Granma* we made a selection according to weight, in the end above all other priorities, what can one do with someone who weighs a lot alongside the lighter, slimmer ones; in the end people were selected according to weight, like boxers. So he could have, for one reason or other, known about this individual and not taken him with him. [...] This book sounds spectacular and sensationalist, send me a copy. He said he worked in the Cuban intelligence. That could have been possible. There are many people who aren't necessarily working for the Revolution, but rather people who work with it — and defend and inform it — and therefore may have been some kind of intelligence officials. I'm not sure, I have no way of knowing, or asking him what was or wasn't, whether he worked or not; a long time has passed since then. But I really don't know, and I didn't want to mention this person.

In the world of revolutionaries, there are many fine people, and perhaps he was one of them. There are also many people in this world who desert, and I wouldn't be at all surprised if he worked with other intelligence services. You can't rule out that possibility. For example, why did he write all these things? What was his objective? Who encouraged him to write it? Who paid him? If he's the kind of person who wants publicity, who is he? I can't say if he's one thing or another. So many books have been written, so much rubbish, but I can certainly say that the first thing you said was completely untrue; I can't deny the other thing because I don't know whether or not he worked for Cuban intelligence. One would have to find people who have information from that time and who would say who this man is, whether he worked with Caamaño, whether he was trained, if we trained him, if he was trained intensively. In our country, in the mountains …

*Félix Reyna (Rahintel)*: For the final part of this interview, since it's the year before the elections in the Dominican Republic, we'd like you to give — I don't know — some kind of message to the Dominican Republic.

*Fidel Castro*: Do you want to get me into trouble? I shouldn't do that, it wouldn't be wise to do that. Only messages of brotherhood, of affection and good will.

*Félix Reyna (Rahintel)*: Not necessarily about a particular candidate, in a year's time that could make things complicated.

*Fidel Castro*: What should I say, vote for this or that party? I can't do that; I can wish you good luck and progress: that you overcome your difficulties, that the country moves forward, that it grows. You deserve it, you deserve it so much that I can even wish for it in the name of our people. I must abide by my principles and not interfere in internal matters. We will not try to influence and nor do you need us to at all. I think that we would cause more harm than good if we begun to declare ourselves in favour of one party, or one candidate. For this reason I can't do that.

## References

Ayuso, Juan José (1967) 'De la Revolución a un campo de polo, La Gólgota Constitucionalista', *¡Ahora!*, 4 Dec.

Cline, Raymond (1978) *Secrets, Spies and Scholars: The CIA from Roosevelt to Reagan* (New York: Acropolis).

Debray, Régis (trans. Rosemary Sheed) (1977) *Critique of Arms* (London: Penguin).

Mankiewicz, Frank and Kirby Jones (1974) *With Fidel: A Portrait of Castro and Cuba* (New York: Random House/Ballantine).

Mañón, Melvin (1989) *Operación Estrella: con Caamaño, la Resistencia y la inteligencia cubana* (Santo Domingo).

# PART II

# OFFICIAL DOCUMENTS, UK AND USA[1]

## (i) British Foreign Office Documents

### 1. British Embassy, Washington 4 May 1965

From Washington to Foreign Office

**Addressed to Foreign Office telegram No. 1187 of 4 May**

Repeated for information to: UKMIS New York [UK Permanent Representative to the United Nations]

Your telegram No. 3702: Dominican Republic

When I saw Mr. Rusk this morning I reiterated our thanks for United States to help in evacuating British subjects from Santo Domingo. I then gave him the gist of Santo Domingo telegram No. 36, emphasising its extremely confidential character. Mr. Rusk commented that it was very interesting although subsequently he added that he thought it unlikely that the Rebels would launch an all-out attack on American troops in view of the latter's overwhelming superiority.

2. Mr. Rusk talked at length about Bosch, emphasising that he was personally progressive, liberal and democratic. Unfortunately he was also a poet and had no political sense and American hopes that he would survive in 1963 had quickly been dashed. In power he had been inept and indecisive and his downfall had been caused by a combination of economic disorder and his indifference to the penetration of his administration by various subversive elements. The movement against Reid Cabral appeared to have been genuinely inspired at the start by Bosch's party, the PRD but they had been joined immediately by the two Communist parties and the 14th June party which raised some possibility of collusion with the PRD but in general the United States did not think that Bosch was committed to the Communists. After three days' fighting, violent left-wing elements had taken control of the rebels after driving out elements of the PRD. Caamaño was something of a thug who was prepared to work for almost anybody. He had no strong political orientation but was a not very

---

1     These documentary sources are at times incomplete, and parts of some transcriptions were indecipherable. Some of the Foreign Office documenta have acronyms which are not clear. Some newspaper reports are pure propaganda or at best inaccurate, having been based on rumour and conjecture.

attractive opportunist. Mr. Rusk emphasised however that the United States was not hostile to the PRD. If the party were elected in, say, September the United States would [...] them. It should be possible to form a government from the spectrum of political forces stretching from the PRD and Left to elements on the Right. Mr. Rusk seemed to [...] a Balaguer-Bosch government might provide the best [...] he added that such a combination was highly unlikely [...] concluded this part of our conversation by saying [...] seemed to be out of contact with the realities in [...] imagining that his people were in control, which they were not. Neither Bosch nor Balaguer should go back to the Dominican Republic at this stage because it would be unsafe.

3. As regards the Communist role in the revolution [...] thought that the United States may have over-emphasized aspect a little in public statements in the past few [...] But the brittle political structure of the Dominican Republic had been shattered and a situation had arisen in which [...] determined armed group could get a long way very quick. [...] was the potential threat from the extreme Left (which [...] active) which was particularly worrying to the United States. [...] Mr. Rusk undertook to provide us as soon as possible with American evidence of Communist involvement in the revolution. I said that we also would be passing to him any information which we had on this, but warned him that we were unlike to come up with anything not already available to the Americans.

4. Mr. Rusk was clearly hopeful that the OAS Committee in Santo Domingo would be successful in its efforts to [...] proper cease-fire and the beginnings of a settlement and [...] was not disposed to consider at this stage what would happen if they come back empty-handed. He was not unduly [...] by the critical public remarks of several members of the [...] Privately they expressed their understanding of United States action. There had been no movement to censure the United States on the grounds that their action had been against Article [...] of the Charter and there seemed to be a strong similarity between OAS requests and recommendations and the action taken by the United States troops, such as the distribution of food and medicine. In conclusion Mr. Rusk remarked that the question "why did you do this?" was always easier to answer than "why did you not do this?".

ADVANCE COPIES:
Private Secretary
Sir G. Harrison
Mr. Greenhill
Hd American Dept.

**2. British Embassy, Santo Domingo 15 January 1966**

From Santo Domingo to Foreign Office

**Addressed to Foreign Office telegram No. 15 of 15 January**

Repeated for information saving to: Washington, UKMis New York

Your telegram No. 4

Following particulars of Caamaño (supplied by United States Embassy) are in addition to those given in my despatch No. 26 of 20 December 1965.

Born Santo Domingo 11 June 1932. Graduated Riverside Military Academy (Georgia) 1947 and joined Dominican Navy. Attended Dominican Naval Academy for 18 months and later returned to United States about six months. Trained in Marine Corps techniques and amphibious warfare. Has served in all branches of Dominican armed forces, including police, as Commander of riot control troops. He is now nominally on Air Force strength.

### 3. British Embassy, Santo Domingo 3 February 1966

British Embassy, Santo Domingo.

I am constantly being asked by various Dominican friends how Caamaño is making out in London. I have told them that until our next bag reaches us I have really no means of knowing, but I hope to hear soon. It is possible that the bag which will be opened tomorrow will bring a letter on the subject, but our own outward bag has to be closed this evening and I hope you will not mind my writing to ask you to let me have any information available about how he is spending his time and how he is getting on.

2. I had hoped to be able to talk to him quietly and at some length about what he wanted to do in England, but right up to the last moment he was exclusively concerned with what was going to happen to his officers and men who were staying behind and I had no chance to do so. He was going to come to our house for a small party I had laid on for the evening of Saturday 22 January; but at the last moment Hector García Godoy decided that he and the others (Montes Arache, Lachapelle and Peña Taveras) should leave at 12.30 pm on that day, instead of on the Sunday, so the party fell through. Ruth and I went to see him off at the helicopter base near the Embajador Hotel and we then went in a helicopter ourselves to the airport. So we did what we could in the circumstances, but I did not manage to get him by myself as he was at all times being got at by his own people or by hordes of journalists. He told one of the latter, in reply to a question about how he liked the idea of going to London, that he was looking forward to it but had really had no time to think about what he was going to do there, as all his thoughts had been for what was going to happen here. Perhaps by now he has been able to think about it.

3. I have no idea whether you have seen or are going to see him or, if so, how he strikes you. By Dominican standards he is rather a remarkable fellow, and I do not think there is any doubt that, unless he is bumped off by one or other of his enemies on the extreme right, he will be one of the leading personalities in this country for quite a long time, whatever he decides about staying in the Armed Forces or resigning and going into politics. Anything that can be done by us to make his stay in London enjoyable and useful from his point of view will be very well worth the effort from ours. As you know, Stafford Campbell knows him pretty well and, as in this kind of case personal relations make a great difference, I hope you will not mind my having asked that he should be alerted about Caamaño's arrival. I also hope, needless to say, that arrangements can be made for Caamaño to see whatever he wants in the way of parliamentary procedure, administration, economic activity and so on, in addition to what he would see in the normal run of being a Military Attaché.

4. I cannot at the moment give you any idea about how long he is likely to remain in London. I suppose, if things get bad here again before the elections, he will come back, but I hope this will not happen not only for obvious general reasons but because the longer he stays in London, assuming he likes it, the more useful his time there will be.

(I.W. Bell)

R.M.K. Slater, Esq,, C.M.G., [Companion (of the order of) St Michael and St George]
American Department,
Foreign Office,
LONDON

**4. Foreign Office, London 7 February 1966**

Colonel Francisco A. Caamaño

Colonel Caamaño seemed in excellent spirits when I had him to dinner on 25 January with Major General Rikhye of the United Nations. As you know, he had a good press the following day and according to News Department rather more coverage than President Frei on his state visit. Since then he has had influenza but now is reported fit. He has been found a good flat and he and his family from that point of view seem to have no problems.

2. Bill Harding put him in touch with Colonel Cassels at M.O.D. [Ministry of Defence] for M.A.'s [Military Attachés] visits to defence establishments. This unfortunately appears to be a slow process and nothing can happen in this sphere for three weeks. Caamaño now has time hanging on his hands and I gather is a little disappointed that he cannot get around the British scene a little more quickly. As he is more a political figure than a military one I wonder if it might not be a good thing to put him on the social/educational/industrial/ welfare net for visits such as I believe J.H. Moore copes with so adequately in Visits Section of I.S.D. [Information Services Division]. I recommend this because Caamaño is going to Paris soon and will certainly be given the treatment there (including, I am told, an unofficial interview with de Gaulle). If it could be arranged, I think it would be worth it — he is almost certain to be President of the Dominican Republic within the next five years anyway.

3. He keeps in touch with the Dominican political pot by telephone several times weekly.

S.F. Campbell

7 February 1966

Mr. G.C. Mayhew,
American Department.

*It might be worth pursuing the proposal in para 2 of Mr. Campbell's minute though I am not sure what I.S.D. can offer to a resident M.A. Moreover there must be a large number of potential presidents of small countries masquerading as M.A.'s in London at present. On balance, therefore, I am inclined to think that we should leave this as it is subject to any views that I.S.D. may have.*

*Draft to Mr. Bell.*

*C. Mayhew 9.2*

*We have in the past arranged programmes of visits for members of foreign Embassies in London and I see no reason at all why we should not offer the same facilities to*

*Col. Caamaño. But, as we usually do in such cases, we should have to ask him to be responsible for his hotel expenses if (as we would hope to do) we took him out of London for a while. Would this be acceptable?*

*JH(?) Moore 21/2*

*American Department (Mr. Mayhew)*

*This is encouraging. Would you care to sound Col. Caamaño on the question of expenses?*

*W. Harding 25/2*

*Mr. Campbell [word indecipherable]*

*Payment for his hotel expenses would be quite acceptable to Col. Caamaño.*

*[signature indecipherable] 2/3/66*

*Then let us offer him some visits. Would I.S.D. be good enough to arrange this?*

*W. Harding 4/3*

*Received to-day… We generally like to keep in step with Protocol Dept in offering visits facilities of this kind, and we should be grateful if they could see these papers before Col. Caamaño is approached. Incidentally, shall we approach him? Does he need an interpreter?*

*(JH?) Moore 10/3*

*American Dept (Mr. Harding)*
*Protocol Dept (Mr. Stow)*

*After speaking to Mr. Stow I tried to arrange a meeting over lunch with Col. Caamaño with a view to discussing with him his form and content of one or more visits. I had in mind that he might be interested in Local Government, Police, Social Services, Education, Housing and possibly some aspects of Industry. Unfortunately, he proved, and is still proving, elusive. I still have hopes of meeting him at Senor Cabral's home (Dominican Embassy) before Easter; but in case I do not succeed, would Mr. Campbell be good enough to raise this question again when next he sees him?*

*W. Harding 29/3*

*I.R.D. [Information Research Department] Mr. Campbell*

*With pleasure, but the form and content is already known. This is, as Mr. Harding says, above but I would definitely include industry because (a) he wants to see it (b) he might be a Minister one day and should leave this country with a high opinion of British industry.*

*I think we can go ahead on Local Govt, Social Services, Education, Housing, Industry, Police etc. I will ascertain when he will be free.*

*26/4 Mr. Harding [signature indecipherable]*

## 5. Foreign Office, London 11 February 1988

Foreign Office, SWI
11 February, 1966

Thank you for your letter 01/1/2 of 3 February about Caamaño's activities in London.

2. You will have seen from the press cuttings we have sent you that he had a good press here. Indeed, according to News Department, he received rather more coverage than President Frei on his State Visit. We have also been looking after him. Bill Harding met him ten days ago and gave him some good advice on whom to meet and whom not to meet in London and Stafford Campbell had dinner with him on 25 January with General Rikhye. Since then he has had influenza but now is reported fit. He has been found a good flat and he and his family have no problems from that point of view.

3. Bill Harding also put him in touch with the office at the Ministry of Defence responsible for Military Attaché's visits to Defence establishments and we hope that something will be arranged in this sphere in the next week or so. In the meantime we are looking into the possibility of seeing whether we could inject him into the Foreign Office Visits net.

4. All in all, therefore, I think we can rest assured that Caamaño is being well looked after. He is in constant touch with Stafford Campbell and we in the Department are on the look out for suitable opportunities to ensure that his stay in this country is as happy and productive as possible. He is, as you probably know, and as we know from him, in touch with his friends in Santo Domingo by telephone several times weekly.

(R.M.K. Slater)

I.W. Bell, Esq., C.B.E.
SANTO DOMINGO

## 6. British Embassy, Santo Domingo 16 February 1966

BRITISH EMBASSY,
SANTO DOMINGO.

Various people here have told me that Caamaño and Ramfis Trujillo have been meeting in London. My informants are mostly Americans, but one or two are Dominicans with definite right-wing sympathies. I have therefore treated the report with, to say the least, reserve, and have limited my comments to saying that, as Ramfis has a son at school in England, this is a good reason for his going to London from time to time and that it does not necessarily mean that he has gone there to see Caamaño.

2. This would not be worth passing on were it not for the fact that the other night Tap Bennett raised the subject with me. I asked him whether he really thought there was anything in it, and he replied that in his opinion there might well be. Ramfis and Caamaño had been buddies in the Trujillo days and they might still be friends, to which I replied that that may well be so but that I thought it unlikely that Caamaño would risk his reputation by getting together with him now.

3. Any chance to smear Caamaño, of course, is grist to Tap Bennett's mill. I asked him if he had any evidence for the report and he said no, what Caamaño did in London was more our concern than his provided he behaves himself; and it is certainly not part of my functions to defend Caamaño's political reputation. On the other hand, as this Embassy has fairly consistently taken the line that he is a sincere and, by Dominican standards, incorruptible person, it would be nice to know that this story is untrue. I am not, of course, suggesting that any investigation should be made, but if by any chance anyone in the Department — or Stafford Campbell, for instance — were seeing Caamaño it might be possible to get him on the subject of Ramfis and see what his reactions are.

*Yours ever,*

*Ian*

(I.W. Bell)

R.M.K. Slater, Esq., C.M.G.,
American Department,
Foreign Office,
London, S.W.1.

*The sense of what Caamaño tells his friend in his Consular Section (not his Consul himself, I think) is getting through to Washington. I do not think that we ought to push them into a more profound dialogue if they are not ready for it.*

*W.Harding 29/3*

*Mr. Campbell*

*P.U.S.D. [Permanent Under Secretary's Department] (Miss McNab) E.M. 17/S*

*I will have an opportunity of putting more questions, I hope, during April.*

*2. Regarding the dialogue between Caamaño and the US Consular Office, I believe that this has stopped. Has it now begun again? It had not been done so last Thursday (24 Mar.). My impression was that it needed restarting.*

*S.R. (?) Campbell 29/3*

*I spoke accordingly to Mr Lowery (US Embassy) who was grateful for this tip and will arrange for it to be followed up.*

*2. I think I have met the Vice Consul concerned, whose name is Gwynne or some sort, at Victor Cabral's house.*

*W. Harding 1/4*

*Thank you. I believe Gwynne is the name you mentioned, but in the Latin American mouth it is one of those names that come off badly! For your information, Mr. Dodds-Parker, Conservative member for Cheltenham, telephoned yesterday asking if I would bring Caamaño to lunch with him. I was away, and the date is not yet fixed.*

*S.R. (?) Campbell 5/4*

## 7. Latin American and Caribbean Section, Joint Foreign Office, Central Research Office, Research Department, Foreign Office, London 22 February 1966[2]

JOINT RESEARCH DEPARTMENT MEMORANDUM

### THE '14 JUNE' MOVEMENT IN THE DOMINICAN REPUBLIC

A. The 14 June Movement, the largest extreme Left group in the Dominican Republic, developed under Cuban inspiration (Paragraph 1)

B. The first attempt at insurrection (Paragraphs 2–3)

C. The relative degrees of Communist and Fidelista influence (Paragraphs 4–7)

D. Activities following the fall of Trujillo (Paragraphs 8–9)

E. The second attempt at insurrection (Paragraphs 10–13)

F. Role during the rising of April 1965; attempt to exploit the revolutionary possibilities of the civil war (Paragraphs 14–17)

G. Struggle within the leadership between Nationalists and Communists; probable future strategy (Paragraphs 18–19)

The Movimiento Revolucionario 14 de Junio, sometimes known as the Agrupación Política 14 de Junio, is the largest and possibly the most important organisation of extreme Left in the Dominican Republic. Its name and history betoken its Cuban inspiration. On 14 June 1959, an expeditionary force of anti-Trujillo Dominicans landed from Cuba with the object of launching a guerrilla campaign which would overthrow Trujillo as Castro's guerrillas had overthrown Batista. The invasion failed, as had Castro's earlier attack on the Moncada barracks on 26 July 1953, which gave his movement its martyrs and its name. The Dominican Revolutionaries sought to turn their initial defeat to account in the same way. A second rising followed in 1963 and proved equally abortive. The upheaval of April 1965 gave the 14 June movement its third opportunity, but here too success eluded them. There is, however, no reason to believe that the movement, or at least its more extreme leaders, have abandoned their original hope of seizing power by armed rising on Cuban lines. Their most recent bid was made in the streets of Santo Domingo, but authentic Fidelista tactics posit guerrilla operations from rural bases. It is possible that the next move by the 14 June revolutionaries may be made from such a quarter. Though the uncertainties of the present situation in the Dominican Republic

2    The *Foreign Office/Central Research Office Research Department* was an autonomous unit based in the Foreign Office which collated material from diplomatic, press and intelligence sources. Established at the beginning of the Cold War, in the late 1940s, its work included background briefing of the press as well as providing information to government officials.

rule out all predictions, a study of the past record of the 14 June Movement may suggest the lines on which it could seek to develop.

## The first insurrection (June 1959)

2. Most of the members of the expeditionary force raised in Cuba were Dominican exiles, though there were also some volunteers of other nationalities. A few of the Dominicans belonged to the PSP (Partido Socialista Popular, the Dominican Communist Party — now known as such — whose leaders had gone into exile in the forties) or the MDP (Movimiento Popular Dominicano, a rival Communist group founded in Cuba in 1956 and led by Máximo López Molina and Andrés Ramos Peguero, a Dominican who had served under Castro with the rank of captain). The expedition's commander was Enrique Jiménez Moya, another Dominican volunteer who had fought as a captain in Castro's forces. There was also a Cuban adviser, Major Delio Gomez Ochoa, who enjoyed the confidence of Fidel Castro and was probably the real leader of the expedition. The revolutionaries flew in by plane (said to have been provided by Venezuela, then on good terms with the Castro regime) from Cuba to Constanza, in the sparsely populated Cordillera Central 60 miles from the capital. They numbered some 50 men. After clashing with the small local garrison, they look to the hills where — though a few held out until 10 July — they were all hunted down. A few days after the arrival of the aircraft at Constanza, a further 150 men landed on the north coast at Estero Hondo and Maimón. They too were rounded up by the Trujillo forces with the help of the local peasants. Jiménez Moya and almost all the captured expeditionaries were put to death. (Gomez Ochoa was held as a hostage for possible bargaining with Castro and survived into the post-Trujillo era).

3. The failure of the invasion did not eradicate pro-Castro feeling in the Dominican Republic and the savage treatment meted out to the expeditionaries may have increased sympathy for them. (Some of the prisoners were said to have been taken to the San Isidro Air Force Base where the cadets were ordered to carry out their execution). In the months following the invasion fiasco, a clandestine anti-Trujillo organisation calling itself Movimiento Revolucionario 14 de Junio took shape throughout the republic. Its aim was to prepare for a further armed rising, but — according to a Cuban account — "its unmasking in January 1960 by Trujillo's Servicio de Inteligencia Militar (SIM) prevented it from carrying out any important action, since most of its leaders were either killed, imprisoned, or forced into exile". When the dictator was finally struck down, on 30 May 1961, it was not by the hand of the 14 June Movement.

## Manuel Tavarez Justo and the Communists

4. The most outstanding organiser of the Movement, and its acknowledged leader until his death, was Dr Manuel (Manolo) Tavarez Justo. His wife, Minerva Mirabal, and her two sisters (one of them married to Leandro Gusmàn, one of the more moderate leaders of the movement) were also active members. The brutal murder of all three sisters by Trujillo's henchmen as they were returning from a visit to their imprisoned husbands outraged public opinion and gave the movement its most celebrated martyrs. Tavarez Justo thus had bitter personal motives, as well as political principles, to feed his animosity against the Trujillo regime. According to ex-President Bosch, "he was a vehement and honest leader, who saw himself obliged to keep his party to a revolutionary line which verged on the extreme Left, to prevent it from falling altogether into the Communist camp. The young 14 June members were frank admirers of Fidel Castro, who had defeated Batista after a prolonged guerrilla war, and this made them vulnerable to Communist penetration. So long as Tavarez Justo lived, the Communist never succeeded in controlling the party. After his death, as was bound to happen, the youth of the middle class, who were mostly 14 June members and, later, Social Christians, were left without a guide".

5. We can only speculate as to whether, had he lived, Tavarez Justo would have kept his movement to revolutionary but non-Communist lines. His Marxism-Leninism, at that time, appears to have resembled the romantic brand of Marxism-Leninism professed by Fidel Castro before 1962. A speaker at a 14 June rally in Santo Domingo later reaffirmed and justified the non-Communist character of the movement in its early stages in the following terms: "It was a time when the Cuban revolution was still within the framework of representative democracy, and was regarded by all revolutionaries of the continent as the model solution to the age-old problems of Latin America. The revolution of the 14 June heroes would not have been a Communist revolution. The fact that the Cuban revolution later became a Communist revolution does not mean that the glorious June martyrs came to establish on our soil a Communist revolution ... Our revolution is a revolution within representative democracy".

6. It is interesting to compare such statements with the Communists' own assessment of the movement. Writing *Cuba Socialista* shortly after Trujillo's fall, the Dominican Communist leader Juan Ducoudray declared: "The 14 June Movement was the central organisation for the underground struggle against the tyranny. Its leaders have recently been released from prison. It is chiefly made up of young professional people, students, and office workers. It represents the interests of the *petite bourgeoisie* and of certain sectors of the well-to-do peasantry. Its programme draws attention to some of the chronic ills of Dominican society and advocates important popular demands, including land

reform. Under the influence of the anti-Trujillista *bourgeoisie*, the leadership of the 14 June Movement has vacillated and has adopted standpoints which are at times progressive and at others reactionary. But it contains a strong Leftist current which is democratic and nationalistic".

7. It was this "strong Leftist current" which the Communists sought to control by infiltrating the movement. Their attitude was defined by a statement of the Central Committee of the PSP put out in January 1964 and quoted in an article in the *World Marxist Review* of June 1964. After describing the 14 June Movement as "the largest movement of the Left ... which enjoys prestige and influence among the masses", the statement goes on to declare that "the Communists were the first to recognize this role which history has allotted to the comrades of the 14 June Movement. If the two parties diverge on some tactical questions, they are in complete agreement on the strategic aims of the revolution. That which unites them is far greater than anything which can divide them. On the basis of this identity of purpose, the People's Socialist Party strives to maintain relations of friendship and close co-operation with the 14 June Revolutionary Movement, as with all revolutionary forces".

### Activities after the fall of Trujillo

8. The fall of Trujillo and the exile of his family permitted the 14 June Movement to operate openly. But its attitude towards the Council of State headed by Licenciado Rafael Bonnelly was ambivalent. The moderates in the movement wished to co-operate with it, and one of them (Dr. Fernández Caminero) was even nominated a member of the Council. But the extremists, mostly young students, plotted with the MPD to start a Castro-style rising in the Cordillera Central and to assassinate a number of important figures. The rising was timed for the beginning of January 1962. The extremists were however dissuaded by the moderates in view of their inexperience, the military precautions being taken by the regime, and the more promising possibilities now offered for constitutional advance. In his public pronouncements, Tavarez Justo tried to put pressure on the Council by threatening direct action unless the Administration gave speedy effect to its promise to introduce radical reforms.

9. The presidential and congressional elections of December 1962 resulted in an overwhelming victory for Juan Bosch and his Partido Revolucionario Dominicano (PRD) over Dr. Viriato Fiallo and the Unión Cívica Nacional (UCN). Whilst the PRD drew its support predominantly from the peasantry and urban working classes, the UCN, which had started life in June 1961 as a non-party organisation formed to co-ordinate the campaign to expel Trujillo's heirs, had by the time of the elections been labelled the party of upper and middle class reactionaries, since it had expelled the PSP agitators who had managed to infiltrate its ranks in the early days. The 14 June Movement, which

continued to exert a strong appeal amongst the professional class and the youth of the middle class as a whole, joined the PSP in boycotting the elections. After President Bosch's victory, they gave qualified support to the Administration, but did not join the Governments on the grounds that the armed forces must first be purged of Trujillo elements. At the same time, at the instigation of the more extremist leaders such as Maximo Bernard (Bernal) Valdez, some sections at least of the movement pressed ahead with para-military preparations, either in expectations of the showdown with the military which they deemed inevitable, or as a means of bringing pressure to bear on Bosch Government, or else themselves seizing power from it. In official statements issued in 1963 and subsequently, the movement continued to declare that "the 14 June movement is not Communist, but a revolutionary anti-imperialist, anti-feudal group", the aims of which were defined as "the defence of the 1963 Constitution, the consolidation of the economic and social gains achieved by the people through its heroic struggle, and the prevention of Trujillo-type dictatorship by the exploiting class".

**The second insurrection (November 1963)**

10. In September 1963 the political scene was radically changed by the military coup which ousted President Bosch. At the end of the following months, the leaders of the 14 June Movement decided to take up arms. This step, apparently taken after a sharp division of opinion, appears surprising. The 14 June Movement was not outlawed and its leaders were under no pressure to seek desperate remedies. They must have been aware of the amateur status of their rank and file for the highly specialized technique of guerrilla warfare. Furthermore, the cowed state of the metropolitan working class, which had just allowed its elected President to be shipped out of the country without a single protest, gave little promise of even moral support. To opt for a guerrilla rising in such unfavourable conditions seems folly, unless the revolutionary leaders were reckoning in decisive help from other quarters. There is some evidence that they did in fact expect such help form two sources: from Cuba, and from large-scale defections from the Dominican Armed Forces.

11. The revolutionaries' Cuban mentors, who had sponsored the abortive invasion of 1959 and no doubt wished to vindicate their creed of guerrilla insurrection, appear to have adhered to their plans even after the disappearance of the Trujillo dictatorship. They continued to provide facilities in Cuba for Dominican revolutionaries throughout 1963, and by the end of that year some two dozen 14 June members were deported to have completed their six-months course of training. A month after the ousting of President Bosch, the Cubans were planning the despatch by sea of a consignment of arms and ammunition. The operation was delayed by bad weather and the arms only

reached the Dominican Republic after the failure of the November rising, most of the consignment being intercepted by the Dominican authorities.

12. The leaders of the 14 June Movement probably set higher hopes on large-scale defections from the Dominican armed forces. Opportunistic deals between the most unlikely partners have been a feature of Dominican politics. The Marxist MPD, for instance, has admitted negotiating with Ramfis Trujillo, son of the Dictator, for the supply of arms to be used against the "Yankees", whom he blamed for his father's death. That the deal fell through has been attributed by the MPD to unreliable elements in the 14 June Movement. The latter, in turn, seem to have had secret links with General Imbert, from whom they had at varying times received arms and funds. There is some evidence to suggest that, after the ousting of President Bosch, and possibly in order to provoke a shadow guerrilla rising and thus persuade the United States to speed recognition of a junta which appeared to be jeopardized by a Castro-type challenge, Imbert duped the 14 June Movement leaders into believing that, once they launched a revolt, they could count on a supply of arms and defections *en masse* from the army and the police force. Whether or not the revolutionaries were tricked into believing that this would happen, the decision was taken that guerrilla bands should go into action at the end of November in six different areas of the country. But the peasantry failed to rise, no supporting movement occurred in the towns, and no defections took place from the armed forces. Some weapons had been supplied to them by Imbert but 90 per cent of them proved to be defective. Though its last group managed to hold out for just over three weeks, the insurrection collapsed. Tavarez Justo was captured. The fact that he and 16 other leaders were then shot in cold blood, and the speed with which the army nipped the rising in the bud, lends credence to the explanation that the military leaders had been privy to the plot and took care that those they had duped should not live to tell the tale.

13. The failure of the second insurrection crippled the 14 June Movement and robbed it of its most prestigious leader. It also exacerbated differences of opinion amongst those who aspired to leadership. The moderates (who now increasingly referred to their movement as the Agrupación Política 14 de Junio) held that their best hope was to explore possibilities of joint action with the followers of Juan Bosch and with the Revolutionary Christian Socialist Party (PRSC). The Communist leaders of the PSP also saw in the failure of the rising a confirmation of their view that a true revolutionary situation did not yet exist in the country, since the people were mainly concerned with re-establishing political liberty and the Constitution of 1963. The extremists, on the other hand, argued that defeat had been due to "subjective" rather than "objective" factors. They diagnosed the former as (1) lack of adequate preparations, (2) the

selection of guerrillas on too romantic a basis, without regard to their physical capacities or training, (3) failure to establish themselves in the zones allotted to them, some detachments getting separated from their peasant guides, (4) unserviceable weapons, (5) failure of supplies and communications, (6) tactical errors in the course of military operations. These, they argued, were faults which arose form the shortcomings of the revolutionaries and did not indicate the absence of a revolutionary situation. It followed that the movement ought to adhere to its tactics of armed revolt and seek a fresh opportunity to carry their plans into effect. The extremists thus favoured co-operation with the MPD who held similar views.

### Role in the rising of April 1965

14. Despite a divided leadership, and the imprisonment or exile of many implicated in the second insurrection, the 14 June Movement still commanded a substantial following in the Dominican Republic. It was particularly strong in the University of Santo Domingo where it captured control of the Federation of Dominican Students. The leaders of the movement now included the following: Jaime Durán (Secretary-General of the Provisional Executive Committee), Roberto Duverge and Norge Botello Fernandez (Secretaries of Organization), Rafael ("Fafa") Taveras, Fidelio Despradel Roque, Dr. Benjamin Ramos Alvarez, Juan B. Mejia, Dr. Rogelio Mejia and Emma Tavarez Justo (sister of the late leader). Several of these had received military training in Cuba, the sentence of exile actually proving for them a blessing in disguise since it enabled them to make their way to that country. In the months preceding the rising of April 1965, a number of these Dominicans trained in guerrilla warfare, either members of the 14 June Movement or of other extremist groups, made their way back to the Dominican Republic.

15. The leaders of the 14 June Movement, however, can claim little or no credit for sparking off the events of April 1965. They appear to have come to the fore only after 26 April when, fearing probably that General Wessin's tanks would win the day, Colonel Caamaño and the regular officers leading the revolt took asylum in foreign embassies, leaving the field to the militant youth who repulsed Wessin's tanks and infantry with well-directed bazooka fire and Molotov cocktails. The opening of the arsenals resulted in the arming of many more 14 June and other militant Leftist groups. Wessin's advance held, Caamaño and the other temporary asylees emerged and resumed the struggle. The 14 June leaders, whose training in guerrilla warfare now stood them in good stead, accepted, somewhat grudgingly, overall direction by Caamaño's military staff in face of the common enemy. Neither they, nor their associates with known Communist antecedents, appeared openly in positions of power in Caamaño's entourage.

16. The 14 June Movement declared in its public statements that it represented the broad anti-feudal, anti-imperialist, and democratic aspirations of the Dominican people, especially the peasants, "the powerful reserve of the Dominican Revolution", and claimed to be fighting "to drive the Yankee invader from our land, enforce the 1963 democratic Constitution and establish constitutional government". The general tone of the movement was however strongly anti-United States and it became apparent that, though there still appeared to be moderates in the movement, the trend of events was strengthening the hand of the extremists. At a large rally held on 14 June and attended by Caamaño and his chief lieutenants, "Fafa" Taveras emphasised that "the Dominican's destiny will not be won at the negotiating table, but only through rifle and war ... We must defeat the United States man to man", and concluded that "there is no other way but to extend the war to the whole people, to take the struggle to the interior".

17. As negotiating proceeded, under the aegis of the OAS, for the end of hostilities and the establishment of a provisional Government, the 14 June leaders became more intransigent. Any provisional Government, they held, would inevitably be a creature of the United States, which would use force if necessary to prevent it from developing in a "progressive" direction. Armed revolution and the expulsion of the American forces thus remained the only goal, and though these might not be feasible to attempt at present, the movement would in no circumstances allow itself to be disarmed. Dr. García Godoy, the provisional President designate, was Deñóunced as a puppet and the Act of Reconciliation a humbug. Their opposition to the proposal that Colonel Caamaño should enter into the negotiations, which led to the formation of the provisional Government, was defeated by the insistence of the PRD and the PRSC that the matter should be put to a "democratic" vote. The 14 June Movement was substantially outvoted on this issue and its relative weakness was exposed. Nevertheless it continued its propaganda in favour of the creation of an "anti-imperialist and anti-feudal front", in which all Left-wing forces, including the Communists and progressive Catholics, would stand shoulder to shoulder "under the leadership of the working class". Such was the attitude of the 14 June Movement when, at the beginning of September, the provisional Government began uneasily to take up the reins of power.

18. During the first three months of Dr. García Godoy's administration, the 14 June Movement has attracted little publicity. It is believed to be going through a difficult period of struggle between its Communist and Nationalist wings. Fidelio Despradel is the leading Communist protagonist, whilst the Nationalist attitude is championed by "Fafa" Taveras, who at present seems to be in the ascendant. The emphasis given to armed action at the Three

Continents Conference in Havana will probably find an echo in the Dominican Republic before long. Some defections have already occurred from the 14 June Movement, and a split is probably inevitable.

**Conclusions**

19. From the above outline the following tentative conclusions may be drawn:

The 14 June Movement was modelled on the Cuban pattern, and its first venture was directly instigated by Castro. Some of its members have received training in Cuba. It is probable however that there remain serious divergence of opinion between moderates and extremists in the movement's leadership.

The appeal of the Movement has hitherto been mainly to the professional classes and white-collar workers, particularly the youth. Its role in the recent disturbances may, however, have widened its support, and it is now making a bid to build up an anti-Government alliance of all Left-wing parties.

The movement is strongly Nationalist and anti-American. It professes to be non-Communist but has collaborated with Communist groups (more closely with the MPD than with the PSP). The latter however is believed to have infiltrated the movement's leadership to some extent. The outlook of most 14 June leaders is probably akin to that of the "new Communists" round Castro, who profess Marxism-Leninism without having acquired a real grasp of it.

The leaders of the movement are likely to do everything in their power to evade or resist the handing-in of weapons by their followers. To what extent they may have set up arms caches in the rural areas is not known. But the Castroite mystique of guerrilla warfare has not been renounced and, despite past failures, there may well be a recrudescence of guerrilla and other subversive actions when circumstances seem more favourable.

Latin American and Caribbean Section
Joint FO/CRO Research Department

## 8. Foreign Office, London 26 March 1966

Recently, I had a long talk with Colonel Caamaño alone. As the result of this, I formed the impression — but I cannot be sure — that he would now not be averse to a private and unofficial exchange of views with someone in the American Embassy here. As I understand that our American friends have been interested in establishing contact with him it occurs to me that my impression might be of interest to them, and, if you feel like doing so, perhaps you could tell your contact in the American Embassy. Previously, as you know, he has shown himself to be wary of overt contact with the Americans here, and I am still sure that he would shy away from anything too obvious such as going in the front door at Grosvenor Square, or anything that might render him vulnerable in the Dominican Republic to charges of betraying the "cause" etc. For this reason a private and unofficial approach, at least at first, would seem to be the best.

2. During our conversation, we discussed the Dominican elections and the chances of getting to some kind of political stability in the future. He said he knew that both the Communists and the extreme Right were as one in not wanting the elections at any price, and were both doing their best to make them impossible. If the free elections planned for June were frustrated by these minority elements he thought a new phase of unrest and violence could not be avoided. In the popular mind the election was their only chance of making a start on the road to some sort of normality, however small. Elections themselves would hardly solve the Dominicans' problems, and maybe would create new ones, but the April revolt and afterwards had been about the constitutional issue, and this theme would come up again and again until, in some way, it was satisfied. Under the surface, public feeling in this issue was explosive. In the final essence, the reason for the failure and removal of Wessin, Imbert, and Rivera Caminero, one after the other, was their open opposition to constitutional government, and as this was what "the people" wanted, these men had eventually ceased to make political sense. Balaguer is aware of the importance of the constitutional issue, as is Bosch. He told me that if he went back suddenly to the Dominican Republic it would be to fight for it. When he said this, he clearly meant with a gun.

3. I said that supposing the free elections came off and a constitutional government followed, the most important factor operating on the future was always the relationship between the Dominican Republic and the USA. A bad relationship would be unrealistic for a Dominican leader because it would keep the Dominican boat rocking dangerously. How did he view relations with the USA in this context? He said that the Dominican Republic, for geographical and other reasons, was part of the American system and that there was no sense

in pretending it could be anything else. This was a fact. A national leader who tried to govern on any other basis would need to have his head examined. Answering my question, he personally had no enmity whatever for the US — some individuals, yes, but they were not the US, by any means. Dominicans looked naturally to the USA for leadership and help. He, personally, accepted American leadership. He was not a fool. The Americans, however, sometimes forgot *dignidad* in their dealings with the Dominicans and this had caused trouble unnecessarily.

4. I asked him if he intended to stand as a candidate for the forthcoming elections and he said he would not. The 24th April Movement however (which was not a political party) would back the PRD candidate whether he be Bosch or anyone else. Beyond the June elections, however, Caamaño clearly sees himself as a potential presidential candidate, and is consciously preparing himself for this role.

5. I asked him if he had met anyone yet from the American Embassy and he said that he had had a private talk with the American Consul recently. It was evident that he thought very highly of this man because he said that dialogues on these lines could remove many misunderstandings on both sides. Answering my question he said at the moment he knew of no plans for more talks of this nature. The way this was said indicated that he would like them.

6. If our American friends still think it would be to their advantage to talk to Caamaño, I suggest that they fix a definite appointment in an unofficial setting and choose someone on their side who can speak Spanish really fluently. The Consul who made a distinct impression on Caamaño is apparently bi-lingual and I should have thought he would be an excellent choice, at least to begin with.

Mr. Harding, American Dept.

S.F. Campbell
28 March, 1966

*This is a useful account of Caamaño's current thinking. Paragraph 4 is particularly important. I hope that Mr. Campbell will be able to continue this close contact. It might be worth putting to Caamaño the question: what if the elections were postponed until next year at Bosch's instigation (as seems by no means impossible?).[3] Would violence and disorder ensue? And might Caamaño run against Bosch in those circumstances?*

*2. We have evidence, which I am (?) for Mr. Campbell to see, that the U.S. Embassy contact with Caamaño is working well, at least in the ... (text ends)*

---

3   See report on US support for this position. p. 169.

### 9. American Embassy, London 19 April 1966

G.F. Hall Esq.,
Assistant Head,
American Department,
Foreign Office, Whitehall, S.W.1
*With the Compliments of the American Embassy*

Our Mr. Gwynn (junior officer in the Embassy's Consular Section) has had another chat with Caamaño — results attached.[4] I gather you have heard about Gwynn's earlier talk with the Colonel through other channels.

Arthur Woodruff

SUBJECT: *details of the meeting with Colonel Caamaño on 11 April*

*This contact with the US Embassy should act as a useful safety-valve for Caamaño. Mr. Gwynn is a fluent Spanish speaker with some years of experience in Latin America.*

2. Caamaño and Guerra left by air for Brussels on 15 April and are returning this evening.

*W. Harding 19/4.*

*I.R.D. (Mr. Campbell)*

---

4   For text, dated 13 April, of US State Department report on meeting with Caamaño, see section on US Documents below, p. 175.

## 10. American Department Foreign Office, 1 July 1966[5]

SUBJECT: *Col. Caamaño and other Dominicans have been given possession of a flat at 8, Palace Gate, without permission and approval and the matter has been put in the hands of the police.*

*I learned today from a close friend of Col. Caamaño (Señor Henry Molina) that he is fed up with life in a flat surrounded by yelling children and is thinking of trying to find a house with a garden. He apparently has no plans for an early return to the Dominican Republic.*

*2. Can Protocol Dept. advise what steps might be taken to help Col. Caamaño find other accommodation?*

*W. Harding 8/7*

*Protocol Dept.*

*The main practical help we can offer is limited to putting Col. Caamaño in touch with reputable House Agents who can provide something suitable. We do not have any list of desirable properties.*

*I find this letter peculiar. Are the Estate Co. alleging that Col. Caamaño is in illegal possession of the flat and not paying any rent? If so we can take action but if not I do not see how we can forward the points they make to the Ambassador at all.*

*W. Harding 12/7*

*I had an appointment for speaking to the Dominican Embassy about this today.*

*Draft.*

*W. Harding 19/7*

*(Copies forward to Protocol Department 20/7, P.U.S.D 22/7., I.R.D. 3/8)*

---

5   This exchange of Foreign Office correspondence followed receipt of a letter dated 1 July 1966 from Mr. John Clark of the estate agents, Gunn Clark, concerning Caamaño's occupancy of the first floor flat of 8 Palace Gate, London W8. The estate agents claimed that Caamaño had taken possession of the flat without their permission, that 'a considerable group not confined to the Republic of Dominica' was in the practice of visiting the flat, and that the wife of the Australian High Commissioner, whose garden backed onto that of the Palace Gate flats, had telephoned the day before to complain about noise on the flat balcony. The estate agents requested the Foreign Office to contact the Dominican Embassy on their behalf. An interim acknowledgement (no copy in files) was sent by the Foreign Office on 5 July and a more extended letter on 21 July, signed by G W Harding of the American Department, recommending that, if there was a 'breach of the peace', they contact the police and enquiring whether Caamaño's occupancy of the flat was illegal. Harding's letter also recommended that the best way for Gunn Clark to solve the problem was to help Caamaño find other accommodation. No reply from Gunn Clark is recorded.

*A.) Gunn Clark Estates to American Dept 23/7*

*I do not think that this calls for a reply; should Caamaño not after all quit the property by the end of July, Gunn Clark Estates will certainly let me know.*

*J.C.B. 1/8*

*Fascinating!*

*2. Mr Cabral told me that Col. Caamaño might go back to the Dominican Republic in two or three months (2nd August). I personally think this is wishful thinking because it is my impression that recent events have made it even more unlikely that Balaguer let him come back.*

*S.R. Campbell 3/8*

*I.R.D.*

*Jennifer Blagden 4/8*

**11. Foreign Office, 6 February 1967**

**London Annual Review Dominican Republic 1966**

*Foreign Office and Whitehall Distribution*

DOMINICAN REPUBLIC
6 February 1967
Section 1

**DOMINICAN REPUBLIC: ANNUAL REVIEW FOR 1966**

*Mr. Bell to Mr. Brown. (Received 6 February)*

SUMMARY

The politico-military crisis with which the year opened was not resolved until two days before the election campaign opened on the 1st of March (Paragraphs 1–9)

The presidential elections (Paragraphs 10–13)

The withdrawal of the Inter-American Peace Force, and the solution of problems still hanging over from the civil war (Paragraphs 14–15)

Balaguer's emphasis in economic questions (Paragraphs 16–18)

The Opposition, and Balaguer's tactics towards it (Paragraphs 19–21)

-----------------------------

Santo Domingo,
2 February 1967

I have the honour to submit my review of events in the Dominican Republic in 1966.

2. The year fell neatly into halves. The first belonged to the Provisional Government headed by Dr. García Godoy, the second to Dr. Joaquìn Balaguer, who took office as President of the Republic on the 1st July. The change was rather more consequential than the routine transfer of power from one Administration to its successor. It marked the restoration of at least the outward forms of constitutional government and the onset of a more frigid political climate.

3. The year began in the critical aftermath of the "Battle Hotel Matum", at Santiago which had brought the conflict between the civil power and

the military leaders finally into the open. During the first days of January Dominicans — and not only Dominicans — waited anxiously to see what the Provisional President would, or could, do to assert his authority. On the 3rd of January he broadcast his judgment. To the fury of the Constitutionalists, he laid the blame on both factions. Nevertheless, a number of officers would shortly be sent overseas. Three days later he announced their names and destinations. The departure list was headed by the Minister for the Armed Forces, Commodore Rivera Caminero, appointed to Washington as Naval Attaché. Also included were the Army and Air Force Chiefs of Staff (posted as Military Attachés at Buenos Aires and Tel Aviv), and three leading Constitutionalists officers, Colonel Caamaño being appointed Military Attaché in London.

4. Would they go? On the answer hung the fate of Dr. García Godoy's Administration and the chances of the Provisional Government being able to carry out its principal mandate, the holding of general elections in June. Dr. García Godoy's decision looked like a dangerous gamble, but he had a fairly strong hand. On the 7th of January the Ad Hoc Committee of the Organisation of the American States (OAS) issued a forthright statement that any attempt to overthrow the Provisional Government would not be tolerated. The last thing the United States Government wanted, however, was that the Inter-American Peace Force (IAPF) should be called upon to intervene against the Dominican Armed Forces and misgivings felt by many Dominicans that Dr. García Godoy had overplayed his hand were fully shared by the Americans.

5. These misgivings proved misplaced. For Dr. García Godoy the military problem was essentially a Dominican one. A solution imposed by the IAPF would be no solution at all, and he had no intention of calling on it to intervene. Instead, with admirable patience, he gave the military leaders scope and rope enough to tie themselves in such knots as eventually only he could undo for them. He agreed that they should not leave until after the Constitutionalist officers had gone. Colonel Caamaño took some persuading, but after a fortnight's negotiation with the Provisional President over guarantees for his troops still in the "27 de Febrero" Camp, he and the two other Constitutionalist officers left on the 22nd of January. The way was now clear for Commodore Rivera Caminero and the Army and Air Force Chiefs of Staff to follow their good example.

6. Colonel Caamaño's proclaimed philosophy was that soldiers must obey orders. It was not Commodore Rivera Caminero's. This man had been Minister of the Armed Forces in the Imbert "government", and Dr. García Godoy had only reluctantly, and at American insistence, included him in his own Cabinet. Although a member of the Provisional Government he had done his best to overthrow it and had twice tried to organise the Provisional President's

assassination. He believed, mistakenly, that he could count on unquestioning American acquiescence and on the good will of the IAPF. In mid-January changes in the latter's top command removed two of his most highly-placed friends on the spot; and after the departure of the Constitutionalist military leaders American pressure on him increased. Finally, having used every possible pretext for prevarication, he left for the United States on the 11th of February.

7. He would not have gone even then but for pressure from an entirely different quarter. Colonel Caamaño's departure had aroused massive demonstrations of popular sympathy. No sooner had he gone than voices in the streets and on the air demanded that Commodore Rivera Caminero and his two colleagues do likewise. A strike committee was set up. Professor Juan Bosch, however, and other leading members of the Partido Nacional Revolucionario (PRD), concerned lest popular disturbances should give the military leaders another excuse to postpone their departure, succeeded in discouraging more drastic action for the time being. During the days that followed, while Commodore Rivera Caminero's departure was repeatedly announced and postponed, tension increased; and early on the 9th of February it broke. The immediate cause was extraneous. A delegation of some 800 students gathered in front of the National Palace demanding the reopening of the University of Santo Domingo. The police lost their heads and fired into the crowd, killing three and wounding many others. Demonstration followed. Cars were burnt; policemen were savagely attacked and two of them burnt alive. In the afternoon the strike committee declared a general strike.

8. The strike had been triggered off by the folly of a junior police officer, but after the dismissal of the inept Chief of Police on the 10th of February, its main objective had become the departure of the three military leaders. On the 11th of February Commodore Rivera Caminero threw in his hand and went. His place was taken by General Pérez y Pérez, then an unknown quantity. The two Chiefs of Staff, however, "heroically" refused to budge. On the 13th of February Professor Bosch, who had held off as long as he could, at last gave the strike his blessing. Next day Santo Domingo was at a standstill, and the strike began to spread throughout the country. On the 16th of February Dr. García Godoy appealed for a return to work, promising a solution of the "military problem" within a few days. An hour later Professor Bosch called the strike off, and next day Santo Domingo returned to normal.

9. A week elapsed before the solution was announced, and at first sight it did not seem any solution at all. The two Chiefs of Staff, instead of being posted overseas, were made Vice-Ministers. They had, admittedly, been kicked upstairs and removed from the chain of command; but would popular opinion see it that way? Dr. García Godoy, backing his hunch that people were sick of

disturbances, had astutely arranged a diversion for one of the main sources of turmoil by announcing elections in the University for the 28th of February. This kept the students busy during two crucial days, and by the time the dust had settled the two controversial Chiefs of Staff had vanished into the oblivion of their new sinecures. For the time being the "military problem" had been solved.

10. And not one day too soon. The 1st of March had been fixed as the opening date for electoral campaign, the elections being scheduled for the 1st of June. The next three months between the two dates were expected to be particularly turbulent, but they turned out to be remarkably tranquil. General Pérez y Pérez was largely responsible for this. He devoted himself energetically to creating a new image for the armed forces as a non-political body subordinate to civil authority. The new Chief of Police, General Morillo López, did the same, and in a remarkably short time restored discipline and raised morale in a force which had been reduced to a timid rabble.

11. Even so, valuable time had been lost. The previous six months had been far from conducive to a proper climate for elections. On the 1st March Professor Bosch, who had consistently questioned the possibility of holding elections at all, was still unconvinced that it would not be in his own and his party's best interest to boycott them altogether. Two presidential candidates were already in the field. Dr. Joaquín Balaguer, titual President when Trujillo was assassinated, had returned to the Dominican Republic in June 1965, and had long been busy organising on the spot the Partido Reformista (PR) which he had founded during his exile in the United States. In February 1966 Licenciado Rafael Bonnelly, President of the Council of State in 1962 after Dr. Balaguer had gone into exile, announced his candidature at the head of five small Right-wing parties. Thus two former Presidents were already entered; and it remained to be seen whether Professor Bosch, President for seven months in 1963, would make the third.

12. Professor Bosch kept everyone guessing until the Easter week-end when a PRD Convention acclaimed him as the party's Presidential candidate with Señor Antonio Guzman, his Minister of Agriculture in 1963, running for the vice-presidency. For the next six weeks or so most people's odds were on a sweeping victory for Professor Bosch. He had already given a show of strength by the immediate response to his calling the February general strike on and off. With his dynamic personality and the unshakeable PRD majority which he had had in 1962, there could, surely, be no other result. By the beginning of May, however, this prospect seemed less sure. Dr. Balaguer's long preparations and ample funds were important factors. More important still, he was campaigning vigorously all over the country, whereas Professor Bosch

remained immured in his house. He feared assassination and his heart was not in the fight. Vanity made him want to be elected, nervous strain made him shy of becoming President. All he contributed to the campaign was a daily broadcast tape-recorded at home; and his dynamic personality was lost on the voters, who never saw him.

13. The results of the elections — the most orderly free elections that this country has ever known — exploded, too, the myth of the unshakeable PRD majority. Dr. Balaguer was swept in with more than 57 per cent of the pool, while Professor Bosch got less than 40. For the smaller parties on both Left and Right it was total defeat. Only the two main parties had seats in the National Congress, and the PR gained a comfortable majority in both Houses.

14. The 1st of July had been fixed as the date for Dr. Balaguer's inauguration. For Dr. García Godoy, the intervening month was a period of winding up. He was able to round off his Provisional Presidency by getting the agreement of the IAPF by September. Also outstanding was the reintegration of the Constitutionalist troops still in the "27 de Febrero" Camp. This he had to leave to Dr. Balaguer who finally did it in November, without fuss and almost without attracting attention, an indication of the change which had by then overtaken the political climate.

15. The change began on the day Dr. Balaguer took office. In this inaugural speech he announced a thoroughgoing overhaul of the public service; and soon there were sweeping changes in all Government departments but one. His Cabinet, with one exception, was composed of entirely new men (and one woman), some of them quite inexperienced. The exception in both cases was the Ministry of the Armed Forces, which he took over lock, stock and barrel from Dr. García Godoy. He later made one change in the top command and in September, before the last units of the IAPF were withdrawn, he drew the teeth of the San Isidro Air Base by having its tanks and artillery transferred elsewhere — an operation, which, to the surprise of those who knew it to be impending, was performed without any noticeable repercussions. Otherwise Dr. Balaguer astutely left the armed forces alone. During his first six months in power there were persistent rumours of plots involving individual officers and units, but none of them came to anything. The "military problem", if not dead, remained dormant.

16. The essential difference between the first and the second half of the year was that under the Provisional Government military and political problems predominated, whereas Dr. Balaguer was primarily concerned, as he made clear in his inaugural speech, with economic reconstruction and development. The parlous budgetary and balance of payments situation he had inherited, could

only be saved by a regime of austerity. The Budget would no longer be balanced by injections of foreign aid. There would be reductions in the administrative establishment and in the salaries and wages of employees, of the State and State-owned enterprises; reorganisation of the sugar mills; enforcement of taxation; restrictions on imports or non-essentials goods. Meanwhile, the United States Government had made an emergency grant of $40 million, to be applied before the end of the year to development projects; and the jobs thus created would offset dismissals from the Administration and State enterprises.

17. Inevitably performance fell short of the objectives. Administrative confusion and technical incompetence grounded many items on the emergency aid programme. Of the $40 million substantially less than half was actually spent; and while the reorganisation of the State-owned sugar industry went ruthlessly ahead and dismissals of redundant employees ran into thousands, the new jobs available were quite insufficient to absorb them. The problem of unemployment — 25 per cent according to the most conservative estimates — was as serious as ever.

18. Against this, the balance of payments position improved somewhat thanks in part to a windfall increase in the Dominican Republic's sugar quota in the United States. The Budget was balanced. In December the Budget for 1967 was passed by Congress. Inevitably it prolonged the austerity regime well into 1967; but it was a sensible Budget and, in the context of Anglo-Dominican relations, satisfactory in that it provided for repayment of the monthly instalments due to the General Electric Company, of which 14 were overdue at the end of the year. At least it showed that Dr. Balaguer had taken our point that this outstanding debt was harmful to confidence in the Dominican Republic in the city of London.

19. To restore confidence was of paramount importance, but there Dr. Balaguer made little headway. A firm indication of future political stability was needed. Frequent rumours of Right and Left-wing plots created just the reverse. For economic reasons they had to be played down, but Dr. Balaguer often reacted to them politically in such a way as to play them up.

20. A serious criticism can be made of Dr. Balaguer's performance in that he tried to run the country as an economist and paid too little heed to the political repercussions of his policies. When he came to power he had an overwhelming majority in Congress and an Opposition prepared to oppose him constructively. Within three months relations between them had become so strained that for most PRD Senators and Deputies any real co-operation with the Government had become impossible. The PRD were not always innocent but the blame rests mainly on Dr. Balaguer, who showed too little understanding of the role

of a parliamentary opposition. His political education he had received under Trujillo; and his Presidential experience had been first as the "Benefactor's" stooge and then as his undertaker and executor. A "respectable" Opposition he found perplexing and inconvenient, and he set out to make it less respectable. The PRD played into his hand when at their Convention at the end of October the party took a definite step towards the Left by replacing the older and more moderate leaders by younger and wilder men. Professor Bosch relinquished the presidency to become an "adviser", and less than a month later he left on an extended visit to Europe. The post of President was abolished and the leadership of the party entrusted to the Secretary General, a hot-headed 29 year old. Two of the moderate "Old Guard" who had accepted posts in Dr. Balaguer's Cabinet when it was first formed, resigned; only Dr. Molina Ureña, until then Secretary General, remained, and even he was relegated to membership of an unimportant committee. Soon afterwards Dr. Balaguer offered Dr. Molina Ureña the job of Ambassador to the United Nations. Other moderates were tempted overseas. The further the PRD moved to the Left, the better Dr. Balaguer seemed to be pleased: they could be dubbed as Communists and discounted. He appeared also to be deliberately dispersing the moderates to prevent them from forming a new Opposition group Left of Centre.

21. On taking office Dr. Balaguer declared, with apparent sincerity, that the last thing he wanted was to restore dictatorship in the Trujillo model, and he referred frequently thereafter to the genuinely democratic character of his administration. In November a new Constitution, providing for all the accepted democratic safeguards, was promulgated. Within a few days he exposed himself to *prima facie* well-founded charges of violating it. His tactics towards the PRD had a distinctly "trujillista" flavour. At the end of the year it was still too soon to say whether his apparent "penchant" for dictatorial methods originated in himself or in his entourage. It was a disturbing fact that among the latter, some very close to the Presidential ear, were several incorrigible "trujillistas" — men of little breeding and much potential cruelty, who, if they did nothing worse, by their behaviour in the anterooms of the National Palace enhanced the feeling of mediocrity and lack of tone at the centre of power.

22. Who, it was asked, in one of the local newspapers at the end of the year, were the two outstanding Dominicans of 1966? The answer he gave was: first, Dr. García Godoy; second not — as might have been expected — Dr. Balaguer but Miss Dominican Republic, who in the contest in London in December, delighted her compatriots by being placed in the first 15. This, I should say, is fair comment.

I.W. BELL.

# CALENDAR OF EVENTS IN 1966

## January

3. President García Godoy announced his findings on the Hotel Matum incident of 19 December 1965, which included dismissal of Minister of Armed Forces and sending abroad of various military on both sides.

6. Rumours of Right-wing *coup d'état*. Government radio station and telecommunications building occupied by Right-wing troops.

7. United States Government and OAS announced support of civilian Government Officers appointed as new Chiefs of Staff and Minister for Armed Forces refused to accept.

8. Inter-American Peace Force took over radio station and telecommunications building.

10. Call for general strike. Disorders in the city.

11. Caamaño accepted guarantee for safety of Constitutionalist forces in 27 February Camp. First six Constitutionalist officers left to assume diplomatic appointments overseas. General strike unsuccessful and called off. Further street riots.

12. W. Connett, United States Deputy Chief of Mission, left and replaced by J.H. Crimmins.

16. Generals Alvin and Palmer replaced as Commander and Deputy Commander of IAPF by Generals Braga and Linville.

22. Colonel Caamaño and Captain Montes Arache left to take up diplomatic appointments in London and Ottawa. Right-wing forces announced that five senior officers would leave shortly.

## February

9. Police opened fire on students demonstrating outside National Palace. Three killed. Several police killed in incidents in town. General strike called, led by PRD.

10. Chief of Police replaced.

11. Minister of Armed Forces, Commodore Rivera Caminero, finally left for Washington and was replaced by General Pérez y Pérez.

13. Bosch broadcast calling for continuation of strike, by now almost 100 per cent effective in capital and beginning to spread into the interior.

16. Provisional President announced that those responsible for events on 9 February would be punished. Bosch called off strike.

19. Bonnelly announced his candidature for the presidency in the June elections.

25. Vanguardia Revolucionario Dominicano declared its support for Bonnelly.

26. President announced that Chiefs of Staff Army and Air Force would be replaced and appointed as Vice-Ministers of Armed Forces.

27. Independence Day. Amnesty granted to members of attempted *coup d'état* of 16 November 1965. Government announced it would recognise results of University elections due 28 February.

28. University elections. Complete control gained by Left-wing.

**March**

1. Election campaign officially opened. Armed forces announced their intention of remaining apolitical.

**April**

7. 14 June Movement legalised.

8. Dominican Communist Party promises support to Bosch in elections.

9–16. PRD convention nominated Bosch and Guzman as presidential and vice-presidential candidates.

10. Partido Liberal Evolucionario convention nominated Bonnelly and Tabaré Alvarez Pereyra as election candidates.

17. Partido Reformista convention nominated Balaguer and Lora as election candidates. Social Christian Party promised support for Bosch/Guzman ticket. 14 June Movement offered support for Bosch, subject to certain conditions.

19. Bosch rejected 14 June support.

21. MPD (Marxist Leninist) dismissed its president and founder-member, Maximo Lopez Molina.

23. 14 June Movement said it would support Bosch.

24. First Anniversary of 1965 revolution passed peacefully.

28. First Anniversary of United States intervention. Demonstrations outside American Embassy. Two United States soldiers opened fire on a crowd that was provoking them, wounding six.

**May**

17. Bosch announced PRD would withdraw from elections unless terrorist attacks on party workers were halted within 48 hours.

18. Provisional President announced that all armed forces would be confined to barracks until after elections.

19. Bosch accepted this proposal and resumed the campaign.

27. Balaguer said he would withdraw from election unless women could be allowed to vote without identity cards.

29. Electoral Board accepted Balaguer's demands.

30. United States Government announced that negotiations would begin for the withdrawal of the IAPF.

**June**

1. Elections held in an orderly and peaceful manner.

2–3. Many protests and charges of fraud from PRD and supporting parties as election results came through.

5. Bosch announced that there had been insufficient irregularities to influence elections result.

6. Bosch and Balaguer meet in Papal Nuncio's residence, their first meeting since they both returned from exile in 1965.

13. Bosch stated that PRD would not participate in a coalition government but would assume role of constructive opposition.

18. President Johnson announced that Vice-President Humphrey would attend Balaguer's inauguration, and J.H. Crimmins was nominated as new United States Ambassador.

22. Balaguer and Lora officially declared President and Vice-President elect.

24. 10th Consultative Assembly of OAS resolved the withdrawal with 90 days of the IAPF.

28. First contingent of IAPF troops departs.

**July**

1. Balaguer installed as President.

17. Balaguer announced six-month emergency development programme financed by $40 million United States aid.

**August**

19. United States granted a supplementary quota for Dominican sugar of 132,000 tons.

28. Dominican Sugar Corporation disbanded and replaced by State Sugar Council.

**September**

17. General Folch Perez dismissed as Chief of Staff Air Force and replaced by General Alvarez Albizu.

20. Last contingent of IAPF troops left.

29. Hurricane Ines struck south-west corner of the Republic causing over 50 deaths and damage to property and crops.

**October**

30. Bosch resigned as President of the PRD and was replaced by Julio Peña Gómez.

31. Two PRD Ministers in Balaguer's Cabinet resigned from the party.

**November**

9. 204 Constitutionalist troops remaining in 27 February Camp re-integrated with armed forces.

26. Bosch left for Europe.

28. New Constitution promulgated.

**December**

1. OAS wrote off $12 million debt owed by State Sugar Council.

2. IMF agreed compensatory finance of $6.6 million.

3. Balaguer announced that Christmas Bonus would not be paid to Government servants except those earning less than RD$100 per month.

8. 'Committee National Unit', led by extreme left, called for general strike on Christmas Bonus issue.

9. Seven leading members of 14 June Movement left to join MPD.

12. Call for general strike clearly unsuccessful and withdrawn.

28. 1967 Budget passed by Congress.

**12. American Department, Foreign Office, London, 8 February 1967**

Sir D. Allen

New Dominican Ambassador

I attach a short brief on the Dominican Republic and a biographical note on Doctor Porfirio Herrera Baez,[6] whom you are accompanying at his audience of The Queen on Thursday, 9 February at 12 noon.

(G.W. Harding)

8 February, 1967

*Many Thanks. I am sending the credentials to Protocol Dept.*

*(signatures indecipherable) 9/2*


## DOMINICAN REPUBLIC

*General Situation*

The return to constitutional Government has only been partly achieved. President Balaguer, who won a handsome majority in the general elections of last June, has tended to compensate for his weak personality by using the high-handed administrative methods which he learned from Trujillo. Undoubtedly he has to endure continuous pressure from reactionary senior officers in the armed forces to take a firm line with the left-wing opposition, whether Communist or not. But this does not excuse the wholesale arrests of moderate opposition political leaders last month, which Dr. Balaguer has sought to justify as necessary to frustrate a communist plot. Professor Juan Bosch, the unexpected loser in the Presidential elections, has abdicated his responsibility as leader of the main opposition party, the Partido Revolucionario Dominicano, and is now in retreat in Madrid prophesying disaster for his country in the shape of another military dictatorship. (We are considering a suggestion by the Overseas Secretary of the Labour Party that he should be invited to pay an official visit to the United Kingdom).

2. The Americans, who were well pleased with the election of President Balaguer, have admitted their anxiety at the authoritarian flavour of his regime. But whether they like it or not, they are saddled with a heavy moral and material burden in helping the Dominican economy to recover from the gross dislocation imposed on it by the civil war of 1965. At the moment, they would clearly prefer to continue nudging Dr. Balaguer in the right direction rather than to find themselves having to deal with either Professor Bosch or a

6   Not included in the archives.

would-be military dictator. But, whatever happens, we can be sure that they will not be caught out in making the same mistake twice; there will be no second military intervention on the massive scale of April 1965.

**Anglo-Dominican Relations**

i. The United Kingdom was the first foreign country to proclaim recognition of the independent Dominican Republic in 1850. This fact is rubbed into all Dominicans at school and is frequently referred to in ceremonial speeches as Anglo-Dominican occasions.

ii. The frigate H.M.S. "Zest" is to pay a visit to Santo Domingo on 27 February, which happens to be the anniversary day of Dominican independence (1844). The Dominican Government are very pleased about this.

iii. The Dominican Government understandably feel especially vulnerable to Cuban subversion. They have accordingly made representations both in London and in Santo Domingo about E.C.G.D.'s [Export Credit Guarantee Department] insurance of 5 years credit for Simon Carves' forthcoming sale to the Cuban Government of a fertiliser plant worth over £14 million. Dr. Herrera Baez left an aide memoire on the question when he paid his first call on the P.U.S. on 19 January.

iv. Colonel Caamaño, the leader of the Constitutionalist faction in the civil war, still holds the nominal appointment of Dominican Military Attaché in London. He is thought to be on poor terms with the new Ambassador. He is not causing us any trouble.

AMERICAN DEPARTMENT
8 February 1967

## 13. British Embassy, Santo Domingo 11 October 1967

Ministry of Defence,
(D.I. 1 Coord),
Main Building,
Whitehall,
London S.W.1 (3 copies)

Colonel Caamaño — Dominican Military Attaché London

1. Reference my letter NA/570 of 9th October 1967, Annex 1, para 1.

2. During my recent visit as Defence Attaché to the Dominican Republic my Ambassador asked me to find out if anything is known of Colonel Caamaño's activities in London. You will remember that during the civil war in 1965 he emerged as leader of the rebel and leftish "Constitutionalist" forces. Although the US Embassy regarded him and his supporters as communist sympathisers, the British Embassy at the time felt that the Americans had perhaps misjudged the nature of the popular uprising. The British Chargé d'Affaires, Mr (ex-Brigadier) Campbell, who unlike his US colleagues was in personal touch with Caamaño, found his views quite moderate and felt he was a man who had risen to the occasion. After the peace settlement, Caamaño agreed to go into exile as Military Attaché in London in early 1966.

3. His present position must be very awkward since he is loathed by his Ambassador, who is the brother of a Minister in the present moderate right wing regime, and is hated by his former colleagues in the Dominican Armed Forces. He probably only goes to the Embassy once a month to collect his pay — and this pay may not be very great. A pay list I saw in Santo Domingo for other exiles of his rank showed that they were only getting $640 a month which would not go far in diplomatic life in London.

4. It would be interesting to know if our Attaché Liaison Section of the Defence Intelligence Staff has seen anything of him; if he has been an active member of the M.A's [Military Attaché's] Association; if he has gone on any of the official tours arranged for M.A's; if he has taken another job in order to earn some more money; what sort political views he now has; is he now firmly in the hands of the communists and being groomed for an eventual come-back or has life in England given him a taste for the democratic way of doing things, and so on? Perhaps you could ask Brigadier Campbell, who is now working in the Foreign Office again, if he has seen anything of him. [handwritten note in margin re Campbell *No: now in Lima*]

5. During my recent visit senior Dominican officers frequently referred to him as a stupid man who had served in all three services and in the police, making

enemies in each, and as a mere opportunist who thought that by climbing onto the Constitutionalist band-waggon he could retrieve his career and perhaps make his fortune. Such officers are of course biased but certainly it seems unlikely that he could have any future in the Dominican Armed Forces, or could even return in safety to the Dominican Republic as a civilian. However, people like him do have a tendency to pop up again unexpectedly in this part of the world and it would be a pity if his stay in England had embittered him or driven him more towards the left.

6. My Ambassador, however, does not want you to suddenly start paying great attention to him, since such attention could well upset the Ambassador's close relations with the present Dominican Government. We should however be interested to hear anything you know overtly of him.

7. Please copy your replies to the British Embassy, Santo Domingo.

H. SELBEY BENNET
Commander,
Defence, Naval, Military & Air
Attaché
SANTO DOMINGO

Copy to:

H.M. Ambassador SANTO DOMINGO

**14. Defence Intelligence Staff, Ministry of Defence, London 25 October 1967**

T.C. Barker, Esq.
The Foreign Office (American Dept)

Box 500
Parliament Street

**Colonel F.A. Caamaño — Dominican Military Attaché, London**

Reference: DI 1-12806 of 20th October 1967.

1. We have not seen Colonel Caamaño since his first arrival. He made his official visit to us on arrival, and asked for advice on where he could get some pistol practice. He has not been in touch with us since. We used to invite him to the collective visits we organize for the Foreign Military Attaches in London but since he never answers our letters we have given up doing so.

2. If you would like us to continue trying to cultivate him in a quiet way, please let me know.

(BURNHAM)
Lieutenant Colonel
for Director of Management
and Support Intelligence

## 15. British Embassy, Santo Domingo 27 November 1967

Addressed to Foreign Office telegram No. 80 of 27 November. Repeated for information to Washington.

There has been much speculation in Press and elsewhere locally regarding present whereabouts of Colonel Francisco Caamaño, leader of constitutionalist forces during Dominican revolution in 1965 and now exiled to London as Military Attaché. He is reported to have disappeared from his London home and not to have made contact with his wife in Madrid or fellow exiles in The Hague and Brussels.

2. His disappearance may be for entirely non-political reasons but we should be grateful if you could ascertain, if it can be done without going to a great deal of trouble, whether he is still in Britain. If not, do you know when he left and what his immediate destination was?

3. We propose to pass results of your enquiries to United States Embassy here who are very anxious to know what has happened.

Foreign Office pass to Washington 23.

Mr. Bell

**16. Foreign Office, London 28 November 1967**

Priority Foreign Office to Santo Domingo

Telegram No. 82 28 November, 1967 (AAD)

Addressed to Santo Domingo telegram No. 82 of 28 November repeated for information to Washington.

Your telegram No. 80

Colonel Caamaño left London on flight to Amsterdam on 21 October. There is no record of any subsequent movement by him into or out this country up to 24 November.

2. Americans here were informed of this on about 17 November when they queried his whereabouts.

3. Washington Post have made enquiries but have not pressed them. News department said we had had no notification of his movements.

SOSFA

Departmental Distribution
F.O. American Dept
J.R.D.
News Dept
D.D. & P.U.S.D.

## 17. British Embassy, Santo Domingo 1 December 1967

British Embassy, Santo Domingo.

*(This should be copied around)*
*(Mentioned in today's C.I.S. meeting)*

*My dear Chris,*

Colonel Caamaño

Thank you for your telegram No. 82 of 28 November. I am sorry we had to bother you about Caamaño's whereabouts, but his disappearance, whether real or only alleged, has caused a lot of speculation here both in the press and at social functions. It is now, I am glad to say, clearly established that he did not "disappear" in London, and that trace of him was only lost after he had been together with Montes Arache and Lachapelle in The Hague. If anything untoward has happened to him, it has not been in the UK.

2. Among the various suggestions which have been made are the following:

a. He has gone to ground somewhere, probably in France or in Spain, with some lady friend. He has apparently done this before and as a result he has become estranged, though not yet legally separated or divorced, from his wife. The latter is in Madrid and claims to [know] nothing of his whereabouts.

b. He has staged a disappearance in order to attract publicity to himself and away from Wessin y Wessin, on whose behalf the PQD [Partido Quisqueyano Democratico] have been more than usually vocal during the last three weeks or so. This view has been expressed to me by, among others, General Imbert, who also thinks that Juan Bosch has put him up to it.

c. He has actually returned to the Dominican Republic under assumed name. This, I should say, is most unlikely. Caamaño could hardly get through the Immigration controls without being recognised, however much he might disguise himself.

d. He has been put out of the way by right-wing agents either in France or Spain. This is being hinted at in rather oblique terms by the PRD. Again, I should say, this is not very likely; and unless and until his body has been found and identified, I cannot bring myself to believe it.

3. On the whole, I would plump for (a), which is not [of] any political interest, or (b), which is. The PRD, as you will recall from recent reports form here, is in disarray, and there could be elements in the party who are looking round for new leadership. Peña Gomez, however much he may have matured during

the last year, is not a credible presidential candidate; and it may have occurred to some PRD supporters — and even perhaps to Peña Gomez himself — that something must be done to keep the memory of Caamaño alive from time to time before the 1970 election campaign opens. They would hardly, however, go so far as to lend themselves to suggestion (c). If Caamaño were to come back here it would make it just that much easier for Wessin and Wessin to come back too. In other words, the PRD would be playing into the hands of the PQD.

4. The American interest in this affair is quite lively, so much so that I even began to wonder whether they had some idea at the back of their minds that Caamaño might turn out to be a possible successor to Che Guevara. John Crimmins has told me, however, that this is not so, though they do not exclude the possibility that he may have made, or be making, his way to Cuba via Prague and Mexico. He seemed to think that Caamaño would be able to do this without being spotted by the Americans on the way. On the whole, he thought it unlikely that Caamaño would have gone to any communist country since this would ruin whatever political ambitions he might have. The Americans' main concern is that he should not come back here as they are particularly anxious to give Balaguer no pretext for allowing Wessin y Wessin to return to this country.

5. The subject of Caamaño also cropped up in a conversation I had at a dinner party last night with the Foreign Minister. Amiama Tio, too, seems inclined to favour suggestion (b). He is naturally not a little incensed that a Military Attaché at one of his Embassies should have left his post without seeking his Ambassador's permission. He admitted, of course, that Caamaño had done this before, but he was particularly annoyed now because of all the publicity attached to his present escapade which, he said, reflected badly on the Dominican Foreign Service and thus, indirectly, on him personally. He added, however, that he was really more sorry than angry with Caamaño, who, he felt, was a decent fellow at heart but who had been led astray all too often by Hector Aristy. The latter he regarded as Caamaño's evil genius, and he said he would not be surprised if it turned out that Aristy had a hand in his present disappearance.

I.W. Bell

C.E. Diggines, Esq.,
American Department

Hon. R.E.L. Johnstone,
Washington

**18. 12 December 1967** [no departmental origin indicated]

From: M.H. CALLENDER

**COLONEL Caamaño**

1. I am sorry that we have taken so long to answer your NA 570 dated 11th October 1967. We sent copies of it to the Foreign Office, DI-21, and the Security people, and the latter have only just replied.

2. In the meantime, Colonel Caamaño has disappeared (see para 2c), but here is a summary of what we have been told:

DI-21. Have not seen Colonel Caamaño since his first arrival (early 1966). He made his official visit and asked for advice on when he could get some pistol practice. He has not been in touch with DI-21 since and never answered their letters or invitations to collective visits organised for foreign MA's in London.

Foreign Office. Had no comments of their own, except that Brigadier Campbell is now Head of Chancery in Lima.

They did however send us copies of rather lengthy reports they had received from the Americans. I understand that the Foreign Office are using these to reply to letters they have very recently received from our Ambassador in Santo Domingo.[7] Very briefly, the reports (covering June and July 1967) indicated that Caamaño was still very much against the present Government in the Dominican Republic, and hinted that his aides, if not he himself, were playing with the idea of trying to assassinate Gen. Wessin y Wessin.

c. Security. Caamaño has paid frequent brief visits to Brussels, Madrid, Paris and Amsterdam. He departed from Amsterdam on 21st October 1967 and has not returned. His present absence is unusually long by comparison with earlier ones.

He has changed his London address three times since arriving and the owners of his last address are believed to be trying to remove him from his flat owing to complaints from other tenants about his behaviour and that of his many unspecified visitors.

Otherwise the Security report is somewhat inconclusive.

3. I am sending a copy of this letter to the Foreign Office, so that they can forward it to the Ambassador along with their answer to his questions.

Commander Selby Bennett, RN
Naval & Military Attaché
British Embassy
CARACAS.

7    See pp. 96, 98–9.

**19. American Department, Foreign Office, London 2 January 1968**

Thank you for your letter of 1 December about the whereabouts of Colonel Caamaño.

2. The mystery is still not solved and I see there is now yet another theory, said by the Americans to be strongly held by Dominican army officers, that Caamaño is in Cuba. In any event our own information is both slight and dated, but you may care to see for the sake of completeness a copy of Callender's letter of 12 December (about which you will no doubt be also hearing from Commander Bennett) and also of two earlier American reports which only prove that contact with Caamaño was mostly indirect.

(C.E. Diggines)
American Department

I.W. Bell, Esq., CMG
Santo Domingo

**20. British Embassy, Santo Domingo**

30 January 1968
Section 1

### DOMINICAN REPUBLIC: ANNUAL REVIEW FOR 1967

*Mr. Bell to Mr. Brown*

SUMMARY

1967 passed with President Balaguer remaining firmly in control and with
no serious trouble from the military. (Paragraphs 1–3)
The attempted assassination of General Imbert. (Paragraphs 4–5)
Balaguer's handling of the Left. (Paragraph 6)
The outbreak of terrorism in April and May, and the walk-out from the
Congress of the Partido Revolucionario Dominicano (PRD). (Paragraphs
7–8)
The problems of the PRD and its increasing stridency. (Paragraphs 9–11)
Economic progress and problems. (Paragraphs 12–13)
Foreign Policy and relations with Britain. (Paragraphs 14–15)

------------------------------

Santo Domingo, 26 January 1968.

Sir,

I have the honour to submit my review of events in the Dominican Republic
in 1967.

2. By Dominican standards a quiet year. It began and ended with President
Balaguer still in the saddle; and although he had some rough moments, at
no time did he seem in danger of being unhorsed. Dominicans were tired of
upheaval and showed signs of a real desire to get the economy moving in an
atmosphere of political tranquillity, a desire which the President stimulated by
designating 1967 as "Development Year".

3. For once, too, a whole year went by without serious trouble from the military.
The Minister of the armed forces, General Perez y Perez, continued to impose
respect for the principle of obedience to civil authority; and although there
were still officers whose loyalty was not beyond question and isolated lapses in
some of the remoter country districts, as a body they remained firm in their
support of the Administration. The President's authority was strong enough for
him to make high-level changes of command without repercussions; and there
was at least one incident which, if it had occurred at any time in the preceding
five years, would almost certainly have provoked the armed forces into playing
a political role.

4. This was the attempted assassination of General Imbert in the 21st of March as he and one of his aides were driving past the British Embassy residence. Fortunately it was unsuccessful; and although they were both seriously wounded, they recovered. General Imbert spent three months recuperating in the United States, and for the rest of the year after his return in August seemed to have abandoned his traditionally conspirational role in Dominican politics.

5. President Balaguer's reaction to the incident was tactically and chronologically smart. General Imbert was one of the two surviving assassins of Trujillo. There was little love lost between him and the man who had been the dictator's puppet President in 1961 and who now, six years later, was President once more. In the latter's entourage there were undoubted "trujillistas", any one of whom might be suspected of a hand in what most Dominicans assumed was an act of revenge instigated by the Trujillo family in exile. President Balaguer, for his part, justifiably regarded with suspicion a man who, rightly or wrongly, had been associated in the public mind with every conspiracy in the Dominican Republic since 1961. Not even the President's most inveterate enemies, however, would have accused him of complicity in assassination. Even so, the attack on General Imbert faced him with both the need and the opportunity to demonstrate that he was neither a "trujillista" himself nor the tool of "trujillistas" in his entourage. He immediately took the unusual but clever step of appointing Señor Luis Amiama Tío, the other surviving assassin of Trujillo and the leader of a small Right-wing party which had opposed him in the elections of 1966, as Minister of the Interior with the specific task of investigating the incident and the promise of a free hand and the full rigour of the law for the would-be assassins if he could track them down. Señor Luis Amiama Tío made an energetic start by sacking the Chief of Police. Witnesses had agreed that the attackers' car had an armed forces number plate, so he obliged all officers and other ranks with cars answering to the witnesses' description to submit them to expert examination, this arousing considerable resentment in military circles. President Balaguer let him have his head; but beyond setting most of his colleagues by the ears he made no real headway in his main task, which was presumably what the President expected. On the 24th of April he threw in his hand. By then the heat had evaporated and his resignation caused no great stir. Nor did his successor's announcement four months later to the effect that every avenue had been explored without result and that, in the absence of fresh evidence, the case must be regarded as closed.

6. The armed forces did not react as they might have done as they had one good reason for not rocking the boat. This was their satisfaction with the President's firmness toward the Left wing. He had already demonstrated this in the second half of January by ordering the arrest of a large number of Left-wing supporters

throughout the country on the grounds that there was a Communist plot to overthrow the Government. The operation was clumsily carried out. Among those detained were several locally respected citizens, and widespread criticism obliged the President to apologise to them publicly. The police were taken to task for exceeding their instructions and all those against whom there was no evidence were immediately released. On the 4th of February in a television broadcast, he divulged the information on which he had acted. A Dominican agent of Fidel Castro had been arrested in Venezuela in December 1966. Documents in his possession, which the Venezuelan Government had passed on, revealed detailed plans of subversive activities in the Dominican Republic. The President's explanation met with general acceptance, though many Dominicans objected strongly to the way he had acted on the information received. Foremost among the political parties to complain on this score was the Left-of-Centre Partido Revolucionario Dominicano (PRD).

7. Relations between the PRD and Government grew steadily worse throughout the year, the PRD becoming progressively more militant. Organisational changes towards the end of 1966 had brought younger and more aggressive men into the leadership. The arrests in January were only the first of several incidents which convinced them that their party was being victimised in a systematic campaign of persecution by Government agents and Right-wing political parties. By no means all of them, however, were directed against the PRD. There was a revival of terrorism on the 28th of April, the second anniversary of the landing of the United States Marines in 1965, when a young American teacher was killed by a grenade thrown at his house. Other incidents followed, and in three of these the victims were members of the PRD. On the 4th of May, Senator Casimiro Castro and two companions were seriously burned when an incendiary grenade was thrown at the jeep in which they were driving in Santo Domingo. On the 10th of May a PRD official and his driver, and on the 12th a PRD youth leader were shot. The Government Partido Reformista (PR), however, was also a target. On the 7th of May the Director of Telecommunications and two others with him were badly burned by an incendiary grenade thrown at their car. For all these incidents, according to President Balaguer, the Communists were responsible; but the truth of this assertion was never proved.

8. The attack on Senator Castro threatened to develop into a serious political crisis. Both Houses of Congress passed resolutions condemning the attack, but this was not enough for the PRD. On the 8th of May its Senators and Deputies announced their withdrawal from Congress until a better political climate had been restored. After a fortnight or so of uncertainty, during which conditions in the city showed signs of returning to what they had been in the

dark days and dangerous nights of the winter of 1965–66, the President offered guarantees of safety to members of the PRD in all their legitimate activities. The guarantee was accepted and the PRD Deputies and Senators resumed their seats in Congress two days before it rose for the summer recess. The "minicrisis" was over.

9. The PRD's predicament, however, was not. During the Parliamentary crisis its Secretary-General, Señor Peña Gomez, had appealed to all Left-wing parties to unite against the Government. Two of the Communist Parties (MPD and PCD) had responded. The other Left-of-Centre party, the Social Christians (PRSC) had not. The latter had joined with the PRD in supporting Professor Bosch in the elections. Since then their alliance had fallen apart with the Leftward drift of the PRD. President Balaguer had contributed to the break by affecting to treat the PRSC, despite its complete lack of representation in Congress, as the only Opposition party with whom he could deal. That the President should in effect choose his own Opposition was regarded by the PRD as an affront and intensified its leaders' sense of frustration. The May crisis had left the PRD in greater disarray than ever, and a new doctrine was needed to give it fresh life and coherence. This doctrine, first enunciated in June by Professor Bosch in his self-imposed exile in Europe, received little publicity at the time; but in August, after a visit to Europe where he had conferred with Professor Bosch, Señor Peña Gomez announced it as the settled policy of the PRD. Professor Bosch had called it "popular dictatorship", which implied a political system on Cuban lines, though both he and Señor Peña Gomez were at pains to declare that it had nothing to do with Communism. Its general effect within the PRD was divisive. It posed the possibility of unconstitutional action from which the more responsible members shrank. Even for those who supported it the word "dictatorship" had an ugly ring, and by the end of the year both the doctrine and its title were being played down.

10. Meanwhile the PRD faced a more immediate practical problem: whether or not to participate in the municipal elections due in May 1968. Abstention might mean extinction. Participation would probably mean ignominious defeat. Added to its own disarray was the danger of increased activity on the extreme Left. The Communists were still fragmented but in May the three main parties had between them gained a majority in elections to the Council of the University of Santo Domingo. Later in the year, when the Government was embroiled with the University over finance and for a time all the faculties were closed down, the Soviet-orientated PCD made the running. PRD influence in the University had dwindled to virtually nil. The same process, less marked, was at work in the trade unions. They were also faced with a new enemy of the extreme Right. In July a new party, the Partido Quisqueyano Democratico

(PQD) had been formed under the aegis of the exiled ex-General Wessin y Wessin, a fanatic whose anti-Communism embraced all Left-wing parties, including the PRD; and by December it had made considerable strides in the country districts. The sapping of the PRD's position by the extreme Left, fear of intimidation by the extreme Right, the Government's hostile disregard, plus its own disarray — all these factors seemed to argue in favour of abstention.

11. The increasing stridency of the PRD brought many people by the end of the year to the point of wondering whether Señor Peña Gomez and his more hot-headed supporters were seriously contemplating violent action. There was some speculation as to whether, if they had such plans in mind, they were connected with the mysterious disappearance in October of Colonel Caamaño the erstwhile Constitutionalist leader and subsequently Dominican Military Attaché in London. Although there was no evidence of his whereabouts since he was last seen at The Hague, he was generally believed to have gone to Cuba; and the possibility of his being prepared for some future guerrilla operation was not excluded. Whether his disappearance was relevant to the aggressive stand of the PRD was anybody's guess, but the fact that in the last two months of the year its leaders made no public reference to it struck many Dominicans outside the party as significant. With or without Colonel Caamaño, however, nobody rated the chances of success for any violent action on the part of the PRD very high. They had enough power, however, to create disturbances in the capital on a large enough scale to shatter the image of political tranquillity which President Balaguer had been at great pains to build up in order to attract private investment from overseas. The patient labour of transforming the "Development Year" from an idea into some sort of reality could thus be nullified at a single stroke.

12. In economic terms "Development Year" was a moderate success. The austerity period initiated when President Balaguer assumed office in 1966 had been extended to the 30th of June 1967, and was later extended for a further year. In July new restrictions on imports and private travel abroad were introduced; and although these were subject to relaxations, the foreign exchange position was held to the extent that the adverse trade balance of $30 million forecast by President Balaguer in June turned out to be less than half that figure. Much of the development was financed by AID [Agency for International Development] but there were signs of Dominican expatriate capital being tempted back and of private foreign investors showing less timidity. Only one major investment, the American Can Corporation's project for a plant for the manufacture of metal containers, crystallised into a hard and fast contract; but more important projects seemed just round the corner at the end of the year, notably the Falconbridge nickel processing plant which

represented an investment of some $150 million. Expectancy had also built up around the proposal for an oil refinery; and it looked as though a start would at last be made on the Tavera Dam project in the new year. Finally, there was considerable progress in housing in Santo Domingo and in road construction all over the country.

13. On the debit side the Government's budgetary position remained as tight as ever, and the budget for 1968 held out no hopes of more funds available for settling outstanding debts. In 1967 the Government cleared most of its current obligations but did next-to-nothing about those it had inherited. Among the many foreign firms to suffer in this respect was the General Electric Company, which received only one of the monthly instalments due under the compensation agreement of 1965. For the economy as a whole the prospects seemed bright enough for President Balaguer to designate 1968 as "Production Year" which, since the country was just then suffering from one of the worst droughts on record, struck many people as rather risky. There was real and widespread optimism, however, over the medium-term outlook and solid hopes that, given political stability, the Dominican economy would in 1970–71 be reaping the benefits of the large-scale investments already in the pipe-line.

14. For the first time since 1961 the internal situation was calm enough to permit the President to leave the country, which he did in April to attend the summit meeting in Punta del Este. It also enabled the Government to devote more attention to foreign affairs. A new Foreign Minister, Señor Fernando Amiama Tío, brother of Luis and a man of more diplomatic experience than his predecessor, was appointed in January. Under him the Ministry became a more effective department, and it was possible to detect what looked like a Dominican foreign policy. Financial dependence on the United States was a paramount factor, though not one to be paraded in view of the strong anti-American feelings in many sectors of the population. For under the American umbrella there were moves [towards] closer relations with Caribbean [countries]. Some progress was made in [establishing] a "common market" [with regional states] though this was [complicated by requests for] special status vis-à-vis the United States. Close links were developed with Venezuela over the issue of Cuban subversion and, later in the year, over technical assistance. There were tentative feelers in the direction of the Central American Common Market. The nearest and most difficult neighbour was, as always, Haiti. For much of the year Dominicans were preoccupied with the possibility of convulsions across the border and their probable repercussions in the Dominican Republic. Illegal immigration and contraband were another problem and were the official reason given for closing the land frontier in October. Diplomatic relations continued, but the Government's policy was to treat Haiti as far as possible as though it did not exist.

15. The election of the Dominican delegate to the United Nations to one of the Vice-Presidencies of the General Assembly, was achieved with the support of the Latin American bloc. Gratitude for this was the reason advanced by the Foreign Minister for his failure to live up to his earlier promise of support for us over Gibraltar. This was disappointing for us but did not reflect any change in the Dominican Republic's traditional friendship towards Great Britain. Apart from President Balaguer's protest to me at the beginning of the year over credit facilities for the installation of a fertiliser plant in Cuba and the tiresome necessity, on our part, of having periodically to badger the Dominican Government about its debts to British firms, our relations ran smoothly enough; and the highly successful visit of HMS *Zest* at the end of February proved a most effective lubricant.

I have, &c.
I.W. BELL

Enclosure

## CALENDAR OF EVENTS IN 1967

**January**

9. President Balaguer delivered official protest to Her Majesty's Ambassador regarding the proposal to sell, with a British Government guarantee, a fertiliser plant to Cuba.

22. Wave of arrests of persons of Left-wing sympathies on grounds of subversive activities.

26. Balaguer inaugurated new Catholic University in Santiago.

27. Year of Development inaugurated by Balaguer.

**February**

3. PRD expelled two leading members for accepting posts in Balaguer's administration.

4. Television speech by Balaguer announcing discovery in Venezuela of Castro-inspired plans for subversive activities in the Dominican Republic.

5–11. Dr. Felipe Herrera, President of Inter-American Development Bank, visited Santo Domingo to sign various loan agreements and discuss future development plan.

23–27. HMS *Zest* visited Santo Domingo.

**March**

21. Attempted assassination of General Antonio Imbert.

22. Luis Amiama Tío appointed Secretary of Interior and Police and head of a commission to investigate the attempt on Imbert's life.

28. Chief of Police dismissed.

29. All military and police personnel owning or using Chevrolet cars ordered to report for investigation.

**April**

3. Two Under-Secretaries of Finance dismissed for unpunctuality and absenteeism.

7. Important changes in military high command in preparation for Balaguer's departure for the OAS summit meeting.

11. Balaguer departed for Punta del Este.

15. Balaguer returned.

24. Amiama Tío resigned as Secretary of Interior and Police.

26. Lic. Carlos Goico Morales appointed Secretary of Interior and Police.

27. 16,000 workers at La Romana Sugar Corporation started go-slow.

28. American school-teacher killed by hand grenade.

**May**

3. 83 men dismissed at La Romana, including entire Communist leadership of trade union.

4. Normal working resumed at La Romana. Phosphorous bomb attack on PRD Senator Casimiro Castro and two PRD companions, seriously burning all three.

7. Hand grenade thrown at Partido Reformista Director of Telecommunications and two companions, wounding all three.

8. PRD withdraw from Congress demanding re-establishment of order and guarantees for personal safety of party members.

10. PRD official and driver shot and killed in outskirts of Santo Domingo.

11. Secretary-General of PRD proposes union of all Left-wing parties to oppose Balaguer.

12. PRD youth leader shot and killed in outskirts of Santo Domingo. PRD call for Left-wing solidarity accepted by two main Communist parties, rejected by Social Christian Party.

15. Balaguer appoints high-level commission to investigate charges of terrorist activities in the police.

17. United States Government announces supplementary sugar quota of 166,134 tons for Dominican Republic.

23. Student body elections in Santo Dominican University, won by extreme Left group amid inter-student rioting.

25. Balaguer offers guarantees for safety of PRD members.

26. PRD return to Congress. Seven students expelled from University.

**June**

14. Balaguer announces that balance of payments deficit for 1967 is estimated at RD$30 million [Dominican pesos].

20. Captain Francisco Rivera Caminero, Minister for Armed Forces in

Provisional Government until sent into diplomatic exile by President García Godoy, returns from United States.

27. Electoral board withdraws recognition from all political parties participating in 1966 election except for PR and PRD, on the grounds that none of them secured 3 per cent of the vote.

## July

1. Some change at Cabinet and lower levels.

2. Balaguer states that ban on return of General Wessin y Wessin and Colonel Caamaño is to be maintained.

10. Monetary Board imposes wide ranging restrictions on imports.

11. Balaguer issues decree moderating some of the restrictions on imports but authorises Central Bank to withhold foreign exchange for all private and much business travel.

## August

4. General Imbert returns from treatment in United States.

7. Secretary of Interior and Police announces closure of investigation in the Imbert case.

23. Senator Casimiro Castro returns from treatment in United States hospital at Panama.

29. Period of austerity extended by Congress.

## September

6. Chief of Police and Air Chief of Staff dismissed.

## October

21. Colonel Caamaño leaves London for The Hague and disappears.

## December

9. Central Bank passes resolution stating that it will retain profits on monies paid [in form of] remittance to Britain before the devaluation of the pound, but not yet remitted.

29. Balaguer states in a public speech, without consulting United States Embassy, that United States Government will never allow the establishment of a Communist regime in the Dominican Republic or other Caribbean countries.

## 21. British Embassy, Santo Domingo 8 March 1968

BRITISH EMBASSY,
SANTO DOMINGO

I was talking to John Crimmins last night and in the course of conversation he raised the subject of Caamaño.

2. He said that he was being continually badgered by senior Dominican Army officers about his whereabouts. The line they usually took was that everyone assumed that Caamaño was in Cuba and that he, Crimmins, must know whether he really was but that he was just being secretive. John said his stock reply was that he did not know — which, he assured me, was the literal truth. He was personally inclined to believe that he had gone to Cuba, (a) because that seemed the most likely place and (b) because that was what various member of the PRD had repeatedly intimated to members of his staff. The PRD attitude towards Caamaño struck him as somewhat ambivalent. On the one hand, they said that, if he really was in Cuba, that would be the end of Caamaño as far as they were concerned. Peña Gomez had made a vague reference to the need for Caamaño to "identify himself politically", which might or might not have been intended as a declaration of dissociation. On the other hand, he felt that some of the PRD preferred to sit on the fence for the time being on the remote chance of Caamaño popping up from somewhere as the leader of a successful revolt.

3. Meanwhile rumours about Caamaño keep on coming up. The latest one, which John Crimmins said he had not heard when I told him about it, was that he had landed on the island of Tortuga with 164 men! This report reached me through a succession of female mouths and the source was said to be the Dominican chief of Air Staff. It undoubtedly gained some currency because of repeated statements in the press by the Secretary of the Armed Forces that military manoeuvres being carried out in the North of the Republic were only routine and had no political or defence significance. I just mention this as an example of how the Caamaño mystery is still a topic of conversation.

4. John Crimmins told me that the State Department had assured him categorically that they had all their lines out and were doing everything possible to track Caamaño down. He said that he supposed that they must have taken the most obvious first step, which was to ask you to ask your Embassy in Havana whether they had any information. He asked me whether I could throw any light on the subject — meaning, of course, had I had a repeat of any communication from you to Dick Slater? — and I told him I had not. He then said he might tackle the State Department again.

5. I assume, from the fact that you have not repeated anything about Caamaño to me, that you have not been approached. It is just possible that, as a result of my chat with John Crimmins, you now may be. Hence this letter.

(I.W. Bell)

Hon. R.E.L. Johnstone, Esq.,
WASHINGTON

cc. to C.E. Diggines, Esq.,
American Department

## 22. Canadian Embassy, Santo Domingo 27 March 1968

The Canadian Embassy,
SANTO DOMINGO, Dominican Republic

Under-Secretary of State for External Affairs,
OTTAWA, Canada

**Caamaño**

It will interest you to learn that Lt. Cmdr. Ubiera recently told Lt. Col. Paul A. Mayer (formerly of the UN team in the Dominican Republic) that Caamaño is in Southern Spain and that Ubiera had spoken with him by telephone only a few days earlier. We are not in a position to assess this report, but Mayer is convinced on the basis of his personal knowledge of Caamaño that the information is correct. According to Mayer, Caamaño is not a Communist and is fully aware of the damaging effect which any Cuban association would have on his prospects for returning to power.

C.S. GADD
(for) Under-Secretary of State
for External Affairs

## 23. Research Department, Foreign Office, London 20 August 1968

Mr. Denison-Edson
American Dept

You may like to see (and have entered if you find them useful) these two cuttings on the situation in the Dominican Republic.[8]

2. The rumours about Caamaño's presence in Cuba have been current a long time. I do not know whether the *El Mundo* article produces any evidence on which to base the assertion that he is there: I have not seen any evidence from other sources.

3. It seems to me quite on the cards that Caamaño is in Cuba (where else could he have gone to?) without having to postulate that Castro has singled him out as successor to Guevara. This strikes me as most unlikely. Castro's intimates remain a close-knit group, and it seems unlikely that Castro would go outside it for choosing a leader with guerrilla responsibilities (which Caamaño has never exercised) or as a hemispheric leader. Caamaño might one day play a role again in the Dominican Republic: perhaps he is being held in reserve for this: but I should be surprised if he were to be entrusted with any functions in e.g. Venezuela, Columbia.

4. I find the references in the *Elite* article to Bosch's popular (?) dictatorship interesting. It was certainly puzzling that Bosch who has stood so long for the idea of a reformist democracy in LA, should have come publicly in favour of dictatorship — even a 'popular' one. It seems to me quite possible that he had Caamaño in mind as the [writing unclear] that could embody it. The account of the meeting of the Dominican exile leaders at Benidorm is interesting — if true.

5. IRD may have some views of these matters.

S. Clissold,
Research Dept
20-8-68

*Mr. Swan*

You may wish to see. Although it is speculative, the "Elite" article does show that both Bosch and Caamaño may return to the Caribbean arena before too long.

P.W. Denison-Edson 22.8

I.R.D.

8   *El Mundo, Elite* articles, reproduced pp. 204–8

We agree that Caamaño may be in Cuba, although definite confirmation is lacking. The PRD are set to publish a new policy statement shortly: this may throw light on Bosch's views after the municipal elections on 16 May.

(signature indecipherable) 28/6

## (ii) Documents from the US Archives

### 1. Central Intelligence Agency Report, 1 May 1965

OCI No. 1234/65

CENTRAL INTELLIGENCE AGENCY
Office of Current Intelligence

INTELLIGENCE MEMORANDUM

**Situation in the Dominican Republic**
(As of 0400 EDT [Eastern Daylight Time])

1. There has been no important change in the situation as of 0400 EDT. Sniper fire continues into the US Embassy grounds. Former US Ambassador Martin is scheduled to meet with rebel leader Colonel Caamaño later today.

2. The Chilean Foreign Minister has handed the US Ambassador in Santiago a statement requesting the withdrawal of North American military forces from the Dominican Republic, "thus enabling the OAS Council to adopt the collective measures called for according to the OAS charter". Chile will probably press this line at the OAS Foreign Ministers' meeting which is to convene later this morning.

3. The Foreign Ministry of Mexico has also called for withdrawal of US forces "at the earliest date", saying that the Dominicans themselves should solve their internal problems without any foreign intervention. Other Latin American governments have been critical of the US for the "unilateral" nature of the US decision to send in troops.

**2. Central Intelligence Agency Report, 6 May 1965**

OCI No. 1603/65

CENTRAL INTELLIGENCE AGENCY

Office of Current Intelligence

INTELLIGENCE MEMORANDUM

**Situation in the Dominican Republic**

(Report No. 162 — As of 10:00 am EDT)

1. French President De Gaulle today expressed his disapproval of "foreign troops" in the Dominican Republic and said they ought to be withdrawn, according to a French cabinet minister's comments in a subsequent press conference. The French minister added that the De Gaulle government was considering recognizing the Caamaño "government" and the French ambassador in Santo Domingo had already been in contact with the rebel regime. No definite decision on recognition had yet been made, however. Foreign Minister Couve de Murville added his observation, according to Reuters, that Colonel Caamaño "seemed to benefit from the support of the Dominican parliament".

2. An anti-American mob, most of them members of the Communist-led university student federation, battled police last night in Buenos Aires in what the US press calls "the worst outbreak of violence in Argentina in years". An undetermined number of persons were injured in the rioting, and one person died of a heart attack apparently brought on by the excitement.

**3. Central Intelligence Agency Report, 6 May 1965**

OCI No. 1615/65

CENTRAL INTELLIGENCE AGENCY
Office of Current Intelligence

INTELLIGENCE MEMORANDUM

**Situation in the Dominican Republic**

(Report No. 174 — as of 10:00 pm EDT)

1. The rebels are moving from the southern part of the rebel-held Ciudad Nueva section and are concentrating in the Independence Park area of downtown Santo Domingo.

2. Earlier information that the Guatemalan Embassy in Santo Domingo was under attack was apparently incorrect. The Embassy, which is in the International Safety Zone, was only subjected to sporadic sniper fire this afternoon.

4. Rebel-held Radio Santo Domingo carried three statements by Juan Bosch this evening. Bosch exhorted the Dominican people to support the "constitutional" government headed by Francisco Caamaño. Bosch stated that behind Caamaño is the "will of the democrats and my political and personal desire to help him with the last drop of my blood". Bosch, quoting an editorial in today's New York Times, stated that the US is not omnipotent, though some Americans would wish it to be. He said that the Times "demanded the withdrawal of US forces as soon as possible in the name of the US people".

## 4. Unsourced US Intelligence Report, 10 May 1965[9]

### THE COMMUNIST ROLE IN THE DOMINICAN REVOLT

### Summary

It seems clear now as it did in the last days of April that a modest number of hard-core Communist leaders in Santo Domingo managed by superior training and tactics to win for themselves a position of considerable influence in the revolt within the first few days. Their influence within the movement grew day by day, and following the collapse of Molina's Government on 27 April there appeared to be no organization within the rebel camp capable of denying them full control of the rebellion within a very few days.

At the same time, the rebel cause, enjoying as it did the backing of Bosch and the continued support of several thousand military personnel, seemed likely to prosper in the face of the ineffective and dispirited countermeasures of the loyalists military.

Thus the prospect at the time of US intervention clearly was one in which a movement increasingly under the influence of Castroites and other Communists was threatening to gain the ascendancy in the Dominican Republic.

### Introduction

1. The insurrection that began against the Reid Government on 24 April was touched off by a group of junior and middle grade army officers, most of whom were nominally sympathetic to exiled former President Juan Bosch with whom they were in contact. "Constitutionalism", the slogan of Bosch's Dominican Revolutionary Party (PRD), was used by these officers as a convenient rallying cry to attract quick popular support for their effort. Indeed for a short while the rebellion had a heavy PRD flavour.

2. The PRD flavor soon began to fade, however. Within a few hours known Communists and extreme leftist civilian leaders were setting up their own paramilitary organizations. The early days of the revolt were critical. To understand fully how and why the Communists were able to react so swiftly, and how, as the intensity of the fighting increased, they were able to assume control of much of the rebel movement, it is necessary first to examine the background of the revolt.

9   This long document reproduces the text of the report found in the British archives, undated, but in its title and first paragraphs corresponding to a summary in the US archives dated 10 May 1965. No authorship is given for the text, but from textual evidence ('flavor', 'Peiping') it would appear to have originated in the USA. Given the very strong pressure that was coming from the Johnson Administration for evidence of 'communist' involvement in the Santo Domingo events, this is probably an INR (US Bureau of Intelligence and Research) or CIA document prepared to meet White House requests.

3. Juan Bosch's landslide election to the Presidency in December 1962 was a measure of the popular revulsion to the years of Trujillo tyranny and of the thirst for reforms of the social and economic fabric of the country. Despite his popularity the idealistic President survived for only a stormy seven months in office. He never had the confidence of the conservative elements of the economic oligarchy primarily because of his reform proposals. He rapidly lost the confidence of the military establishment because of his permissive attitude toward the growth of Communism in the country, and his inept administration. The armed forces were also concerned because of Bosch's obvious distaste for the military.

4. The Communists and their allies flourished under the Bosch administration. It was in this period that what had earlier been tiny groups of malcontent intellectuals began to expand and to improve their organization techniques. The Moscow-oriented Dominican Popular Socialist Party (PSPD) was the most professional of the Communist groups and along with the Dominican Popular Movement (MPD), a self-proclaimed Marxist-Leninist party with affinities for Peiping, still today provide the hard core of Communist militants. On the eve of the current rebellion it was estimated that the PSPD had about 1000 or more well-indoctrinated members and the MPD some 300.

5. Also beginning to expand at this time was the Castroite 14th of June Political Group (APCJ). This organization is the mass-based party of the extreme left. It now boasts some 3000 members plus perhaps 20000 sympathisers. Largely because of its origin as a patriotic and nationalist movement fighting the Trujillo tyranny, the APCJ still retains many non-Communist members. However, it came under effective Communist leadership as Bosch assumed power.

6. The atmosphere of the Bosch administration was naturally conducive to Communist growth. Soon after his inauguration, for example, leading Communist exiles began returning to the Dominican Republic and openly conducted party operation. Communists and Castroites were allowed to travel freely to and from Cuba and the Bloc. Dato Pagan, a leading crypto Communist theoretician, was permitted to conduct a school in a government-owned building aimed at creating a cadre of ideologically-trained young Communists, despite US pressure on Bosch to close the school.

7. Bosch himself was apparently convinced that his own democratic and moderate revolutionary program had such popular support that it could not be seriously threatened by the Communists, and that they would remain a harmless and isolated minority. He never had an opportunity to prove his point. After repeated warnings that he should take steps to curb the Communists, the military overthrew him in a coup headed by General Wessin y Wessin in September 1963.

8. The Junta which replaced Bosch ultimately became the Reid Government. It was the target of all leftist groups from the PRD to the Communists. Two extremist groups actually took up arms against the new regime. In December 1963 members of the Dominican Popular Movement (MPD) launched a guerrilla operation in the hills of the interior. They were joined by members of the pro-Castro 14th of June Political Group. The guerrillas were rooted out by the Dominican armed forces; one of the most effective extremist leaders, Manuel Taracez, was killed; and many other leaders of the MPD and the APCJ were exiled. Many of the exiles found their way to Cuba where a number of them received training in guerrilla warfare and in other subversive tactics. The extremists began infiltrating back into their country in the latter half of the 1964 and by early 1965 at least 45 had clandestinely re-entered the country.

9. During 1964 and early 1965 Juan Bosch's party, the Dominican Revolutionary Party (PCD), was pressing its demands for the return to constitutionalist government. During this period there were growing contacts between members of Bosch's party and the MPD, the APCJ, and the Moscow-oriented Dominican Popular Socialist Party, all of whom say the advantage of pressing for the return of Bosch and his constitutionally-elected government. Although the leadership of Bosch's PRD claimed to be strongly opposed to any agreement with the extremist, there was evidence during March and early April of this year that middle-level PRD officials had approached the APCJ for support. A group of 33 new PRD leaders sworn in on 3 February 1965 included four of the former leaders of a now-defunct extremist party, the Nationalist Revolutionary Party (PNR), as well as several other persons known to have been associated with or to be in contact with elements of the extreme left. In short, the three extremist parties had effectively aligned themselves with the PRD's platform which demanded the return of Bosch to the Presidency and at the same time were attempting, with at least some success, to infiltrate and influence the PRD.

10. The regime which succeeded Bosch in power never developed a base of popular support. Despite the efforts by Reid to cope with some of the country's more pressing economic problems, his government was regarded by a large segment of the politically aware population as being merely the instrument of the old economic oligarchy exploiting the population.

11. In this atmosphere, Bosch retained a large following in the Dominican Republic and plotting for his return gradually intensified. Bosch's own involvement in this plotting is reliably established. A Dominican army officer with good contacts at the general staff level in mid-April, less than two weeks before the coup began, said that Bosch was organizing a plot to overthrow sometime between 18 April and 1 June. He accurately reported that Lt. Colonel

Miguel Angel Hernando was to be one of the plot leaders and added that Hernando had travelled to Puerto Rico to discuss the coup plans with Bosch.

12. There had been information from other sources prior to the coup on Bosch's involvement in the planning. A high ranking Dominican army officer told a US Embassy officer on 16 April — eight days before the coup — that PRD leader Peña Gómez had returned from Puerto Rico on 15 April with funds to buy support for a coup from units of the Duarte, Mella and Sanchez battalions of the army. The units that did, in fact, launch the coup effort. On 14 February of this year, a US military source who has good contacts in the Dominican Republic and among Dominican politicians abroad reported that Bosch had been holding meetings in Puerto Rico and New York concerning plans for a coup. Bosch's activities reportedly were financed by Diego Bordas, a wealthy businessman and former member of Bosch's cabinet. Another source, untested — but with good Dominican military and political connections — reported on 8 February that Juan Bosch and associates among whom were Nicolas Silfa, Gustavo Espinal, Jacobo Majluta, Pedro Rodriguez Echevarria, and Rafael Fernandez Dominguez, were plotting to overthrow the Reid regime.

13. In its earliest moments then the rebellion appeared to be a coup of anti-Reid officers, some of whom had old scores to settle with Wessin y Wessin, and some of whom were intent on returning Bosch from exile in Puerto Rico. Many PRD members who had not been involved in the plotting quickly threw in with the rebels; a provisional government headed by PRD member Rafael Molina Urena was proclaimed and Bosch was asked to return.

14. It now appears, however, that extremist and Communist groups also had advanced word of the revolt. One report states unnamed PRD leaders approached the Peiping-oriented Dominican Popular Movement on or about 23 April, the day before the coup, and asked MPD leaders for support in a coup attempt. The source, a member of the MPD who had furnished reliable information in the past, added that the PRD leaders had assured the MPD that the PRD would furnish the arms. Juan Bosch was identified as one of the leaders of the plot.

15. In any event, once news of the revolt became public on the afternoon of 24 April, these groups moved quickly to participate. Leaders of the three Communist parties began collecting arms, organizing their forces, and establishing strongpoints in Santo Domingo. The PSPD established its principal strongpoint, or garrison, at the house of party leader Buenaventura Johnson Pimentel at No. 5 Calle Espaillat. A known paramilitary center of the PSPD was the residence of Buenaventura Johson Pimental, Calle Espaillat. PSPD activists were observed at the house on 25 April, engaged in stockpiling

efforts. It was reported on 28 April that the PSPD, under cover of the darkness of the previous night, relocated the headquarters at a party member's house elsewhere. However, Johnson's residence continued to be an apparently important command post and arsenal.

16. A building on the corner of Arzobispo Portes Avenue and Sanchez Street also served as a PSPD stronghold during this period. Diomedes Mercedes Garcia, Jose Rodriguez Acosta, and other PSPD leaders were observed there and were seen leading a paramilitary force armed with submachine guns and rifles, Molotov cocktails and hand grenades.

17. The APCJ is known to have established a strongpoint during this same period on Jose Gabriel Street near the Malecon in the Ciudad Nueva section of the city. A heavily armed paramilitary force was seen using this building as a base. A headquarters and strongpoint of MPD guerrillas was established on Benigue Street in the Ciudad Nueva area.

18. On the first day of the rebellion the military rebels, fearful that the high command would move rapidly against them, opened the arsenals of Santo Domingo and began passing out weapons to civilians. One such arsenal was at the "27 February" camp on the outskirts of the city where Colonel Francisco Caamaño directed the release of the stocked weapons. This and similar actions elsewhere on subsequent days provided the leaders of the various Communist and extremist groups with the material they needed to supplement their own collection of arms and become a significant factor in the rebellion.

19. Buenaventura Johnson Pimental, Juan Ducoudray Mansfield, Jaime Duran Hernando and Fidelio Despradel Roques were particularly active in acquiring weapons and equipping their followers in both the PSPD and APCJ. The last of these, Despradel, had been trained in Cuba, and according to reliable informants, had received funds from the Chinese Communist Embassy in Paris prior to his return to the Dominican Republic in October 1964. All these men appeared to be responsive to direction from Manuel Gonzalez Gonzalez, a Spanish Communist veteran of the Spanish Civil War.

20. By the afternoon of Sunday, April 25, the situation in Santo Domingo had become chaotic and confused. Violence had begun but there was more feinting and jabbing than significant action. Some of the rebels, particularly among the military, were tempted by offers from the loyalists for the establishment of a new Junta which would seek a solution, presumably along traditional compromise lines. The Wessin forces, apparently taken by surprise, were reacting slowly and not very effectively. In this situation the Communists were intent on strengthening popular participation in the revolt. Public address cars

manned by identifiable PSPD members prowled the city directing the crowds to tactical positions.

21. At this point the PRD leaders appeared to share the initiative with rebel officers; the Communists were busying themselves with organizing the distribution of weapons to "reliable" groups and rounding up manpower for civilian militant units. It was in this period that the various Communist parties established their weapons depots and set up disbursing controls.

22. As they established their organizations to assume the military effectiveness of the civilian rebels, the Communists apparently also began to turn their attention to the political ends of the revolt. On the night of April 25 and the early morning hours of April 26 rebel leaders consulted in the captured Presidential Palace on strategy and on the composition of a provisional government. To these meetings came PSPD leaders Ariosto Sora, Milvio Perez, and Silvano Lora, as well as a Cuban trained guerrilla fighter of the APCJ, Facundo Gomez.

23. These conversations in the palace showed for the first time not only that the Communists were intent on winning influence in the rebellion, but that they already had a degree of bargaining power.

24. A lawyer and retired army officer, Rafael E.Saldana Jimenez, was acting as legal adviser to the rebel military officers occupying the national palace between 24 and 27 April. Saldana is closely connected to the APCJ and is reported to have used his military connections during 1963 to obtain weapons for the APCJ. APCJ and MPD leaders are known to have been in communication with Saldana on 27 April and at other times.

25. Thus by the night of April 26 the rebellion was undergoing a rapid evolution. The Communist militants among the rebel had established their credentials as effective and ruthless leaders. They were recruiting supporters with sound tracks and manufacturing Molotov cocktails for use against Wessin's tanks. This latter task was a specialty of PSPD members. APCJ activists organized in patrols were arresting "political prisoners" and often meting out rough justice on the spot.

26. At the same time the loyalist forces who had been badly disunited and disorganized were finally beginning to buckle down to the business of blasting out the rebel-held areas of the city. The rebellion had turned a corner, or rather two corners: the pressure on the rebels was becoming more intense — and the political character of the rebel movement was moving left.

**The Rebellion — Second Phase — April 27/29**

27. Monday, April 26, was the last day of the short-lived Molina rebel government. The day began with vigorous bombardments of the downtown area of Santo Domingo by loyalist planes and naval guns. While heavy casualties were being sustained in the rebel sectors, members of the PSPD were meeting at the home of Nicolas Richardo Vicioso to plan the destruction of the city by fire if Wessin's troops entered. This was apparently characteristic of the Communists' doggedness during this bleakest hour for the rebels. Before the night was over it had become the dominant mood of the workers' quarters embittered by the bombing raids. Some of the military rebels apparently had had enough, but they were relieved of their weapons by rebels before being allowed to defect to the loyalists.

28. The principal defections at this stage of the rebellion besides that of Molina were those of Jose Pena Gomez, Colonel Hernando Ramirez, and Antonio Martinez Francisco, the Secretary General of the PRD. After he had withdrawn from the rebel camp and taken refuge, Jose Pena Gomez, a prominent PRD leader, informed US Embassy officers that he considered his movement to have been defeated. He admitted that the Communists who joined the rebel force had infiltrated into positions of importance and that it was very difficult to stop them. Molina, who took asylum in the Colombian Embassy, is reported to have said on 5 May that he wanted to get the truth of Communist infiltration across to the world, but that he could not face further jeopardizing his and his family's safety. He reportedly said that he was already under intense attack by the Communists for opposing them. Also, he was reluctant to make any statement that would force him to give up asylum.

29. Martinez made his way out of the rebel lines and on April 28 addressed the nation over San Isidro radio, controlled by the forces of General Wessin y Wessin. In that broadcast, Martinez said "I beg all to lay down their arms; turn them in to the nearest military post, because this is no longer a fight between political parties".

30. The various Communist organizations now were definitely setting the tone of the rebellion. The Communists led attacks on police barracks in a drive to win control of available weapons and supervise their disposition. It was the MPD which spearheaded the attack on the police fortress on the Ozama River. The fall of the fortress on 29 April meant a fresh supply of arms and ammunition for the Communist and extremist groups. Executions of captured police and other loyalists were undertaken without trial, and Communist literature was turned out on the presses of the newspaper Prensa Libre. Foreign banks were looted. Most importantly for the rebels, the loyalists began to falter. Indeed the rebels were gaining the upper hand in Santo Domingo when the marines landed and the situation stabilized.

31. It seems clear now as it did in the last days of April that a modest number of hard core Communist leaders in Santo Domingo — 83 have so far been identified as active participants by US observers and other sources — managed by superior training and tactics to win for themselves a position of considerable influence in the revolt within the first few days. Their influence within the movement grew day by day, and following the collapse of Molina's government on 27 April there appeared to be no organization within the rebel camp capable of denying them full control of the rebellion within a very few days.

32. At the same time, the rebel cause, enjoying as it did the backing of Bosch and the continued support of several thousand military personnel, seemed likely to prosper in the fact of the ineffective and dispirited countermeasures of the loyalists military.

33. Thus the prospect at the time of US intervention clearly was one in which a movement increasingly under the influence of Castroites and other Communists was threatening to gain the ascendancy in the Dominican Republic.

34. Following the arrival of the first US Marines on the evening of 29 April and the subsequent build-up of US forces over the next few days the rebels lost hope of a military victory. Their emphasis then shifted to propaganda and political moves designed to discredit the US and to enhance their claims as the "constitutional" successors of Bosch. This activity culminated in the "election" on 4 May of Colonel Caamaño as "President". Communist actions during this period displayed several tendencies. Some of the trained guerrilla fighters began to slip out of Santo Domingo. Some were seen driving toward Santiago and others were reported moving out to points in the interior where they were said to be caching their arms and planning the initiation of guerrilla warfare at some more propitious time. Still others, including top PSPD leaders, were said to have gone into hiding in the capital.

35. Other Communists remained active in the city inciting the people to continued resistance and provoking the sniping fire at US forces and buildings in the international safety zone. Although there is no hard information, it appears likely that some of these actions may have been intended to provoke US forces to take bloody reprisals that could then be exploited to inflame OAS and world opinion against the US.

36. Still other leftist leaders remained close to the military leaders of the revolt, advising on tactics and propaganda. For example, a usually reliable source reported subsequently that the resolution signed by the rebel "legislature" proclaiming the new government established by the rebels had actually been written on 3 May by lawyers with Communist sympathies.

37. Other sources have reported that APCJ leaders were energetic during this period in urging Caamaño to accept the Presidency when he was at first reluctant. One report from an untested source claims that the Communists extracted a promise from Caamaño under duress to consult with them and follow their advice if the rebel cause should succeed. According to the source this promise was made at a meeting attended around 1 May by several leading members of PSPD and at least two ranking members of the APCJ.

38. Although the patterns of Communist activity after the US intervention have shown various tendencies, as indicated above, the predominant tactic has been one of withdrawal from the center of the stage. Thus, the Communists apparently made no efforts to place any of their known leaders in Caamaño's cabinet, although some of the appointees have unsavoury reputations.

39. Concurrently, as the physical danger diminished and as rebel prospects appeared to grow in the political phase, PRD leaders have returned to the rebel camp. For example, Francisco Martinez, who left the rebels on 27 April, rejoined the rebels in early May. Other PRD leaders, including Jose Pena Gomez, Maxione Lovatio and Jorge Yeara Hasser came back to the rebel camp on 4 and 5 May.

40. As the Caamaño government deals with the OAS commission and seeks recognition abroad, therefore, it presents to the world the picture of a moderate leftist regime dedicated to the fulfilment of a popular revolution — an image that is likely to have considerable appeal in many parties of Latin America. There may be only a few Communists in sight when negotiations with the OAS begin, but had it not been for the Communists' early role the rebels would not have won even the strong negotiating position they now hold.

Two unclassified Annexes as described below to follow:

Annex A: Cuban involvement in Dominican revolutionary activities.

Annex B: Communist participation in the Dominican rebellion consisting of names and summary information of 83 Communists and extreme leftists who were all active participants in the rebellion.

## 5. Notes of a White House meeting, 30 April 1965

On April 30, 1965, from 8:30 to 10:45 a.m., a meeting on the Dominican Republic took place in the White House Cabinet Room. Until 9:40 a.m., when President Johnson entered the meeting, Rusk, McNamara, Raborn, General Wheeler, Bromley Smith, Bundy, Valenti, Moyers, Ball, Martin, Dick Goodwin, Mann, and Vance discussed the April 29 OAS meeting (see footnote 2, Document 45); U.S. efforts to send an OAS contingent to the Dominican Republic; and the possibility of sending Martin to the Dominican Republic. Valenti's handwritten notes of the remainder of the meeting follow:

*Martin:* Has doubts about the Communists in charge? CIA has no doubts. Rebels are not all of the same stripe. With [American] troops in the country it is difficult to talk with the rebels.

*LBJ:* I am not willing to let this island go to Castro. OAS is a phantom. They are taking a siesta while this is on fire. How can we send troops 10,000 miles away and let Castro take over right under our nose. Let's just analyze. We have resisted Communists all over the world: Vietnam, Lebanon, and Greece. What are we doing under our doorstep. We know the rebel leaders are Communist, and we are sitting here waiting on OAS. We know Castro will hate us. We got rid of the dictator and we will now get a real dictator.

*Rusk:* We can move through the OAS and achieve what you want. Martin can communicate on two levels 1) with rebels, and 2) with groups who can oppose rebels.

*LBJ:* (to McNamara) Why don't you first find out what we need to take that island. Rusk, why don't you determine what it takes to make this take on the right color.

*Bundy:* We have no international cover. We have no real legitimacy.

*McNamara:* Danger of rebel troops and uprising in the countryside.

*Ball:* Danger of junta renouncing us because they sense anti-Communist sentiment.

*McNamara:* One to two divisions can clean up the island. We can have one division in 30 hours.

*Bundy:* We ought to wait a day. By that time we can have some legitimate cover.

*LBJ:* 2 dangers: 1) wind up with [illegible] support with Castro government, 2) or Castro-dominated in a short time. We have done little in the past several days.

*Bundy:* We have done a great deal. We are talking about a division going in and we couldn't do that several days ago.

*LBJ:* I think enough leaders are there to make it Castro. Not all Cubans were Communist. I am ashamed of the little we have done.

*Ball:* But we have done considerable ...; we have put men ashore without real angry response.

*LBJ:* I want McNamara to get ready so that Castro cannot take over.

*McNamara:* Before we move, open press corps .... show evidence of Castro takeover, evidence irrefutable. Until we act, Castro will be in command of the island, China Reds. Call on Latin American countries to join us in support to crush Communist threat. Call on Dominican Republic citizens to organize their own government. Must have some government to get behind. Asked us to come in to save their island from communism.

*LBJ*: I want us to feverishly try to cloak this with legitimacy. We cannot stand with our hand in our pocket and let Castro win. Military get ducks in a row. Diplomats see if we can do anything to get observers in here or troops from other Latin American countries. We are willing to do whatever is necessary to put the pistols down. We will have one of 3 dictators: 1) U.S., 2) Moderate dictator, 3) Castro dictator.

*Bundy:* Here are some thoughts that may or may not be helpful to you. One thing is clear: a Castro victory in the D.R. would [be] the worst domestic political disaster we could possibly suffer. But in order to quash Castro in D.R. we need above all else to get hemispheric public opinion on our side. We can do it this way: Before we move call an open press conference. 1. Show indisputable evidence that Castro-Communists are in control in the D.R. (CIA ought to prepare full dossiers). Vital that this [be] proven without a doubt. If can be linked to Chinese reds all the better. 2. Call on D.R. citizens to rise up (if at all possible, a group of responsible D.R. citizens should cry out for us to save them from Castro). 3. Call on Latin-American countries to join with us? (if we can announce 2, 3 or 4 countries who are with us all the better). 4. Give the choice: stand by [and] do nothing, let Castro take over or with the OAS and local entreaties move in to quell the Castro people and save this island from black darkness. We must lay the public opinion base — a clear choice: freedom versus Castro; citizens cry out for help versus Castro reds." (Johnson Library, Office of the President File, Valenti Meeting Notes).[10]

---

10  Sections of Valenti's notes were included in an April 30 report to the President on
    the Dominican Republic. (*Ibid.*, National Security File, Defense, ND 19/CO 62,
    1/1/65/5/5/65).

### 6. US Congress Debate, 14 May 1965

CONGRESSIONAL RECORD — SENATE

**THE SITUATION IN THE DOMINICAN REPUBLIC**

Mr. CLARK. Mr President, first I should like to offer for the Record a recent editorial published in the New York Times entitled "Government in Crisis". I ask that it be printed in the Record at this point in my remarks.

There being no objections, the editorial was ordered to be printed in the Record as follows:

GOVERNMENT IN CRISIS

The Dominican and Vietnam troubles disclose a serious weakness in this country's management of its foreign affairs. This weakness has been a long time developing and it will not easily be set right, but its many-added nature and its implications deserve exploration.

The weakness is simply stated. Congress control of the warmaking power has been eroded almost to the point of invisibility. This development is readily understandable insofar as the waging of thermonuclear war is concerned. If the President learns that hostile atomic missiles have been launched against the United States, he has no time and no choice except to act in his unique capacity as Commander in Chief.

But it is guerrilla wars, undeclared wars, civil wars, and wars by subversion that now plague the world and are likely to continue as the chief difficulties in the years ahead. It is in this area of policymaking that the people's elected representatives in Congress have largely abdicated their constitutional responsibilities.

Speed is not the overriding consideration in making policy in these diverse difficulties. The war in Vietnam, for example, has been dragging on for several years and US activity there has been intensifying for 9 months. Yet Congress has not conducted a full, serious debate on American participation.

It is true, of course, that Congress has gone on record not once but twice, President Johnson has seen to that. Last August, after a now almost forgotten air strike in the Gulf of Tonkin, and again last week, Congress dutifully countersigned what came close to being a blank check. In the case of the August revolution and of last week's $700 million appropriation bill, there was a suddenly announced television speech by the President. Then came the submission of a hastily drafted proposal which the relevant committee of Congress approved with the flimsiest of hearings and which both Houses approved with no real deliberation.

From initiation to Presidential signature, each of these manoeuvres took only 3 days. That is not constitutional procedure: it is a caricature of such procedure.

The Dominican trouble exemplifies congressional default in a different form. In October 1963, after a military junta overthrew President Juan Bosch in the Dominican Republic, Senators [...] of New York and [...] of Oregon, introduced a resolution intended to put forth the sense of Congress on Latin-American dictatorships.

No action was ever taken on this resolution. Nor did the relevant House and Senate committees develop any congressional judgement on American policy in the event of future revolutions and coups in Latin America. When civil war erupted in the Dominican Republic, President Johnson acted in a vacuum, one partly of Congress' own making.

The problem long predates Mr. Johnson's Presidency. It first became evident in the failure of Congress to clarify its own responsibility for the waging of war in Korea, where war was never actually declared.

There are many present contributing influences to the diminution of congressional authority in policymaking, quite apart from Mr. Johnson's forceful assertion of leadership. One is Senator [...] of responsible bipartisanship into something that often approaches coalition government. Another is the reluctance of Senator [...] to follow his independent ideas by asserting his full authority as chairman of the Foreign Relation Committee.

But beyond these transient personal factors, there has been an institutional failure on the part of Congress to develop the new procedures and tradition necessary to protect its role in the making of foreign policy in a new age of international political warfare.

The nature of the cold war, the speed with which minor engagements can escalate, the extent to which secret information must help shape vital decisions — all these and many other factors have made the development of new procedures and practices difficult. But they have also made them essential if there is not to be a total erosion of Congress' authority in this field and an atrophy of democratic debate.

Mr. CLARK. Mr. President, the editorial points out that both the Dominican and the Vietnamese troubles disclose a serious weakness in this country's management of its foreign affairs.

The editorial points out:

The weakness is simply stated. Congress control of the warmaking power has been eroded almost to the point of invisibility.

The editorial continues:

There has been an institutional failure on the part of Congress to develop the new procedures and tradition necessary to protect its role in the making of foreign policy in a new age of international political warfare.

I am in complete accord with that statement in the editorial. I do not believe we have done our job in Congress. I believe we should resume an active interest in terms of our historic power of advice and consent in determining the course of our foreign policy. The day-to-day conduct of foreign policy is, of course, in the hands of the President of the United States. I support him in his efforts to restore and maintain peace. However, Congress has an obligation which I believe we have been slow and perhaps loath to fulfil.

I hope that we will be more active in fulfilling that constitutional responsibility.

Another excellent editorial recently appeared in the New York Times. It is entitled "The Dominican Morass". I ask unanimous consent that it may be printed at this point in my remarks.

There being no objection, the editorial was ordered to be printed in the Record as follows:

## THE DOMINICAN MORASS

The United States is getting more and more deeply involved inside the Dominican Republic, politically as well as militarily. What began as an uprising has become a civil war in a state of suspended animation. Whether there was or was not a genuine threat of a Communist coup — and US correspondents are emphatic in casting doubt on Washington's assertions that there was — it is clear that Dominican and Latin American communism has been strengthened in reaction against the American intervention.

What may have seemed to the American public to be a simple operation when President Johnson first sent in marines on April 28 has become a complicated, confused, and potentially explosive act of force majeure, with profound effects on the whole inter-American system. Some of the United States' best friends in Latin America are included among the anti-Communist governments and peoples whom American intervention has alienated. The man in whose name the rebellion was started, the strongly anti-Communist Juan Bosch, may yet prove correct in his bitter comment that the United States, by its intervention, will create far more Communist sympathizers in the Dominican Republic and Latin America than were on hand — whatever their number — when the revolt began.

The Dominican situation is proving that the best intentions mean little or nothing in the face of contrary realities. No one could doubt the sincerity of Under Secretary Mann when he stated in an interview with the Times that the United States does not want to dictate the kind of government the Dominicans choose. But the fact is that the US intervention bolstered a rightwing military coup against a movement that, while it had some Communists within it, was for the most part democratic in spirit and intention. The idea of supporting the Bosch elements against the Communist minority in the rebel ranks was apparently never even entertained.

When it became clear that the military junta's first leader, Gen. Wessin y Wessin, was adamantly opposed in the Dominican Republic and throughout Latin America, Washington came up with another — but equally unpopular and rightwing — protégé. American correspondents on the spot agree that General Imbert, now head of the junta, was chosen, groomed, and put in by the Americans and is being kept in power by Americans.

US representatives refused even to talk with the rebel group headed by Lieutenant Colonel Caamaño until yesterday although Colonel Caamaño clearly has a considerable following throughout the Dominican Republic. In his enclave in Santo Domingo, surrounded by American troops, he has thousands of fanatically dedicated and well-armed followers.

In present circumstances the stalemate can be broken in only two ways. One is a cleanup by the American troops of the rebel enclave in Santo Domingo, with inevitable slaughter and destruction. The other is continued negotiation with the Caamaño-Bosch group. Of the two methods, it is a peaceful settlement that holds the best hope — we believe the only hope — of controlling ultimately the Dominican Communists.

In the long run, even if the marines once again stay on for years, it is the Dominicans and not the Americans who are going to decide the fate of the Dominican Republic.

Mr. CLARK. Mr President, the editorial points out — and I share the view — that there is a very grave question as to whether or not there is now or ever was a genuine threat of a Communist coup in the Dominican Republic. It points out that the US correspondents on the scene are emphatic in casting doubt on Washington's assertions that there were. It is clear, as the editorial points out, that "Dominican and Latin-American communism has been strengthened in the reaction against the American intervention". It has certainly not been weakened.

In my opinion, for every Communist in the Dominican Republic that we rout out or kill or capture or scare back to Cuba, we make 100 and perhaps

1000 other Communists by the ruthless methods of our intervention in the Dominican Republic, in violation of our treaty commitments.

In this connection I should like to make a few comments. In my opinion, the greatest contribution that we in the Senate can make to the day-to-day course of events in the Dominican Republic is to urge that the United States maintain a strictly neutral posture between the so-called rebel government, which is actually the only government with a surety of constitutional authority behind it, in the Dominican Republic, and the various military generals and juntas with whom, in my opinion, our Armed Forces have become entirely too friendly.

Note should be taken of the fact that it was a high ranking naval officer and not a representative of the State Department who first made the announcement on the scene in the Dominican Republic that our purpose in sending the marines, and later Army troops, into the Dominican Republic was not only to protect American lives — and let it be noted parenthetically that not one single American civilian has received as much as one scratch either before or after our troops went in — but also, as this high ranking anonymous naval officer was quoted as saying, to prevent a Communist government from taking over in the Dominican Republic.

I am concerned that day-to-day military operations are overtaking diplomacy in the Dominican Republic. I am concerned that our Ambassador has apparently been panicked into believing that we were faced with an overriding emergency under which a takeover by a Communist government in the Dominican Republic was imminent. I am distressed that he felt that he should rely to the extent that he did on the "Dominican Joe McCarthy", General Wessin y Wessin and the assassinator of Trujillo, the former civilian Imbert, who, in reward for his assassination, was made a general.

One difficulty with the situation in the Dominican Republic is that as a result of 30 years of tyranny, torture, death, and assassination, most of the brains and most of the ability in the civilian population in the Dominican Republic has been murdered or chased out of the island by Trujillo and his minions. It would be a great tragedy if we were to aid and abet the military junta in resuming power in that country.

I am happy indeed that the President was so quick to call in the Organization of American States. I note with pleasure that he has taken as his advisers a select group of very able Latin Americans who are friendly to our country — individuals such as former President Betancourt of Venezuela, former President Jose Figueres of Costa Rica, and other high officials who happen to be American citizens, such as former Assistant Secretary of State Morales, who is now working with the OAC, and that magnificent colonial administrator, former Governor Muñoz-Marín of Puerto Rico. I hope that advice of those people will be listened to with great interest and followed in the White House, and I have every hope that it will.

I should like to make another suggestion in connection with the situation in the Dominican Republic. The sooner we can get our troops out of there, the better. The sooner we can turn the military situation over to contingents from the other countries which are members of the Organization of the American States, the sooner we shall prove to the people of Latin America, whose friendship and respect we so desperately want, that our action is not a return to gunboat diplomacy, and that our intervention was merely to protect lives and to prevent chaos.

I wonder what justification we can give for housing as many as 22000 troops in the Dominican Republic in the environs of Santo Domingo? It should also be noted for the Record that there has been no uprising of any sort in that country. Outside Santo Domingo everything is quiet. So I would hope that we would be able in short order to bring back the majority, if not all, of our troops in order to reestablish our belief in collective action, and our repudiation of that gunboat diplomacy — that dollar diplomacy — which got us into so much trouble with our neighbours in the early days of present century.

I should like to make one final suggestion in that regard. The unrest in the Dominican Republic is not entirely political. A great deal of it is economic. In a country with perhaps no more than 3 million people there are at least 500000 who are totally unemployed. Perhaps the most effective gesture we could make to restore and pacify the country, to take people's minds off of political issues, and place them in a situation where they would be thankful for American intervention instead of antagonistic would be to organize a program of needed public works which could give employment to vast numbers of unemployed in the Dominican Republic.

I believe we ought to look pretty carefully in the Senate — certainly in the executive arm — to the charge which has been widely repeated that the real force behind the counterrevolution which threw out the constitutionally elected President Juan Bosch, and which is now attempting to crush the rebellion headed by his deputy Caamaño, are economic interests, American and Dominican alike, and particularly sugar interests; which are concerned lest a liberal government come into office with power to enforce a badly and long needed land reform, to see that adequate taxes are collected from the very rich who are making money out of agriculture and industrial operations in the Dominican Republic, and to assure that in due course we can have a

Government which is not controlled by a military junta, but by a Government which has substantial support from the civilian population in the Government.

Mr. President, I ask unanimous consent to have printed at this point in the Record an editorial entitled "Our Dominican Objective", published in the Washington Evening Star, issue of May 4.

There being no objection, the editorial was ordered to be printed in the Record, as follows:

## OUR DOMINICAN OBJECTIVE

Among a mass of falsehoods, there was one grain of truth or near truth, in Nikolai Fedorenko's remarks to the Security Council. The United States, the Russian representative declared, is determined to use its Armed Forces to suppress Communist-supported national liberation movements not only in Latin America, but in Asia and other parts of the world as well.

Had he said Communist dominated, this would have been substantially true. Certainly we are fully committed to use our Armed Forces to prevent the forceful emergence of another Communist regime in this hemisphere. And in certain situations in Asia, where we have treaty or other commitments, as in Vietnam, we also will use our Armed Forces to cope with these so-called wars of national liberation.

The true nature of these wars should be understood. No one, except in the last extremity, intends to fight an all-out nuclear war. The cost would be prohibitive. It also seems doubtful that there will be another large-scale conventional war. Hence, the war of liberation. The Communists can foment this kind of war at small cost and little risk to themselves. And where an indigenous revolutionary movement, as in Vietnam, can be encouraged and eventually taken over, a war of liberation can be a very difficult thing to deal with. But Mr. Fedorenko is right in saying that the United States will resist them to the best of its ability. If we don't, who will?

The principal effort in the Dominican Republic at this time, however, is on the attempt to find a formula for peace, not on war. Our troops are not fighting the rebels in any meaningful sense. Instead, they are "containing" them while the OAS commission presses its search for acceptable terms.

Obviously, this search may be quite difficult. One must hope, however, that it will succeed. The President has repeated that we will pull out our forces as soon as a peace plan is developed which offers some hope of stability of government. The inference, of course, is that the troops will stay where they are until some such peace plan emerges. Hence, the sooner an agreement is reached the better it will be for all concerned.

**7. House of Representatives, Statement by Congressman Donald Rumsfeld 18 May 1965**

**Fidel's Sister Warned Dominicans of Revolt**

EXTENSION OF REMARKS of HON. DONALD RUMSFELD of Illinois in the House of Representatives

Mr. RUMSFELD. Mr. Speaker, to those who doubt that the Communist threat in Latina America is very real, I call attention to the following story carried in the American edition of the Times of Havana, April 1965, of the warning given by the sister of Fidel Castro to the Dominicans that a revolt was being planned in their country. This is a timely reminder of the well-known Communist strategy for political takeover in countries undergoing social, economic and political change.

The article follows:

FIDEL'S SISTER WARNED DOMINICANS OF REVOLT

"I know that Castro wants to take over this country".

The speaker was Fidel's sister, Juanita, and the country she had in mind was the Dominican Republic. She should know.

Early in April Juanita Castro spoke to the Dominican people at Santo Domingo, the capital city. Three weeks later the tragic revolution against law and order began.

"The Cubans", Juanita said, "do not want the Dominican Republic to travel along democratic paths so that it will become a happy and progressive people".

BROKE WITH FIDEL

She recalled that her brother, Fidel, had been very happy about 3 years ago when he told her that his agents had "cleared the path" for the future.

Juanita fled Cuba about a year ago. She went to Mexico and since that time has travelled throughout the hemisphere.

Some Cuban sources in the underground used to count on her help even while she was still in Cuba. It was long suspected that she would come to a final break with Fidel. This finally happened about a year ago.

WARNING

Less than a month ago she warned the Dominicans that "He has tried to take your country several times. This is not the first time. It will not be the last time that Communist imperialism will use its Caribbean puppet".

She reported that Castro had ordered his agents "to infiltrate all sectors, professional, economic, labor, agriculture, and among students since communism always tries to find allies to reach power and then eliminate".

To block democratic processes at Santo Domingo "many of the local leaders of the Dominican Popular Socialist Party received training in subversion in Cuba.

"The Castro Communists have many tactics. They capture prospects and turn them into fanatics. What Lenin used to call useful idiots. They fall for false promises and are soon used for subversion. In the end they are jailed or shot".

EXILE OPINION

Miami's Cuban colony knows that only quick US action kept the Dominican Republic from taking Castro's road to Communism.

They have been through it once. They know it when they see it a second time. Where, they ask, did the thousands of Castro [end of text]

## 8. Central Intelligence Report, 2 June 1965

OCI No. 1744/65

CENTRAL INTELLIGENCE AGENCY

Office of Current Intelligence

INTELLIGENCE MEMORANDUM

**Situation in the Dominican Republic**
(Report No. 256 — As of 7:00 am EDT)

The rebels have not yet reacted to Imbert's proposal calling for elections supervised by the Organization of American States (OAS).

Imbert's plan is likely to meet with an automatic veto by Caamaño unless it can be presented in a wider context and not carry an exclusive Imbert stamp. As it now stands, the proposal does not deal with the key question of getting Caamaño's agreement or with the nature of a provisional government. Presumably Imbert and his Government of National Reconstruction (GNR) plan to hold the reigns of power until elections are held.

Both sides agreed yesterday to the neutralization of the area around the National Palace. The agreement, which will go into effect at 12:00 noon EDT today, has lessened the possibility of renewed fighting in the area. Several blocks around the palace will be demilitarized and armed forces of both sides are precluded from entering or using its limits. The loyalists will be allowed to retain a symbolic force of 25 men in the palace.

Meanwhile, a group of Santiago and Santo Domingo civic leaders is continuing to seek a compromise formula to the political stalemate. Although the group primarily represents conservative banking and business interests, it hopes to devise a progressive program of government which would meet the country's aspirations. The civic leaders are concerned about the country's deteriorating economic situation and the possibility of trouble in the interior if the impasse in Santo Domingo continues.

Santo Domingo remained quiet during the night. Yesterday evening the rebels freed three US soldiers who strayed inadvertently into the rebel-controlled area earlier in the afternoon. Caamaño told reporters that he believed the men crossed into his territory by mistake.

The Organization of American States (OAS) voted early today to send a three-nation committee to the Dominican Republic to assist in mediation efforts. The committee will be composed of representatives of the United States (Ambassador Bunker), Brazil (Ambassador Ilmar Penna Marino), and

El Salvador (Ambassador Ramon Clairmont de Duenas). The committee will probably leave for Santo Domingo sometime today.

Despite rumors of incipient troubles in Santiago, La Vega and Bani, the countryside remains quiet though uneasy.

In Santo Domingo, employee turnout for jobs in the GNR continues at a disappointingly low level. The number of employees actually at desks varies from about 10 to 50 percent. Dominican government workers are traditionally a lackadaisical group and the absence of organization and essential services, such as mail, has resulted in an almost complete absence of work. From 40 to 70 percent of the employees show up to sign attendance sheets and then go home. With the OAS handling salary payments, the link between work and pay has been broken. The GNR, not daring to dismiss absent employees for fear they will join the rebels, is virtually helpless.

## 9. Central Intelligence Agency Report, 16 June 1965

OCI No. 1951/65

CENTRAL INTELLIGENCE AGENCY
Office of Current Intelligence

INTELLIGENCE MEMORANDUM

### Situation in the Dominican Republic

(Report No. 278 — As at 7:00 am EDT)

The fighting that was initiated by the rebels yesterday morning continued most of the daylight hours until a hastily arranged cease-fire went into effect at about 9:30 pm EDT.

The night hours were apparently generally quiet except for sporadic explosions in rebel territory — the result, according to the rebels, of mortar shells being fired into the area from loyalist positions.

Twenty-four US military personnel were wounded in action yesterday, as was one Brazilian lieutenant. The rebels lost at least 16 killed and an unknown number wounded. Among the rebel dead was the French soldier of fortune Andres Riviere who is believed to have been one of the closest advisers to rebel Defence Minister Montes Arache.

A rebel force of between 30 and 40 began firing against the US troops at about 8:30 EDT yesterday morning. US forces did not begin returning the fire until they had suffered casualties. At about 9:15 am EDT the rebels attached US forces at another point from the eastern side of the rebel-controlled area and at about 1:30 EDT in the afternoon rebel attacks were made from the other side of their zone in the National Palace which is guarded by Brazilian troops.

Starting about noon EDT, US forces, with the endorsement of General Alvim, advanced into rebel-held areas several blocks in order to outflank the rebels and better protect US-held areas. By late afternoon, troops of the Inter-American Force had established a new line which, in effect, widens the International Security Zone by two city blocks along the southern edge of the corridor.

The rebel attacks seem to have been motivated in part by a desperate rebel effort to obtain more direct United Nations intervention in the Dominican Republic — a development which they have reason to believe would benefit their cause.

Within an hour after the initial rebel attacks, their radio was broadcasting an account of the "yankee attacks" complete with inflammatory allegations that US forces were killing Dominican women and children. The Caamaño government immediately lodged a protest with the UN observer team and the rebel foreign minister cabled a detailed protest to the UN secretary general. As a result, the UN Security Council has scheduled a meeting for 3:00 pm EDT this afternoon to discuss yesterday's events in the Dominican Republic and to consider the probable requests from the USSR and others for an expanded UN role in the Dominican crisis. The Soviet delegate is likely again to charge that the renewed fighting once more demonstrates that the OAS is incapable of dealing with the crisis.

Another and perhaps equally important factor behind yesterday's rebel action is the increased influence of hard-line extremist groups and particularly of the pro-Castro Fourteenth of June Political Group (APCJ) which is reported to be dominant among the armed units defending the rebel areas. The APCJ issued a publication during the big rebel rally on Monday which clearly spelled out its position that "armed struggle", not negotiation, is the only proper means of consolidating the "popular revolution".

The APCJ publication clearly indicated that there has been a strong difference of opinion between rebel factions as to the best tactics. It declared that "others believed that by conversing with the imperialists victory could be achieved. Now they concede that we are right and there is talk of incorporating the entire country into the armed struggle". The publication urged the immediate extension of the struggle to the towns and cities of the interior.

The extremists may, in fact, have calculated that an intensification of fighting in the capital would spark uprising in the interior. There have as yet, however, been no reports of any such renewed violence in the interior.

The line of the APCJ is similar to that proposed in a letter from an exiled leader of the Marxist-Leninist Dominican Popular Movement (MPD) which was intercepted by loyalist officials as it was being carried into the country. The letter proposed that "the right road, which we should have taken long ago — without talking to the OAS or to Bundy or to anybody — is that of declaring a great patriotic war against the interventionist enemy, carrying the war to all corners of the country, and condemning to death all those who collaborate with the foreign troops".

There were further indications yesterday that the rebel government may be losing control of the extremist-led armed units defending rebel territory. UN observer Mayobre told Ambassador Bunker yesterday afternoon that Caamaño had advised him that he had given orders that the shooting should cease, but was not at all confident that these orders would be obeyed. The embassy was also informed by General Alvim's chief of staff that he has received several telephone calls recently from top rebel military commanders seeking to excuse recent sporadic firing by rebel units on the grounds that these were unauthorized and committed by forces not under full rebel control.

Meanwhile, the loyalist government of Antonio Imbert has remained generally isolated from the day's main developments. He did inform the special OAS committee yesterday afternoon, however, that he had ordered his forces so deployed as to reinforce Inter-American forces in case of need. Imbert's radio stations during the day engaged in a major psychological warfare effort against rebel areas by seeking to create the impression that the Inter-American forces were moving in to wipe out the rebels once and for all.

**10. Central Intelligence Agency Report, 17 June 1965**

OCI No. 1952/65

CENTRAL INTELLIGENCE AGENCY
Office of Current Intelligence

INTELLIGENCE MEMORANDUM

**Situation in the Dominican Republic**
(Report #279 — As of 7:00 am EDT)

Inter-American troops in Santo Domingo came under moderate to heavy rebel fire again yesterday and last night as evidence continues to mount that hard-line extremists have increased their influence in the rebel movement.

Total US casualties in the two days since the rebels initiated their stepped up firing are three dead and 37 wounded. Five members of the Brazilian contingent have also been wounded.

During the day yesterday, US troops consolidated their newly gained positions in the expanded OAS-controlled corridor and in the area of the power plant on the west bank of the Ozama river.

Rebel leader Caamaño claimed during a press conference yesterday that 67 persons in rebel territory had been killed and 165 wounded during the two days. Caamaño and other rebel leaders charged the US with "indiscriminate bombardment", expressed their determination to continue the struggle, and indicated that there will be no compromise in their basic demands.

The rebel radio continued yesterday its inflammatory allegations against the US "occupation forces", charging them with "renewed inhuman acts of violence" and repeating the slogan "death to the Yankee troops". The thrust of the rebel propaganda now is that the Organization of American States, and principally the US, is the main enemy. This is the line that has been promoted by the hard line Communist-led Fourteenth of June Political Group (APCJ).

There are some divisions reportedly aggravating the differences among the three Communist parties. The Moscow-oriented Dominican Popular Socialist Party (PSPD), which has usually been the most cautious of the three parties, is said to be under fire from the hard-line groups — the Fourteenth of June Political Group (APCJ) and the Dominican Popular Movement (MPD).

[seven lines deleted]

In general, it appears that the PSPD members have grown progressively more discouraged and less willing to take action in recent weeks, while the APCJ and the MPD have grown more militant.

**11. US Congress, House of Representatives 17 June 1965**

CONGRESSIONAL RECORD — HOUSE

**DOMINICAN Caamaño PARALLELS CUBAN CASTRO**

(Mr. ROGERS of Florida asked and was given permission to address the House for 1 minute)

Mr. ROGERS of Florida. Mr. Speaker, the strength and support of rebel forces in the Dominican Republic has been grossly overrated.

Present estimates show the rebels to number 2500 to 5000 fighting in a country of 3.3 million people. Despite these small figures the rebels claim they have wide popular support, yet have refused to accept free elections supervised by the Organization of American States.

If these Dominican rebels claim to represent over 3 million people, why should they fear free elections?

It is the same old story we heard when Fidel Castro came to power, and in many respects the circumstances surrounding Cuba and the Dominican Republic run a shocking parallel. For example, both Cuba and the Dominican Republic are island nations, easily infiltrated along the shoreline; have the Communists using similar guerrilla tactics; have widespread poverty; and have lived under harsh military dictatorships.

But there is another aspect to the parallel, and that concerns reports circulated about the rebel leader, Col. Francisco Caamaño Deñó. We keep hearing, for example, that Caamaño is not a Communist. We heard that about Fidel Castro not being a Communist, that only those around him were Communists, and I hope we have learned a lesson about that by now.

However, there are some facts about Caamaño which need to be brought out. He claims to be a champion of the Dominican people, yet his own father was chief of the armed forces under the brutal Trujillo regime. In addition, on December 27 1962, Colonel Caamaño participated in a massacre of his fellow Dominicans at the village of Palma Sola, near the Haitian border. The entire village was burned, and the mission left a large number of Dominicans either dead or wounded.

It is clear that had the United States acted as swiftly in Cuba as was done in the Dominican Republic Castro and communism would not be in Havana today. It is also clear that we must pursue a firm policy in the Dominican Republic to curb Castroism in the Caribbean.

## 12. Central Intelligence Agency Report, 24 June 1965

OCI No. 1960/65

CENTRAL INTELLIGENCE AGENCY
Office of Current Intelligence

INTELLIGENCE MEMORANDUM

### Situation in the Dominican Republic

(Report No. 286 — As of 7:00 am EDT)

The Caamaño and Imbert governments both formally indicated their approval "in principle" of the OAS formula, but both responded yesterday with counter-proposals unacceptable to the other.

The rebel response, delivered to the special OAS committee yesterday morning, began with a long preamble reasserting the rebel claims that the US military intervention was an illegal act that had prevented a rebel triumph. Similarly, the OAS was condemned in the rebel statement for ratifying the US action and participating in the armed intervention.

Two of the rebel counterproposals would significantly reduce the role which the OAS expects the Inter-American Peace Force to perform in the coming months. The Caamaño regime would have the Inter-American Force evacuated within one month of the installation of a provisional government. It also insists that the weapons now controlled by its irregular forces be turned in to the provisional government, rather than the OAS.

The Caamaño regime also insists that all regular military personnel on its side, as well as all those who were dismissed after the September 1963 coup against Bosch, be reinstated in their previous ranks. The rebels also propose that the "institutional act" that the OAS would have serve as a temporary constitution include the sections on human rights from the 193 constitution and that the entire "institutional act" be ratified by the rebel congress.

The rebel counterproposals, while clearly unacceptable to the Imbert regime, do represent some important concessions from earlier rebel demands. The rebels have now abandoned their earlier insistence that they form the government to stay in power until the expiration of the term to which Bosch was elected in 1962. They also are now willing to disband their congress. The rebels may well expect to be obliged to make further concessions and the pressure of the deteriorating conditions within the rebel camp could bring them to it.

The Imbert government informed the OAS committee yesterday afternoon that it too approved the OAS formula "in principle". It insisted, however, that it has the basic attributes of the provisional government which the OAS has suggested should govern the country until after elections. It therefore insists that there is no need for it to be replaced by another provisional government. The Imbert government did indicate, however, that it would be willing to consider certain changes in its structure designed to give it a broader representation.

The statement by the Imbert government also stresses the urgent need for the "normalization" of the city of Santo Domingo and the restoration of public services and economic activity there. It also suggests that all persons identified as Communists be deported.

Meanwhile, other political and civic leaders of the country have been expressing their views on the OAS proposals. One point which many have made independently is the suggestion that elections be staggered so that the congress is not elected at the same time as the president. They point out that too often in the past — and specifically during the brief Bosch tenure — the simultaneous election of both branches of government resulted in a rubber-stamp congress. Many have also suggested that it would be advisable for a constituent assembly to be elected and a constitution promulgated prior to the installation of an elected government.

Meanwhile, the extremists in the rebel camp have all but given up on their much touted general strike effort, which has been an almost complete failure. Only the sugar mill at the La Romana sugar complex remained on strike yesterday and there were indications that the workers might return today.

## 13. Defence Intelligence Agency Report, 1 July 1965

DCI BRIEFING FOR RIVERS' CIA SUBCOMMITTEE OF HOUSE ARMED SERVICES COMMITTEE

DOMINICAN REPUBLIC (pages B1–5)

I. Communists and extremists are protesting Caamaño's decision to negotiate with the OAS, and the outbreak of fighting in San Francisco de Macoris indicates that they are attempting to take the struggle into the interior.

- Elements in the extremist camp are divided in their response to Caamaño's decision to negotiate with the OAS and accept many of its proposals.

  1. The orthodox Dominican Popular Socialist (Communist) Party generally approves Caamaño's actions, as does part of the pro-Castro Fourteenth of June Political Group (APCJ).

  2. Opposition to the Caamaño response is centered in the pro-Chinese Dominican Popular Movement (MPD) and a section of the APCJ. The MPD went so far as to mobilize 150–200 youths to demonstrate against Caamaño in front of rebel headquarters. Caamaño was reportedly planning a meeting with MPD leaders on 29 June, probably in an attempt to gain their support for his position.

  3. Available evidence indicates that the MPD and part of the APCJ were involved in the violence which broke out in the interior town of San Francisco de Marcoris on Friday. Loyalist police and army forces repulsed an 80-man group led by Communists and pro-Castro extremists. XXX had indicated for some time that the rebels were sending arms and men into the interior and pointed to San Francisco as a likely target for attack. A few days after the attack, a small rebel band unsuccessfully tried to storm a police post in the nearby town of Pimentel.

- There are many reports and rumors of future violence in the interior.

  1. The town of Moca is mentioned frequently as a possible target.

  2. The police and army are nervously on the alert and have tended to overreact to any provocation. This, in turn, has led to charges of brutality.

  3. However, one indication of a possible lessening of tension in the interior is the fact that strict curfews are no longer being enforced in some towns.

II. The extremists' actions have strengthened the Imbert government's desire to wipe out the rebels and heightened its resistance to accepting the OAS proposals.

- Uprisings in the interior have heightened Imbert's criticism of the US for not allowing him to "clean up" the rebel zone in Santo Domingo. He has hardened his attitude toward the US and the OAS, and initially refused to allow the Inter-American Human Rights Commission to investigate conditions in San Francisco. Some elements in the loyalist military, who are distressed over alleged police atrocities, hold Imbert responsible for them and would like to see him step down when a provisional government is formed.

III. Meanwhile, the return of ex-President Joaquin Balaguer has focused attention on his possible role in any political settlement.

- Balaguer returned to Santo Domingo on Monday to visit his dying mother, and his supporters are flocking to see him. It is not known how long he will stay, as Imbert has reportedly stated that he cannot assure Balaguer's personal security.

- Balaguer is a widely-known political figure in the country and has considerable support from a broad spectrum of Dominican society. He announced on his arrival that he endorsed the OAS proposals but would not take a post in a provisional government because he wanted to run for president for free elections.

IV. The OAS committee is continuing its discussions with leading Dominicans, representing a wide range of political thinking, aimed at acceptance of the committee's proposed solution to the ten-week-old crisis.

A. Although the Caamaño regime and, to a lesser extent, Imbert's government of National Reconstruction have at times appeared amenable to negotiations, both sides have also remained firmly committed to demands which the other side unequivocally rejects.

B. It now appears that the OAS committee is making progress on the formation of an acceptable provisional government. The leading contender to head the provisional government is Hector Garcia Godoy, a career diplomat and member of Balaguer's Reformist Party.

## 14. Secret OAS Report, 2 July 1965

THE LATIN AMERICAN TIMES

**SECRET OAS REPORT**

Revealed below for the first time are verbatim statements made verbally in the closed session of the Organization of American States Tenth Meeting of Consultation called at 10:30 pm on May 7 to hear the first report of the first Special OAS Committee sent to the Dominican Republic.

The five-man committee made a formal written — and much less specific — report of their investigations at the height of the crisis. Parts of this written report were released. The international press has been criticized for ignoring it.

The following statements, here translated, have not been polished by the Latin American ambassadors who made them — or edited. The statements come directly from the classified stenographic records made of each OAS session.

Three members of the five-man committee spoke. The other two did not comment to differ with them.

The verbal statements answer questions put in the secret OAS meeting about the degree of communist activity and or influence in the Dominican crisis.

The Latin American Times presents them as a valuable documentary contribution to the great debate over the drama of Santo Domingo.

STATEMENT BY the Special Delegate of Colombia, Ambassador Alfredo Vazquez Carrizosa:

With regard to the sector led by Colonel Francisco Caamaño, many diplomats accredited in the Dominican Republic, and I didn't include my country's diplomatic representative, feel that, if not Colonel Francisco Caamaño, whom I do not know to be personally a communist, there are indeed numerous persons on his side that, if they are not members of the Communist Party, are actively in favor of Fidel Castro's system of government or political purposes.

There is such a tendency in the opinion of many diplomats I spoke to, and I do not mention other countries in order not to commit countries represented here.

They are firmly convinced that on that side there are many persons, I do not say members registered in an officially organized Communist Party, but persons who do have leanings toward a well-known trend that is prevalent in Cuba.

STATEMENT BY the Special Delegate of Argentina, Ambassador Ricardo M. Colombo:

I am going to add very little, of course, to what the Ambassador of Colombia, with his accustomed brilliance, has just said, by saying that this report, affirmed by a large number of representatives of the Dominican Corps, is public and well known to anyone who cares to make inquiry.

But despite the respect that I owe to the opinion of the Diplomatic Corps, in order to establish this in precise terms — for I was concerned as much as was the Ambassador with being able to verify this question — I wanted to go to the source; and we spoke with the different men who were in this rebel grouping, and, a notable thing, from the head of the revolution, Colonel Caamaño, to someone known as Minister of the Presidency, they recognized that they were their great problem, they explained to a certain extent briefly the process of the history of the Dominican Republic, they confessed to us how gradually a number of elements were being incorporated with them whom they called communists, and that their problem was to avoid infiltration for the purpose of springing a surprise and seizing control.

They said this clearly, and even at one point — I in the sometime difficult task of dividing this formal nomination of the chairmanship in which there is no merit greater than that of anyone else, because perhaps in the other four members there is much talent for doing what the chairman did — I spoke with Colonel Caamaño and asked him in a friendly way whether he honestly believed that such infiltration existed.

He confirmed this to me, but he gave me the impression that he had the courage to face it.

He said to me: "They are not going to grab the movement, and my concern is that in their losing the possibility of control, they have stayed behind as snipers; today there are those that do not wish a solution for the Dominican Republic", and already he put the political label on a good part of the snipers on both sides.

It should be said, Mr. Ambassador, that you will understand the extent of responsibility of the answers and the depth of the questions, and I would like to satisfy your own concern; but I have fulfilled with loyalty by reporting the conversation to you objectively, telling you that I believe that those who have the answer to this question are to be found among the actors, the protagonists of this hour who are living in the Dominican Republic.

This is what I wanted to say, Mr. Chairman.

STATEMENT BY the Special Delegate of Brazil, Ambassador Ilmar Penna Marinho:

Mr President, I should like to corroborate the statement made by my colleagues from Colombia and Argentina, and add one more aspect that I believe could help to clarify the approach that could be given to the problem.

I should like to add, gentlemen, that with the complete collapse of public authority — since neither the forces of the Government Junta of Benoit Santana, and Saladin nor those of Colonel Caamaño were in control of the situation — the Dominican state practically disappeared as a juridical-political entity.

The disoriented population of adolescents and fanatics was taking up modern automatic arms, in a state of excitation further exacerbated by constant radio broadcasts of a clearly subversive character.

Neither do I believe that I am, nor do any of the members of this Committee believe that he is in a position to state with assurance that the movement of Colonel Caamaño, inspired by the truly popular figure of former President Bosch, is a clearly communist movement.

But one fact is certain: in view of the real anarchy in which the country has been engulfed for several days, especially the capital city, where bands of snipers have been killing and obeying no one, any organized group that landed in the island could dominate the situation.

For that reason, and our understanding coincides with that of a majority of the depositions of the chiefs of diplomatic missions accredited there, all of the members of the Committee agree in admitting that the Caamaño movement, fortunately truly democratic in its origins, since none of us sincerely believes that Caamaño is a Communist, could be rapidly converted into a communist insurrection; above all it is seen to be heading towards becoming a government of that kind, susceptible of obtaining the support and the assistance of the great Marxist-Leninist powers.

Therefore, Mr President, we do not believe that Colonel Caamaño and his closest advisors are communists.

Meanwhile, as the entire Caamaño movement rests upon a truly popular basis, by certain areas escaping from the control of that democratic group of leaders it would be quite possible for that movement to be diverted from its real origins and to follow the oblique plan of popular-based movements, which can be easily controlled by clever agents and experts in the art of transforming democratic popular movements into Marxist-Leninist revolutions.

Thank you Mr. President.

**15. 2 September 1965**

MEMORANDUM

SUBJECT: **Cuban subversion in Latin America**

1. The Castro government remains convinced that a Cuban-style revolution is inevitable in Latina America and the "export of the revolution" continues to be a major tenet of its foreign policy. Cuba is willing and able to provide training, money, and propaganda support to subversive groups in Latin America through espionage and subversion organization, the General Directorate of Intelligence (DGI). It now concentrates on those countries — especially Venezuela, Guatemala, Colombia and Peru — where active subversive movements already exist in the field, but it can be expected to capitalize on "targets of opportunity" elsewhere in the hemisphere. The recent events in the Dominican Republic were read by Havana as both a lesson and a warning — a lesson on the importance of having a trained cadre of professional revolutionaries in place, ready to take advantage of a catholic political situation, and a warning that the US is determined to prevent "another Cuba" in this hemisphere.

2. Although Castro never has wavered in his belief that revolution will sweep Latin America, his appraisal of the practical realities in various countries has undergone a change. In the last two years, Castro's policies have suffered reverses in Venezuela, British Guiana, Chile, and Brazil, as well as in the failure of any of the continents' militant subversive groups to overturn Latin American governments. These have served to convince Castro that his "inevitable" revolution is not imminent.

3. Cuba appears to have altered its indiscriminate revolutionary ties in Latin America. An indication of this is seen in the November 194 conference in Havana of representatives of the Latin American Communist Parties. Cuba and the other Communist Parties agreed to aid only those groups endorsed by the regular Communist Parties — with the proviso that such groups adopt a more militant approach to the problem of revolution in their respective countries. It is too early to tell whether this agreement is being carried out. In one country — Guatemala — there are some indications that the official Communist Party is taking a more militant line, probably in the hope that increased Cuban support will follow. In Haiti, Cuba is trying to unify the two Communist Parties and rally public support for a program of violent action against Duvalier. Cuba has also tried to enlist international propaganda support for the "constitutionalist" faction in the Dominican Republic.

4. The main focus of Cuban interest, however, lies in those countries where Havana feels a genuine revolutionary potential exists. As specified in the communiqué of the Havana conference and consistently reiterated by Cuban

leaders, the three most immediate targets are Venezuela, Guatemala and Colombia. Haiti, Honduras and Paraguay were also mentioned as was Panama. In his 26 July speech, Fidel Castro added Peru to the "official" list of countries where a viable and exploitable revolutionary situation exists.

5. A large number of Venezuelans, Guatemalans, and Colombians participate in Cuba's continuing program of providing Latin American subversives with ideological orientation and training in the specifics of revolutionary warfare.

7. In its propaganda, Cuba seems to have turned from its earlier, blatant calls to revolution, and now spends more time in laying the groundwork for revolutionary activity. This includes ostensibly objective reporting of economic and political conditions in Latin America, along with greatly exaggerated reports of the successes of militant subversive groups and calls for unity among revolutionary groups in selected countries. Havana radio broadcast 143 hours a week to Latin America in Spanish, French, Creole (Haiti), Aymara and Quechua (Andean country) and Guarani (Paraguay). Emphasis is on broadcasts to the "top three" — Venezuela, Guatemala, and Colombia — and there is even a special weekly program, "Venezuelan Panorama", although a portion of the Cuban effort is devoted to almost every country in the hemisphere.

8. Recent broadcasts to Haiti provide a case in point. Rene Depestre, a Haitian Communist long resident in Cuba, broadcasts vitriolic commentary on the economic and political deterioration of Haiti and the need for unity among the revolutionary forces. Depressed by the lack of concrete action by Haiti's two Communist Parties, Depestre stated, "It is of the utmost necessity that all honest Haitians gather under the banner of the Unified Democratic Front ... to make Duvalier pay for his treason and all of his crimes". On the practical side of revolution, Havana radio has also been serializing "beautiful and inspiring" sections from Che Guevara's manual on guerrilla warfare and translated some speeches that were given in Cuba by the representative of the Venezuelan Armed Forces of National Liberation (FALN).

9. Cuba's role in the current Dominican situation points up several aspects of its subversive activities. Cuba provided training to more than 50 of the rebels in Santo Domingo. The majority of these were members of the pro-Castro 14th of June group (APCJ). In December 1963, Cuba was involved in an abortive attempt to land weapons in the Dominican Republic for the violence oriented Dominican Popular Movement (MPD).

10. When the revolt began in April, Havana apparently decided that, tactically speaking, the achievement of popular support for the Caamaño forces demanded that the Communist and Cuban-trained participation in the revolt be overshadowed by its proconstitution, pro-Bosch, anti-Imbert cast.

As a result, Havana at first did not refer to Communist Participation, did not extend diplomatic recognition to Caamaño, and used its propaganda media to concentrate on the "evils" of the Reid Government, the Imbert junta, and the OAS and US presence. The APCJ, on the sixth anniversary of its founding, was lauded as a popular, nor specifically a Communist, group. Havana played as a straight news item the decision of the orthodox Communist group to change its name to the Dominican Communist Party and did not take advantage of the opportunity to show that Communists were leading supporters of the Caamaño forces. The degree to which US and OAS countermeasures prompted these tactics cannot be determined. However, they do show Castro's realization that tagging a "Communist" or "pro-Castro" label on a movement is not always useful to Cuban interests.

11. In sum, while Cuba may be in the process of altering its tactics, it has changed neither its desire nor its willingness to aid subversion in Latin America. Havana will continue to offer training and propaganda support — and probably monetary assistance — to active revolutionary groups throughout the hemisphere.

## 16. Santo Domingo Radio, 29 November 1965

### SANTIAGO PLOT PARTICIPANTS ARRAIGNED IN COURT

Santo Domingo Radio Universal in Spanish 11:30 GMT [Greenwich Mean Time] 26 November 1965

A total of 38 persons charged with having participated in the plot prepared in Santiago de los Caballeros to overthrow Dr. Hector Garcia Godoy's provisional government last Monday, were placed yesterday in the hands of the justice courts by the national police. Among the persons charged with plotting against the government are: Dr. Tomas Alcibiades Espinosa who was proclaimed democratic revolutionary president by the movement, businessman Jose Rafael Espailliat Gonzalez, Luis Ramirez Subervi, (Abonito Pastias Foreta — phonetic) Ponce Perez Moralez, Homero Gonzalez Mera, Mejia Santos Reyes, Nicolas (Contrae — phonetic) Rodriguez, Lorenza Taveras Burgos, Pedro (Barria — phonetic) Caraballo, Candido Polanco de la Cruz, Juan Caraballo Guzman and others.

The new attorney general, Luis Gomez Ceara, yesterday said that one of his first actions was to ask the police chief to arraign the prisoners and that the police had promised it would be done yesterday. Gomez Ceara said he made this request because the prisoners had been under arrest more than 48 hours and the law states that a person must be arraigned within that time. He also said that the competent court to judge the prisoners involved in the plot is the court of Santiago de los Caballeros where the incident took place.

(Editor's note: Santo Domingo Radio Comercial in Spanish 17:00 GMT 26 November adds that the attorney general of the republic ordered an extensive investigation to clear up the situation facing judicial officials in Barahona. The attorney general was specifically referring to a complaint that a group of persons involved in the Santiago de los Caballeros unsuccessful subversive movement had been released due to pressure exerted by military men, the report said).

(Santo Domingo Radio Universal in Spanish 11:30 GMT 26 November says that a total of 14 persons under arrest on charges of allegedly being involved in the 22 November short-lived Santiago coup were released 24 November).

(Santo Domingo Radio Universal in Spanish 11:30 GMT 27 November adds that provisional President Dr. Garcia Godoy on 26 November visited Santiago de los Caballeros to obtain more information on the recently frustrated coup).

### DELEGATION AT RIO SUPPORTS COLOMBIA PROPOSAL

Santo Domingo Radio Comercial in Spanish 10:30 GMT 26 November 1965

(Excerpt) Rio de Janeiro — The Dominican delegation stated yesterday that it will support Colombia's resolution which reaffirms the principle of non-intervention. This was the first position adopted by the Dominican foreign minister, Jose Ramon Rodriguez, who previously told the conference that his delegation would reserve for the constitutional government which the Dominican people will elect next year all statements on reforms to the OAS chapter.

A statement issued yesterday by the delegation, on behalf of the Dominican foreign minister said: "The proposed resolution introduced by the Colombian delegation regarding non-intervention is a reaffirmation of basic principles of the OAS charter and not a change of the charter. Therefore, the Dominican delegation cannot object to the reaffirmation of that principle inasmuch as my government and my country oppose any manifestation of intervention because of historic reasons. In this sense, our tradition has always been invariable. On 4 November 1965, President Garcia Godoy told the national and foreign press that his government would oppose the creation of an Inter-America Peace Force because it feels that the principle of non-intervention is a sacred concept. I make this clarification now because when I quoted the statements setting forth the Dominican provisional government's position, the Colombian resolution had not been circulated".

IAPF PAY CHECKS — It has been disclosed that the provisional government has been making efforts to have the IAPF troops stationed in the Dominican Republic receive their pay checks in Dominican pesos. Official circles said that there is a government law issued in 1965 during the time when the dollar black market reached its highest peak, which authorizes the Central Bank to withhold all the dollars that enter the country. (Santo Domingo Radio Universal Spanish 11:30 GMT 26 November 1965)

NEW DOMINICAN AMBASSADOR — The new Dominican ambassador to the Vatican Atilano Vicini Perdomo on 25 November presented his credentials to the Pope in a brief ceremony. (Santo Domingo Radio Universal Spanish 11:30 GMT 26 November 1965) The new Dominican ambassador to Spain, Emilio Rodriguez Demorizi, 25 November presented his credentials to Generalisimo Francisco Franco in the Presidential Palace. (Santo Domingo Radio Universal Spanish 11:30 GMT 26 November 1965)

TEENAGE VANDALISM — Private School Principal Luis A. Parada has stated that a group of teenagers on 25 November threw rocks at their school building, breaking windows and damaging roof tiles. (Santo Domingo Radio Universal Spanish 11:30 GMT 26 November 1965)

THIRD FORCE — An article published by the newspaper La Hoja says: For several days we have heard strange broadcasts from Radio Pueblo, broadcasts which evidently have political overtones. With a series of slogans, this station has been calling attention to the formation of a third political force. One of these slogans says: "Neither one nor the other. Wait for the third political force". (Santo Domingo Radio Universal Spanish 20:10 GMT 26 November 1965)

CONTRACT WITH LA NACION — The government has dissolved all contracts with the newspaper La Nacion which heretofore was printed at a government plant. The government will use the printing plant to print textbooks, especially for primary school children who cannot buy their own. The La Nacion plant was confiscated at the fall of the Trujillo regime on the grounds that most of the shares were owned by the Trujillo family. (Santo Domingo Radio Universal Spanish 16:30 GMT 27 November 1965)

BURNING OF FLAG — According to reports from (Monsenor Noel — phonetic), college and high school students burned a US flag in a demonstration against foreign military intervention. The demonstrators chanted the revolution anthem. No incidents were reported. (Santo Domingo Radio Universal Spanish 10:30 GMT 27 November 1965)

BOSCH ON INTERVENTION — Former constitutional President Juan Bosch said 26 November speaking over Radio Universal that the US unilateral military action in the Dominican Republic was a return to the international jungle law. The PRD leader said it had been understood that there was an Inter-American law which prohibited any sort of intervention, especially military intervention. Bosch said that US Secretary of State Dean Rusk had ignored the international law publicly, before the world, and concluded "We have been the first victims, but the United States will be the last victim. It is impossible to attack without being attacked in return some time". (Santo Domingo Radio Universal Spanish 11:30 GMT 27 November 1965)

RESUMED MAGAZINE PUBLICATION — The Ahora magazine, bombed last October, resumed its activities on 26 November. The magazine will reappear on the market very soon. (Santo Domingo Radio Universal Spanish 10:30 GMT 27 November 1965)

NEW PUBLICATION — A new book entitled El Judas de Bosch, by newsman (Gino Feliz — phonetic), will be on the Santo Domingo market in the week beginning 28 November. The book refutes some ideas by Bosch in his book El Judas. (Feliz) is editor of the daily El Caribe. (Santo Domingo Radio Universal Spanish 10:30 GMT 27 November 1965)

DOMESTIC SERVICE CONVERSION — The Dominican education minister has confirmed the possibility that next year Radio Santo Domingo Television will become an exclusively cultural station. The minister said he had had official word on the matter. (Santo Domingo Radio Universal Spanish 10:30 GMT 27 November 1965)

INSTALLATION OF MINISTER — The new finance minister, Lic. Enrique Tarazona, took office on 26 November. (Santo Domingo Radio Universal Spanish 10:30 GMT 27 November 1965)

ANTIELECTION PLAN — A Reformist Party spokesman yesterday Deñóunced a plan to alter the public order in Santiago de los Caballeros when Dr. Balaguer, president of the party, visits that city. The informant said that several persons are planning to explode bombs in their own homes to leave the impression that the time is inappropriate for electoral campaigning. (Santo Domingo Radio Universal Spanish 11:30 GMT 27 November 1965)

CITIZENS' COMPLAINTS — Many citizens complained on 26 November against the firing of rockets and other artificial fireworks in Santo Domingo. Those complaining said that the continual explosions have created a tension among the occupational troops, and that they feared disagreeable results. (Santo Domingo Radio Universal Spanish 11:30 GMT 27 November 1965)

IAPF DEPARTURE DEMAND — The delegation appointed by the negotiating committee of the government presided over by Colonel Caamaño on 26 November suggested a nationalist movement to demand that the provisional government be the one to decide when the Inter-American Peace Force should leave the country. The delegation sent a cablegram from Rio de Janeiro, where they have presented a valuable document on the Dominican crisis. (Santo Domingo Radio Universal Spanish 11:30 GMT 27 November 1965)

POLITICAL ACTIVITY RESTRICTION — The Government 24 November issued a law prohibiting political activities and the illegal suspension of work in public offices. The law also prohibits all labor union propaganda promotion in government offices as well as meetings of public employees during working hours. Persons who promote agitation among employees will be severely punished. (Santo Domingo Radio Universal Spanish 11:30 GMT 25 November 1965)

REOCCUPANCY OF CENTER — Leaders of the Social Christian Revolutionary Party (PRSC) on 24 November reoccupied their party center formerly used by Inter-American Peace Force Brazilian troops. The PRSC leaders said they found boards nailed to windows and doors, damaged furniture and pillaged files. (Santo Domingo Radio Universal Spanish 11:30 GMT 25 November 1965)

ARMS COLLECTION — Last week the government paid out 35,982.55 pesos for firearms turned in voluntarily by Dominican civilians. This week 13,346.40 pesos have been paid out for weapons of varied calibre and manufacture. (Santo Domingo Radio Universal Spanish 11:30 GMT 25 November 1965)

POLITICAL PARTY CRITICISM — The Christian Democratic Progressive Party (PPDC) has charged in a communiqué that the provisional government has done nothing to pave the way for the forthcoming elections. PPDC said that the matter was of utmost importance. The communiqué was signed by Ramon A.Castillo, president; Dr. Rafael Solano, general secretary and Juan Bautista Carrion, secretary of public relations. (Santo Domingo Radio Universal Spanish 10:30 GMT 24 November 1965)

DISSATISFIED PUBLIC WORKERS — The National Association of Workers and Employees of the Public Works and Communication Ministry have said that the Christmas bonus should be paid to all government workers and employees. The association said the bonus was a social benefit for which they will struggle untiringly. (Santo Domingo Radio Universal Spanish 10:30 GMT 24 November 1965)

YOUTH DEMONSTRATION — Using tear gas grenades, a patrol of Brazilian soldiers dispersed a group formed by several hundred youths who were staging a demonstration to commemorate the fifth anniversary of the Mirabal sisters' death. The demonstrators, belonging to the Dominican Communist Party, the Republica de Argentina and Salome Urena high schools, paraded through several streets before going to the nation's altar. (Santo Domingo Radio Universal Spanish 17:00 GMT 25 November 1965)

HIGHER COFFEE QUOTA — The Dominican Republic will try to obtain a higher coffee export quota during the conference of the Inter-American Coffee Council slated for 30 November in London. The Dominican Republic feels that it could export annually approximately 550.000 60-pound bags to foreign markets. (Santo Domingo Radio Universal Spanish 11:30 GMT 25 November 1965)

EL SALVADOR AMBASSADOR — The new Salvadoran Ambassador to the Dominican Republic Roberto Castillo will present his credentials to provisional President Hector Garcia Godoy on 25 November. (Santo Domingo Radio Universal Spanish 11:30 GMT 24 November 1965)

CONDITIONS FOR NEGOTIATIONS — The University Provisional Council director, Andres Maria Aybar Nicolas, 23 November presented the conditions under which the council is willing to negotiate a solution of the current university crisis. The conditions establish that no reforms will be accepted other than those aimed at strengthening the law of autonomy of the university. (Santo Domingo Radio Universal Spanish 11:30 GMT 24 November 1965)

NAVAL TRAINING CRUISE — Dominican navy frigate "Gregorio Luperon" on 29 November left for a 10-day around-the-island training cruise which includes a weekend stopover in Puerto Rico. The frigate is commanded by Capt. Manuel Antonio Logrono Contin and carries a new crew of 15 officers and 96 enlisted men. Aboard the frigate are 16 coast guard cadets accompanied by the naval school commandant. (Santo Domingo Domestic Spanish 16:30 GMT 29 November 1965)

ANTIPOLIO VACCINATION PROGRAM — The Health and Social Welfare Ministry on 29 November began a nationwide antipolio vaccination program. A total of 26 vaccination centers began operations in the National District. (Santo Domingo Domestic Spanish 16:30 GMT 29 November 1965)

UNINTERRUPTED OPERATIONS — The operations of the Central Electoral Board have not suffered any interruption due to the government's delay in naming replacements for the two resigning members. An electoral board spokesman on 29 November said that there is no foreseeable interruption in the board's activities to prepare for the May or June 1966 elections. It is expected that the two replacements will be appointed this week. (Santo Domingo Domestic Spanish 16:30 GMT 29 November 1965)

BAN ON FIREWORKS — Interior Minister Manuel Joaquin Castillo has issued orders prohibiting the use of fireworks during the Christmas holidays. Castillo, during a brief press conference on 29 November, said that he has requested the annulment of all import permits for fireworks. He said the police will be instructed to prevent any act that may possibly cause intranquility and anxiety to the Dominicans. Castillo said that the prohibition is aimed at preventing confusion during the tense situation prevailing the nation. (Santo Domingo Domestic Spanish 16:30 GMT 29 November 1965)

JOSE JOTTIN CURY — The former Dominican Constitutionalist foreign minister charged in Rio de Janeiro that the so-called Inter-American Peace Force that is occupying the Dominican Republic constitutes a parallel government to the provisional government of Hector Garcia Godoy. Jottin Cury is now in Rio de Janeiro at the head of a Dominican Constitutionalist delegation that tried to speak at the OAS conference to request the withdrawal of foreign troops from the Dominican Republic. The delegation was denied admission to the conference by the Brazilian dictatorial regime under the pretext that it does not have the necessary credentials to attend the conference. In statements to the Rio press, the former Dominican foreign minister said that "if the Inter-American Peace Force does not withdraw from the soil of our country, we shall be subjected to a long and cruel war in Santo Domingo". (Havana Spanish Americas 12:00 GMT 28 November 1965)

LA NACION CLOSURE — The Dominican provisional government issued a decree definitely closing down the newspaper La Nacion whose premises were occupied by the foreign interventionist troops. The government decree transfers La Nacion's premises to the Education Ministry to be used for printing government publications. (Havana Spanish Americas 00:00 GMT 29 November 1965)

## PRESIDENT'S OFFICE COMMUNIQUE ON SANTIAGO

Santo Domingo Domestic Service in Spanish 20:30 GMT 29 November 1965

(Communiqué from the Office of the President)

In connection with the recent events which took place in Santiago and in other places, the Office of the President reports the following facts to the citizens: according to reliable reports in possession of the government and judicial officials, a well-known group of persons intends to carry out a plan which includes terrorist and violent actions, attempts against people's lives, murders, kidnappings, and similar acts, to create a chaotic situation which will cause the fall of the government. The insurrectional movement launched in Santiago on 22 November was part of that terrorist plan. That movement was immediately stifled by the timely and vigorous action of military and police authorities who arrested several of the leaders and other persons involved in the terrorist plan have been arrested. Others whose names are not mentioned for obvious reasons are also involved. Therefore, we are not dealing with individuals who act peacefully, moved by democratic ideals, but with groups whose main objective is to create an abnormal situation, to disturb public order, and to obstruct governmental activities. The government has in its possession all details of the plan and has taken necessary measures to prevent the materialization of said plan so that all persons involved may be brought before the courts. The Armed Forces and the National Police, fulfilling their functions to guarantee public order and safeguard peace, and pursuant to orders issued by the Office of the Presidency, are on the alert to repress any other subversive attempt or terrorist acts carried out in the national territory. Santo Domingo National District, 29 November 1965.

## JOAQUIN BALAGUER CALLS FOR AUTHENTIC ELECTIONS

Santo Domingo Domestic Service in Spanish 10:30 GMT 29 November 1965

Reformist Party President Joaquin Balaguer yesterday declared in Santiago that in the Dominican Republic strong governments are no longer those which rely on the backing of the bayonets but rather acquire their strength through the backing of people. Balaguer made his statements to thousands of his followers who met yesterday morning in the Cibao football stadium. Balaguer said that an authentic election will be the only action through which we will achieve the beneficial results the nation needs for its pacification. Our efforts must seek to oblige the political parties to respect the laws or eliminate them if they do not produce the desired results.

Balaguer added that he would give his backing to a crusade against misery and foreign intervention. He also referred to other problems affecting the Dominican nation.

## FRANCISCO Caamaño, ARISTY DEPARTURE RUMORED

Santo Domingo Public in Spanish 17:00 GMT 29 November 1965

Unconfirmed rumors heard by the newspaper La Hoja indicate that Col. Francisco Caamaño and Mr. Hector Aristy, the president and presidential secretary of the Constitutionalist Government, have departed from the country, reportedly to assume diplomatic posts. La Hoja reporters are seeking a confirmation or denial of this report.

## DEMOCRATIC UNITY FRONT TO PICKET PALACE

Santo Domingo Radio Comercial in Spanish 10:30 GMT 29 November 1965

The National Front for Democratic Unity (Frente Nacional de Unidad Democratica) will picket the National Palace today at 15:00 hours and will request the release of those implicated in the Santiago uprising. The group published a communiqué in this morning's papers urging the general public to take part.

## REVOLUTIONARY STUDENT UNION BURNS US FLAG

Santo Domingo Radio Comercial in Spanish 10:30 GMT 29 November

Students of the Ercilia Pepin school and of the San Vicente de Paul college, along with numbers of the Marxist-Leninist movement and the Dominican Communist Party, burned a US flag and demonstrated yesterday in San Francisco de Macoris. The demonstrators reportedly chanted slogans such as "Quisqueya, si! Yankees, no!" and "With the Maul and the Gun. We Will Struggle Till Death".

The demonstration was in protest against the presence of the Inter-American Peace Force and its intervention in the past revolution. According to reports, most of the school children were in a meeting with the school director when the incident took place in the school yard. Only the Revolutionary Student Union took part in the burning of the flag.

## PRD OUSTS MEMBER FOR ANTI-BOSCH STATEMENTS

Santo Domingo Radio Comercial in Spanish 10:30 GMT 29 November 1965

Former PRD leader Angel Miolan was definitely ousted from the party yesterday. He was charged, among other things, with having said that "Prof. Juan Bosch had cooperated with Dominican communists". Miolan was also charged with having violated several articles of the PRD bylaws, such as "squealing on a fellow party member; opposing the moral, political and material interests of the party; disobeying party regulations; falsely Deñóuncing a fellow member; and refusing to contribute to the clarifying of a disciplinary matter".

A tape recording and other documents — including clippings from magazines and newspapers — were presented against Miolan. These clippings included statements allegedly made by him in which he says that Bosch and Wessin y Wessin struggled against each other for control of the government during the past revolution; that PRD organizers had received financial aid from the Triumvirate in 1964 and that he continued to be the president of the Dominican Revolutionary Party.

**17. Central Intelligence Agency Report, 12 January 1966**

OCI No. 0475/66

CENTRAL INTELLIGENCE AGENCY

Office of Current Intelligence

INTELLIGENCE MEMORANDUM

**The Dominican Republic Situation Report**
(As of 8:30 PM, EST [Eastern Standard Time])

2. The contending forces in the Dominican Republic have been granted a brief breathing spell with last night's departure of six "constitutionalist" military, and the cancellation of the last day of the relatively unsuccessful general strike. There is still no indication that former rebel leader Francisco Caamaño and his chief military aide, Manuel Montes Arache, are preparing to leave the country, and the regular military is adamant in refusing to consider its own departure until these two men have left.

## 18. Central Intelligence Agency Report, 17 January 1966

Central Intelligence Agency

CENTRAL INTELLIGENCE BULLETIN

Rebel leader Caamaño refuses to leave the country until the provisional government assures the safety of his rank-and-file followers who are to remain.

A strike by telephone workers has disrupted international and domestic long-distance service. The shutdown began on 13 January when employees of the US-owned Dominican Telephone Company failed to report for work following the firing on 12 January of five principal union leaders. Company officials had charged the union leaders with aiding last week's illegal general strike.

Statements calling for armed action and criticizing scheduled elections in the Dominican Republic by Dominican delegates attending the Tri-Continent Conference in Havana have generated increased Dominican public interest in the conference. Last week the government barred the return of the Dominican delegation, numbering at least five, presumably on the grounds of violating passport restrictions on travel to Communist countries.

On 14 January Radio Havana broadcast a speech by Guido Gil, who identified himself as president of the Dominican delegation. Following a short diatribe against the United States and the "imperialist puppet government in the Dominican Republic", Gil vowed that "we will return and we will fight".

**19. Central Intelligence Agency, 5 February 1966**

3. CENTRAL INTELLIGENCE BULLETIN

Current Intelligence Relating to National Security

Dominican Republic: The proposed solution to the present civil-military crisis contains many potential complications.

Minister of Defense Rivera has agreed to a formula whereby he will depart if the other service chiefs stay and if he obtains other concessions. Rivera's major demand is the dismantling of the rebel military camp on the outskirts of Santo Domingo.

President Garcia Godoy has said that he and Rivera have discussed a possible solution that would "theoretically" integrate the rebel military into the armed services. The rebels would then go on leave with pay for five months. Thus, the emotion-charged problem of actual integration would be left to a new and probably very weak elected government.

Garcia Godoy appears unwilling to guarantee under all circumstances that if Rivera leaves no other command changes will be made before elections. In fact, the provisional President is very reluctant to limit the current command shift to Rivera and has not specifically committed to this course. He has indicated doubts that the defense minister's departure would solve what he sees as the basic problem — creating an attitude of impartiality on the part of the armed services during the election campaign.

It seems unlikely that Caamaño, Bosch and the rest of the "constitutionalist" camp will accept anything less than the implementation of Garcia Godoy's decree of 6 January calling for the overseas assignment of Rivera, two service chiefs, and a group of "trouble-making" officers. One of Bosch's conditions for running in the elections has been the removal of these military leaders.

As soon as word leaks out of the proposals under discussion, an outcry is probable. Caamaño may see the failure to gain the departure of the service chiefs and the proposed disbanding of the rebel camp as a sellout by Garcia Godoy and advance it as a rationale for the return to the country of several of his exiled colleagues and perhaps for his own return.

At any rate there must be further negotiations between Rivera and Garcia Godoy, possibly in an atmosphere charged by leftist agitation, before the issue can be resolved.

## 20. Central Intelligence Agency, 16 March 1966

OCI No. 0793/66

CENTRAL INTELLIGENCE AGENCY

Office of Current Intelligence

INTELLIGENCE MEMORANDUM

### THE PRE-ELECTION CLIMATE IN THE DOMINICAN REPUBLIC

1. With the resolution of the protracted crisis over command-level changes in the military, a relative calm has been established. Garcia Godoy has moved publicly to repair his relations with the military, and the new minister of defense, General Perez, has sacked one officer for partisan political activity. The country's basic social and political problems remain unsolved, however, and a new period of turbulence seems certain to accompany preparations for the elections.

The Campaign Gets Under Way

2. The provisional government, through its recent public actions, has begun to lay the groundwork for choosing a new four-year administration on 1 June. Arrangements are under way to register voters, and the number of pro-Bosch civil servants is being reduced to alter the partisan character of provincial and local governments.

3. Any number of fortuitous developments, however, could jeopardize the elections. Deep political passions could easily magnify small incidents between the left and the security services into major confrontations. The assassination of leading political figures is an ever-present possibility. The rebel military are a thorn in the flesh to the regular military. The return of Caamaño or a graceless exploitation of the anniversary of the outbreak of revolution on 24 April could easily trigger violence. The general lawlessness characteristic of Dominican society has become a graver problem since the revolution. The disruption of public order is particularly serious now because of the widespread availability of arms and the lack of effective law enforcement. Inter-American Peace Force (IAPF) troops might have to be drawn in to maintain order in Santo Domingo during the campaign.

4. Bosch and his followers have charged that a systematic campaign of intimidation has been directed at them by the military and civilian rightwingers, and that "hundreds" of members of the Dominican Revolutionary Party (PRD) have been killed. Although the PRD really has cause for concern, these charges are greatly exaggerated. The sporadic acts of terrorism that have occurred

against PRD members appear to be the work of a small number of right-wing extremists operating independently of each other.

5. Extreme leftists may also try to prevent the elections. Some already have threatened to do so, but most of them seem to be waiting for Bosch's decision on his candidacy — probably expecting to lend him covert support if he runs.

6. At the present time, it appears that the President is intent on going through with the elections and leaving office on 30 June. It is possible that he may change his mind if he decides that conditions for an orderly transfer of power do not exist or that the elections will result in increased bitterness and hostility. Before taking office he felt a two-year term would be desirable, and during recent weeks he has mused about extending the life of the provisional regime. Although Garcia Godoy has thought about the possibility of standing as a compromise candidate, he is probably discouraged by the legal and political obstacles that would have to be overcome. The Institutional Act itself rules out the candidacy of anyone serving in the provisional government. His recent references to the desirability of having a candidate who would not arouse antagonism and could continue the provisional government's work of reconciliation may stem from some behind-the-scenes activity that could eventuate in the formation of a new political movement, possibly involving the "Santiago Group" of businessmen.

7. Free balloting has not been the traditional method of apportioning political power in the Dominican Republic. Indeed, the elections of 1962 constituted the first truly free referendum in the history of the country. When the Inter-American Peace Force leaves, the Dominican military will once again become the final arbiters of political life. Despite the tumult over command changes under the provisional regime, no basic changes have been effected. The military still consider themselves an elite group not entirely responsible to civil authority.

The Candidates

8. Joaquin Balaguer has been the one predictable element on the Dominican political spectrum. The Reformist Party (RP) leader consistently has urged holding elections on 1 June — chiefly because he is confident of winning. His party began preparing for the campaign almost immediately after his return to the Dominican Republic last June.

9. Balaguer, who held the presidency for a brief span immediately before and after the death of Trujillo, has stressed that he is the candidate of moderation and order. At the same time he has advocated a program of moderate reform — a platform designed to catch the vote of the conservative rural population.

10. However, the mercurial Bosch remains the key to the development of the

campaign, and possibly to the future stability of the Dominican Republic. So far, he has refused to commit himself on his candidacy — on the grounds that terrorism and violence preclude valid elections and that in any case the military will not respect their outcome. He has left himself considerable room to maneuver, and his final decision may be a month or so away. In the meantime, his PRD is preparing for the campaign. Bosch is probably attempting to judge whether he can win and take office if he does win. At the present time he would seem to be leaning to the conclusion that this is unlikely.

11. Bosch's penchant for doing the unpredictable and keeping those closest to him in the dark about his real intentions makes it difficult to forecast his actions. His plans are further obscured by an almost paranoic concern with personal security that has caused him to shut himself off from normal Dominican life.

12. There are likely to be strong pressures on Bosch to avoid having the PRD sit out the election. Many of the party's politicians think their electoral chances are good and do not relish the prospect of a four-year patronage drought. If Bosch does stay on the sidelines, there is a strong possibility that he will lose his influence over the "constitutionalist" movement to someone like Caamaño.

13. Instead of boycotting the elections, Bosch may be seeking to delay the balloting until a more propitious time. Of late, he has hinted that elections should be postponed, and that he would welcome an IAPF pledge to assure his security or a US guarantee to protect his regime in office. He has also proposed that he, Bonnelly, and Balaguer agree on a new provisional president to rule for one year.

14. The several minor candidates and movements that have emerged complicate the electoral picture, but have not really cut into the strengths of Bosch and Balaguer. The most significant of these groups has been Rafael Bonnelly's "third force" — a coalition of minor parties. Bonnelly, president of the Council of State that ruled during 1962, is generally regarded as a conservative and an example of "thwarted ambition", according to the embassy. He may be more interested in using his candidacy to obtain patronage from Balaguer than in actually running for office.

15. On the left, the increasingly militant Revolutionary Social Christian Party (PRSC) has split with the PRD over strategy and tactics, but there is a good chance it will support Bosch in return for political favors. Hector Aristy feels that his nascent organization, the 24th of April Movement, should support Bosch now in return for patronage which will build up the party for the future. Aristy is counting on Caamaño to return and give a boost to the 24th of April Movement, possibly by running for the vice presidency of the PRD ticket. The PRSC and the 24th of April Movement will become more significant if

Bosch does decide to boycott the race, since either one could hoist the banner of "constitutionalism" against Balaguer. Without Bosch, however, a Balaguer victory would seem a foregone conclusion.

16. A Bosch-Balaguer contest in which Bosch employed his undisputed talents as a campaigner could go either way. Although Balaguer is thought to have the edge now, Bosch has several potential advantages. Among these are his skills as a campaigner, his appeal to the country's urban have-nots and youth, his control of an important segment of the country's public administration — including the vital sugar corporation — and his acceptability to important labor unions.

The Post Election Period

17. The fiercer the competition, the greater the likelihood that the winner will be accepted as the country's legitimate leader. If Bosch does not run and no suitable substitute figure, such as Caamaño, emerges, Balaguer will be vulnerable to the charge that he is a puppet, imposed in the country and not deserving of allegiance. In such a contingency, the Communists and associated extreme leftists will find willing allies among the non-Communist left.

18. If Bosch or a candidate of the left is elected, a military coup is likely to occur in short order. Its timing would be more dependent on the disposition of the Inter-American Peace Force and the OAS mission, which have been the real sources of stability for the last seven months, than on the actions of a leftist regime itself. Balaguer would be much better able than Bosch to get along with the military, but even the moderate reforms he advocates probably would cause some dissatisfaction.

19. In addition to the military, the elected regime will face a host of other problems — such as widespread unemployment, extreme poverty, low sugar prices and high production costs, an imbalance in international payments, and increasing inflationary pressures.

## 21. Central Intelligence Agency Report, 25 March 1966

Central Intelligence Agency

## CENTRAL INTELLIGENCE BULLETIN

Colonel Francisco Caamaño's hoped-for visit to the Dominican Republic before the elections in June could jeopardize the fragile political peace.

Caamaño told a US Embassy official in London that he hopes to make a brief first-hand assessment of the pre-election situation and take readings on the views of Dominican military leaders if conditions are propitious. He definitely plans to return after elections, which he said he hopes will take place on schedule.

If Caamaño returns before the elections, he might see some advantage in timing his arrival to coincide with the expected celebrations marking the first anniversary of the Dominican revolt on 24 April. Although Caamaño disclaimed any political aspirations, he probably would like to reassociate himself with the aura of the "constitutionalist" cause which will be revived by the anniversary.

In addition, Bosch's Dominican Revolutionary Party will have held its national convention by that time. If Bosch chooses not to run, Caamaño might reassess his own political prospects and possibly attempt to gain a following for a last-minute presidential campaign. Hector Aristy's nascent 24th of April Revolutionary Movement could provide a convenient vehicle for such a campaign.

## 22. Central Intelligence Agency, 8 April 1966

CENTRAL INTELLIGENCE BULLETIN

Current Intelligence Relating to National Security

Dominican Republic: Juan Bosch's electoral intentions are still obscure on the eve of his party's nominating convention.

Bosch's conduct strongly suggests that he does not really want to take on the job of ruling the country — particularly when he feels he will be faced with the threat of military overthrow — and is looking for a way out of running. Nevertheless, Bosch is highly unpredictable and many of his statements during recent weeks have made him sound very much like a candidate. Meaningful elections will not necessarily be precluded if Bosch does not run.

On 4 April Bosch proposed that he and Balaguer agree on a new provisional government and postpone elections. Bosch made the proposal to a leader of Balaguer's Reformist Party (PR), who made clear that the PR remains fully committed to holding elections on 1 June.

On 5 April Bosch broke off while filming a television interview, saying of the elections, "there is no use going on with this farce; the Americans do not want elections and the situation here is impossible". He made similar statements to the British ambassador, asserting that terrorism was still being practiced against Dominican Revolutionary Party (PRD) members and accusing the US of not being prepared to allow him to govern should he win.

Bosch has suggested that Caamaño be a presidential or vice-presidential candidate on the PRD ticket. However Caamaño replied publicly that he has no political ambitions and privately told Bosch supporters that while he would accept a military post — possibly minister of defense — he would not accept a political position.

Bosch's intentions should be clearer after the party convention this weekend. He has expressed fears that violence will break out, but the US Embassy reports that the new police and military chiefs appear determined to prevent any major flare-up.

## 23. American Embassy, London 13 April 1966

TELEGRAM Foreign Service of the United States of America

## CONVERSATION WITH COLONEL Caamaño

Emboff dined with Col. Caamaño and two Dominican Embassy officials evening April 11 at Emboff's house. Following topics discussed:

Travel Plans — Caamaño still entertaining idea of brief visit to DR prior to elections but stated this depends on how situation there develops. He conveyed impression such as visit, if it transpires, would take place at later date and is not in prospect for immediate future. He also conveyed distinct impression he will be in London during anniversary of revolution on April 24, and will remain here through the end of April. (COMMENT: Dominican Counselor believes it extremely unlikely Caamaño would attempt return DR for April 24 commemoration). Caamaño also stated he considering possibility personal travel in Europe, most probably in May after warmer weather arrives. Stated he hopes visit France and Spain. Various relatives in Spain have apparently extended invitations.

PRD Convention and Bosch nomination — He expressed pleasure at nomination of Bosch as PRD presidential candidate at April 9–10 convention. Stated he was somewhat surprised at reported nomination of Silvestre Antonio Guzman as PRD vice-presidential candidate but added that he thought it a good choice as it would rally Santiago business interests behind PRD. He made no comment with respect to his own oft-rumored candidacy. (COMMENT: Dominican Counselor Cabral, however, claims that Caamaño was offered first the presidential, and then the vice-presidential, candidacies on the PRD ticket but turned down both offers because of his desire to remain in the military at this time).

Elections — Caamaño re-stated his conviction that the June elections must be held as scheduled and that the election verdict must be respected. He said he still entertains serious doubts that the US will permit free elections and will allow the winning party to take office. He believes that Bosch will win by a wide margin if the elections are held as scheduled. Emboff reassured Caamaño that US has committed itself in support of scheduled elections and will respect the verdict. Emboff added our chief concern is that no violence, from either left or right, should disturb election campaign. Caamaño replied somewhat sourly that any violence, should it occur, would be responsibility of US, since US and IAPF troops are present in DR.

General Situation — Caamaño said that he is more optimistic now than he has ever been since the early days of the revolution, and added it appears situation has improved markedly during the past two months. He understands there is to be considerable turnover in staff of US Embassy Santo Domingo, and hopes new people Quote will have an appreciation and understanding of the constitutional principles underlying Dominican revolution Unquote.

Dominican Counselor Amiama and Captain Guerra Ubri recently arrived Assistant Military Attaché and aide to Col. Caamaño, were also present at dinner, as well as wives.

Cabral later informed Emboff that Caamaño plans issue general press statement in very near future. He assured Emboff press statement will contain nothing sensational and will be recapitulation of Caamaño's views regarding forthcoming elections, withdrawal of US troops etc. Cabral said he hoped Emboff and Caamaño would remain in contact.

BRUCE

William H. Brubeck

## 24. American Embassy, London 5 April 1967

From: Amembassy LONDON

Subject: Col. Caamaño

FSO Peter B. Johnson, currently stationed in Bilbao, recently attended a conference in London and following up on his former service in the Dominican Republic, attempted to arrange an interview with Colonel Francisco Caamaño. Mr. Johnson did so after consultation with this Embassy. Col. Caamaño agreed to receive Mr. Johnson at his home, but did not appear for the meeting. His aide, Captain Pedro Julio Guerra, also an exiled constitutionalist, explained that Caamaño had been called away on "an urgent business matter", but that he would be happy to talk with Mr. Johnson himself. Mr. Johnson emphasised throughout that his visit was entirely personal. Caamaño, incidentally, lives in suburban Richmond and apparently has become something of a recluse — at least as far as London contacts are concerned. When in town, he remains largely at home, while Guerra maintains contact for him with the Dominican Embassy. Guerra indicated however, that Caamaño would be amenable to future contacts with the American Embassy, provided the contact was initiated "at an appropriate level" and items for discussion were specified in advance. Guerra was careful to point out, however, that his chief was not seeking contact with the American Embassy but would merely be receptive to an invitation from us. (As the Department is aware, and as Mr. Johnson reminded Guerra, the Minister invited Caamaño to lunch at his home on a tete-a-tete basis on three separate occasions. The invitations were ignored).

As to Caamaño's plans, Guerra indicated that he and his chief regarded their tour in London as a regular two-year assignment and disclaimed any feeling for the political considerations upon which the Colonel's return to the Dominican Republic might be based. He was apparently careful to point out that Caamaño was not in close touch with the Government and admitted being generally out of touch with the current scene at home. Guerra said their information on the home front came from correspondence with the fellow constitutionalists and from Dominican newspapers (El Caribe, Listín Diario, Información). He said some letters from home had been "lost" (extraviado) en route, but he did not elaborate further on this suspicion.

Guerra said he was unaware of the activities of Juan Bosch in Madrid, but seemed interested in what he was doing. When asked about the treatment of ex-constitutionalists in the Dominican Republic, Guerra said they could see from the newspapers that the persecution was still going on. On the other hand, he said that the police under Murillo and his successor had done a fairly effective job, implying that the persecution was not officially inspired.

Guerra asked about the US attitude toward Wessin y Wessin and toward Caamaño himself. Mr. Johnson disclaimed direct knowledge of official US views on either man and sensed, behind Guerra's question, some degree of concern that Wessin might be rehabilitating himself faster in US eyes than his own chief.

Guerra evidently views the Dominican military establishment as the greatest obstacle to his, and presumably Caamaño's return to the Dominican Republic. He asked Mr. Johnson about our attitude toward the Dominican military and was told that we were doing what we could to modernize military attitudes and render the military more professional and more immediately responsive to civilian control. Guerra thought this program had little chance of success as long as the old guard generals and colonels remained in control of the military. He thought the best hope for the Dominican military would be in the hands of people like Col. Caamaño. Guerra, of course, viewed the whole intervention as a terrible mistake from which the US was still suffering in terms of world opinion. He rejected the idea that the communists had been in control of the revolution and thought the US had completely misinterpreted events in this sense. He thought the Embassy in Santo Domingo had not been in touch with the situation or with the aspirations of the Dominican people, especially the younger elements.

The third (and apparently silent) member of the foregoing conversation was one Fernando Pimentel who said he was in London studying English. He said, however, that he had been with the Colonel "during the revolution". Capt. Guerra for his part stated his only ambition was to be a competent career officer. He is 28 years old, married with two children, and has attended US Air Force training courses at Maxwell Field. He is apparently quite devoted to Caamaño. Mr. Johnson described the conversation as informal and friendly.

**25. American Embassy, London 3 July 1967**

Robin Edmonds, Esquire
Head, American Department
Foreign Office
Downing St., S.W.1

Dear Robin:

The enclosed two messages, read in chronological order, are self-explanatory and may be of some interest either to your Department or to others in HMG. As you may know, the State Department has asked us to try to stay in some kind of informal contact with Colonel Caamaño and develop some information on his views, attitudes and future plans. We haven't been at all successful in this, although our Minister has invited him to lunch privately in July 18 and we are awaiting a reply from him.

Best regards.

Sincerely yours,

Arthur H. Woodruff

First Secretary of Embassy

**[no messages in archive]**

**26. American Embassy, London 24 July 1967**

## TELEGRAM TO DEPT. OF STATE FROM AMERICAN EMBASSY LONDON

SUBJECT: MEETING WITH COL. FRANCISCO Caamaño Deñó

1. Col. Caamaño, accompanied by his aide, Captain Pedro Guerra, lunched privately with Minister Kaiser and Emboff at Minister's residence today. Lunch conversation centered mainly on US race problems, but over coffee scene changed to Dominican Republic with little or no prodding from us. Both Caamaño and Guerra seemed quite willing to talk about their personal plans. Conversation was friendly and frank throughout and we feel a fair degree of rapport has been established which can hopefully build on.

2. There was little joy to be derived from the conversation itself, however. Caamaño is evidently no better disposed than he ever was toward Balaguer administration. When we suggested that present government merited support as constitutionally elected regime, he insisted that presence of American troops during election nullified results. We demurred, citing presence of neutral observers, strict impartiality of IAPF and non-campaign conducted by Bosch. Caamaño countered by implying presence of IAPF had allowed right wing activists to bully voters and opposition workers.

3. Equally, he feels present regime in its fourteen months has not even made a start on unemployment and economic development problems which he describes as root difficulty in DR. Again, he blames US. Armed "invasion", he asserts, protected position of Trujillistas who still dominate government directly or otherwise and Balaguer is still influenced by them. As result, US development aid is mis-directed, goes mostly into pockets or oligarchy and any economic progress, like land re-distribution, which would disadvantage oligarchs has become impossible. He and Guerra insisted Dominican people would not wait forever for economic improvement and that sooner or later whole Balaguer regime would have to go. They feel that now people and new structures are needed, evidently at all levels of government.

4. Caamaño was less specific about what he thought US policy should be at this juncture. When he suggested that Dominicans might resent degree of interference needed to control aid program down to the last penny, he implied that US influence was bound to be important everywhere in Latin America, that this was well understood and would be accepted by Latin Americans provided US influence was manifested in the right way.

5. He volunteered no information about his personal activities, nor did we press him on this. He did mention, however, that Juan Bosch had been in London "about a month ago".

# (iii) Press Reports from the US Archives

*The following ten newspaper articles from the period 1965–8 were included in the CIA's Dominican Republic files, as held in the National Security Archive in Washington. Also included, and reproduced elsewhere in this volume, were the report in the London 'Times' of Caamaño's press conference of 26 January 1966 and the interview with Carlos Nuñez published in 'Marcha' (Uruguay) on 25 March 1966. These press reports range from the factual and analytic to the partisan and, as with items 9 and 11, contain what appear to be intelligence service fabrications. They are included to provide relevant background to the content covering public discussion at the time about Caamaño and the Dominican Republic, not as factually or analytically reliable documents.*

1. *Newsweek* 10 May 1965

### 'POWER — AND THE TICKING OF TIME'

Ten thousand miles separate South Vietnam from Santo Domingo, but the US combat troops who marched into the bullet-scarred Dominican capital last week did so in the performance of precisely the same political mission that sends US Marines at Da Nang out on patrol against the Viet Cong guerrillas. That mission is the exercise, wise and correct, hopefully, of the enormous US power to protect its own security and what it conceives to be that of its friends, allies, and the common interest.

Time has yet to prove the decision to use this power in the Dominican Republic wrong or right. But events themselves march apace with the ticking of the clock. Decisions must be made, or not made — and the refusal, or failure, to make a decision is, inexorably, a decision itself.

In this instance, President Johnson first sent in 556 Marines "in order to protect American lives ... [and] nationals of other countries". Then, as evidence of Communist control and manipulation of the revolt increased, Mr. Johnson decided to make clear his determination to prevent a Communist take over. He weighed the inevitable wrath and resentment of other Latin American nations against the embarrassment (or worse) of another Castro in the Caribbean — and clearly decided that the first would be lesser of two evils.

Throughout the week, Moscow and Peking bitterly Deńóunced the US move into Santo Domingo, but their stricture had a ring more of formality than of threat. The Latin American reaction, when it came, was not so sharp nor so broad as expected. Had the lesson of Cuba finally got home?

There seemed little question but that the President's decision to intervene in the Dominican Republic — like the earlier decision to fight in Vietnam, of which it is a corollary — will come in for sharp and heated comment from his critics at home. They include influential intellectuals (*Newsweek*, May 3) who have recently been arguing that the US is trying to be all-powerful everywhere at once, and that it cannot "play policeman to the world". The record of US power exercises since World War II, however, seems to contradict this contention. In Greece, Berlin, Korea, and Lebanon, the US has used its power with wisdom and restraint — in the common interest of its own and its allies' security. And this far with a reasonable measure of success. In the process, four US Presidents — Truman, Eisenhower, Kennedy, and Johnson — have used their awesome power of decision to underscore the abiding truth of Balzac's phrase, said of marriage, but no less true of politics: "Power is not revealed by striking hard or often, but by striking true".

There is no foreseeable end to the chronic turmoil that besets much of the Caribbean. Economics, history, and human pride and passion will see to that. There is also no foreseeable end to the responsibility the US must bear there. Cuba saw that.

It was these political realities that prompted the US to move swiftly and powerfully last week to put down the bloody revolt in the Dominican Republic, the proud but chaotic little nation (population 4 million) that occupies the eastern half of the island of Hispaniola. In the four years since assassins freed the Dominican Republic of the tyranny of dictator Rafael Leonidas Trujillo, the government in Santo Domingo has known one free election, eight different governments, and at least half a dozen assorted coups and countercoups.

Last week's revolt got off to a faltering start, but before it was over more than 2000 Dominicans had been killed or wounded, and US Marines and Army troops had been landed in a Latin American nation for the first time in three decades.

**The Rebels Act**: The revolt began shortly before 3pm on a quiet Saturday, when eighteen soldiers and civilians, led by nominal supporters of exiled president Juan Bosch, stormed Radio Santo Domingo in the heart of the capital. They promised the overthrow of the military-backed Triumvirate headed by Donald Reid Cabral, the return from Puerto Rico of Bosch, and urged Dominicans to turn out in the streets and demonstrate. Simultaneously, the rebels seized two government arms depots outside Santo Domingo and began distributing arms and ammunition to their immediate supporters.

The first call to revolt brought little response. Dominicans had been through it all before, or so they thought at the time. A few hours later they hear Radio Santo Domingo announce that the station had been retaken, and the rebels had been issued an ultimatum to "surrender or die". And that seemed to be that.

But it wasn't. At dawn the next day, a detachment of rebels stormed the National Palace, overpowered the guards, and ousted Reid. The rebels retook the radio station and announced that the ex-President of the Congress would be Chief of State pending Bosch's return from Puerto Rico. "We want", said Colonel Francisco Caamaño Deñó, a rebel leader and a confidant of many Dominican and Cuban Communists, "to return to the people what was taken from the people". In Puerto Rico, white-haired ex-President Bosch did his best to rise to the occasion. He would return, he said, "within the hour".

By now, the rebels totaled about 1000 men, mostly soldiers like Caamaño. Not all the Dominican military units were willing to join in. But scores of pro-Bosch partisans, finally convinced that the revolt was in earnest, and hundreds of youthful hooligans, known locally as "tigers", joined the rebel forces. Arms were passed freely to all comers. They poured out into the streets of the capital, shooting at random, looting and occasionally pausing to link arms with bands of citizens and shout, "Viva Bosch!".

**Counterattack**: Almost from the outset, the rebels were opposed by the navy and air force and, more important, by Gen. Elias Wessin y Wessin. The burly, black-browed son of a Lebanese immigrant, Wessin y Wessin had helped overthrow Bosch in the first place (in 1963) because he was convinced that Bosch's well-meaning but lackluster liberalism was setting the country up for a Communist take-over.

The air force began strafing rebel positions intermittently Sunday afternoon. One prime target: the two-lane Duarte Bridge over the Ozama River. Rebel soldiers at the bridge fired back at the planes; some used mirrors to try to blind the attacking pilots by reflecting the bright tropical sun into their eyes. Now, at his military center at the sprawling San Isidro army base 20 miles east of Santo Domingo, General Wessin y Wessin prepared his infantry and armor for the attack on the rebels' ground positions within the city. There, anarchy was in full cry, and slowly the dead began to pile up at the city's morgues and hospitals.

In Washington, the progress of the coup was watched closely from the first day. The State Department's Dominican desk telephoned US Ambassador W. Tapley Bennett, who had arrived in the capital for consultations only two days before. Tap Bennett, an incisive, quietly brilliant Georgian, had been recalled to discuss the Dominican Republic's worsening economic and political situation. Bennett returned to Santo Domingo, arriving scant hours before the US Embassy there came under fire for the first time. At first, in Washington as in Santo Domingo, the reading was that the revolt would be short-lived, and that General Wessin y Wessin's forces would carry the field in a matter of hours.

**Enter the Navy**: He didn't. On Monday, Wessin y Wessin tried to send his tanks across the Duarte Bridge, and was repulsed twice. From offshore, the tiny

Dominican Navy supported the general's attacks with shells and flares. At the US Embassy, Bennett and his staff prepared for the evacuation of as many of the 2000 US citizens in Santo Domingo as wished to leave.

By now Washington's crisis machinery was in full gear. President Johnson had been notified of the revolt almost as soon as it began. In the US Navy's Pentagon war room, the maps and charts on Vietnam were moved to one side, and the maps of the Caribbean and the Dominican Republic rolled to the center of the stage. Throughout the day, the President met with State, CIA and Pentagon officials. By Monday nightfall, Ambassador Bennett had advised the President he wanted to evacuate Americans, and the aircraft carrier USS Boxer hove to off the Dominican port of Haina, 8 miles from Santo Domingo.

On Tuesday morning, Tap Bennett issued the evacuation order in Santo Domingo. "We were given twenty minutes' notice" said New York Attorney Charles Carroll. "We could take one suitcase. Everything else had to be left behind. At 5:30 am, there were 1000 Americans in the lobby of the Embajador Hotel. Then a group of Dominican civilians drove up. They shouted 'Everyone line up against the wall'. Then they began firing machine guns. I hit the dirt along with everyone else". But no one was hurt. The Dominicans were firing at their opponents on the hotel's roof. Ambassador Bennett, meanwhile, had managed to arrange a temporary cease-fire, and by that afternoon some 1100 Americans had been evacuated by launch and helicopter to the Boxer.

**Across the Bridge**: The fighting raged unabated. Wessin y Wessin's troops finally forced the Duarte Bridge, and fought into the center of the capital. Bosch's deputy fled the National Palace for the Colombian Embassy, but rebel forces fought on, entrenching themselves in Ciudad Nueva, a low-cost public housing project downtown. By nightfall, unofficial reports placed the Dominican dead at more than 400.

Wednesday was the day of decision in Santo Domingo and in Washington. While the fighting continued, Wessin y Wessin swore in a new military junta headed by Air Force Col. Pedro Bartolomé Benoit. The US Embassy evacuated 200 more Americans, and [got] an assurance that US lives and property (total investments of $110 million, chiefly by Alcoa, the Southern Puerto Rico Sugar Corp, and United Fruit) would be protected. But the new junta could promise nothing. That afternoon, Tap Bennett got on the telephone to Washington to recommend that the Marines be sent in. "Even while the Ambassador was talking", an Embassy aide recalled later, "small-arms fire came in, shattering the windows, and the Ambassador was yelling, 'Duck, or you'll get your heads cut off by the glass!'".

President Johnson had already decided to follow his ambassador's recommendation. Though the fog of war prevented any definitive attempts at classifying all the rebels who fought on — the pro-Bosch officers by now had sought asylum — both Defense Secretary McNamara and the CIA's new boss, Adm. William F. Raborn Jr., believed there was clear danger that the Communists were ascendant. Some OAS ambassadors heard reports from their embassies in Santo Domingo that Castro-style uniforms were being worn by rebel leaders. At 8:45 pm Wednesday, President Johnson went on national television to announce his decision to send the Boxer's contingent of 556 Marines in to protect the lives of US and other foreign nationals.

**Rape and Pillage**: Throughout the next day LBJ [President Lyndon B Johnson] conferred constantly. An emergency session of the Organization of American States met at the Pan American Union and ultimately sent in a five-nation peace mission. From Santo Domingo, snippets of intelligence trickled to Washington; leaders of three Communist factions were identified among the leaders of the rebel street fighters. The beleaguered city was now without water or electricity. There were reports of rape, pillage, and mass executions. The dead lay in the streets.

That afternoon, a State Department briefing for reporters was postponed, put off repeatedly into the night, then cancelled at 3:15 am. Soon after 2 am Friday, the White House announced that 2500 combat troops of the US 82nd Airborne division had been landed in the Dominican Republic. Friday night, Mr Johnson went on television again. "There are signs", the President said, "that people trained outside the Dominican Republic are seeking to gain control. Thus the legitimate aspirations of the Dominican people ... are threatened ... Loss of time may mean that it is too late ..."

But in Santo Domingo, the rebels fought on. At a conference held between Wessin y Wessin's troops and the rebels, Papal Nuncio Msgr. Emanuele Clarizio and Ambassador Bennett finally obtained agreement on a cease-fire. But the agreement [...] before it was broken, apparently by both sides. US casualties stood at four or five killed and nearly two score wounded as the week ended.

But the President was determined to bring peace to the Caribbean at any cost. As estimates of rebel fighting strength rose to 15000, US units moved out on the attack; the Pentagon sent in 6000 more US troops and set up an occupation-like US Dominican Command. That put total military strength in the taut little island at some 10000, or almost one-third of the number of Americans already committed to Vietnam.

## "CHALK UP ANOTHER SNIPER"

*Just after 2 o'clock last Friday morning, some 2500 infantry paratroopers of the 82nd Airborne Division of Fort Bragg, N.C. [North Carolina], began disembarking at Gen. Elias Wessin y Wessin's headquarters in Santo Domingo. At 8 that morning, Newsweek Associate Editor John Barnes approached San Isidro in a single-engine red-and-white Piper Cherokee from San Juan, Puerto Rico. His on-scene report:*

The air-base control tower wouldn't give us permission to land, but the pilot John A. Franciscus of St. Louis, put down on the strip anyway, in the middle of eighteen US transport planes. The base was teeming with American troops, hundreds of them guarding the airstrip with antitank guns, mortars, and bazookas.

An armed guard of Dominicans immediately took me to Air Force Col. Pedro Bartolomé Benoit, the small, retiring nominal head of the new governing junta. "The fighting isn't going as well as I would wish", he confessed, "but it is improving. The rebels still hold 3 square miles in downtown Santo Domingo". He predicted that the fighting would only end "when the city has been recaptured house by house".

In his command-post office nearby on the base, Gen. Wessin y Wessin blearily announced as I entered that he had not slept since the revolt began six days before. He is a short, pudgy man whose stomach bulbs out over his belt. He wore a crucifix over his sweaty army fatigue shirt and he had a bust of John F. Kennedy on his desk.

There is not a doubt in the general's mind that the revolt was started by Communist army officers. "It used to be that our soldiers shouted 'Viva la patria'", he said. "Now, those who went with [rebel chief] Col. Francisco Caamaño shout 'Viva Fidel!' But with the help of the American troops who are releasing our own men for fighting, we can end this soon". After the fighting is over, Wessin y Wessin said, "we will make a date for elections". Whatever the date, he added, "my opinion is that Juan Bosch can never return".

From San Isidro to the center of town, the road was guarded by US and Dominican troops. Along the banks of the muddy Ozama, where rebels fought the government tanks, I counted 60 bodies rotting in the hot sun. The center of the city, securely in rebel hands, is a human fortress of men, women, and children armed with weapons (including tanks) taken from the main Dominican ammunition dump. Windows in the center of town are boarded up, and makeshift barricades block the streets. On the river nearby, overlooking the port, stands the Ozama fortress, originally a police stronghold; just before I arrived the rebels stormed and captured it. A few police escaped by jumping the ramparts and swimming across the river; those who surrendered were butchered on the spot. In Santo Domingo, gunfire rattled incessantly.

At San Carlos Church, beyond the US Embassy, six priests are being held as hostages; the rebels have mounted machine guns on the roof. An escaping priest reported that the bodies of three Dominican Air Force men hang in Independence Park, labelled with "traitor" placards. They happened to be on leave when the revolt started, and the rebels strung them up. There are stories of firing-squad executions by rebel bands who shouted the Castro slogan "Al paredón!" (to the wall) and triumphantly bore the head of at least one victim through the streets. Looting appears to have been extremely widespread.

**Friendly Rebels**: The rebels don't deny these and other atrocity stories; they are particularly friendly to American reporters and urge us to "tell them we are not Communists". One rebel insisted: "We are people fighting against Wessin y Wessin, who has killed many of us and deprived us of food and water". Artisans, shopkeepers, well-dressed professional people including lawyers and doctors are fighting alongside soldiers and the mobs of what they — and Bosch — call "the constitutional forces". Always before, city mobs have easily been cowed by police. But the other day, when armed rebels faced the *cascos blancos* — white helmeted riot police, trained in Los Angeles — several hundred police were reported massacred.

On Friday afternoon, I followed an armed personnel carrier and tank convoy of US Marines as they fanned out from their polo-grounds beachhead beside the Embajador Hotel to carve out an International Zone for refugees [map]. As we moved cautiously into a quiet residential suburb with neat, bright-colored homes surrounded by flower gardens, rebel snipers suddenly opened fire from laurel trees and housetops. The Marines returned the fire. They are eager to finish the job, and probed far into the center of the city. One of them was killed with a bullet through his chest as he stepped around a corner.

**Cease-Fire**: Later, as I arrived in front of the sprawling white US Embassy, a Marine nonchalantly strolled out from behind a blood-red flowered bougainvillea bush, spat on a finger, and announced: "Chalked up another sniper". Marines have taken up key positions on the roof; rifle fire is continuous around the embassy. Nearby I met the Papal Nuncio, Msgr. Emanuele Clarizio, just after he negotiated the cease-fire which began officially at 5:45 pm Friday. A tall, distinguished man in white vestments, he was talking with a rebel captain and a captain from the junta forces in the middle of the street, and was full of hope that the fighting would soon stop.

Several hundred American and foreign refugees with children and crying babies spent Friday night in the lobby of the Embajador, sleeping on floor and benches and being fed US Army rations by Peace Corps workers. There is no electricity and little water. The shooting echoed through last night, and now (Saturday) the embassy is still under intermittent attack from snipers. Ambassador Bennett says Colonel Caamaño's brother Fausto admits rebel forces no longer control many bands of fighters. But the cease-fire is not being honored by either side and it looks at the weekend as if junta chief Benoit will indeed only recapture the center of the city "house by house" and bullet by bullet.

*2. Post Despatch* 10 May 1965

**IMMEDIATE PROBLEM FACING US IN DOMINICAN REPUBLIC CRISIS IS TO HEAD OFF ANOTHER TRUJILLO.**

**Presence of American Troops Rules Out Emergence of Red Rule, but Right-Wing Tyranny is a Threat**

By Richard Dudman

SANTO DOMINGO, Dominican Republic, May 10.

THE IMMEDIATE PROBLEM facing the United States is not how to prevent the emergence of another Fidel Castro but how to head off another Rafael Trujillo Molina.

No Communist government could conceivably emerge as long as such overwhelming United States forces remain here. But by the unfortunate logic of Caribbean politics, there is a strong possibility that efforts to head off another Castro will lead to another right-wing tyranny like the 30-year dictatorship that ended with Trujillo's assassination in 1961.

Worse, the next step in this particular logic would be massive growth of the anti-Americanism and left-wing extremism that the present military intervention is intended to prevent.

THIS is the dilemma in which the United States finds itself. The United States is still mainly alone in the affair.

Leading Latin American figures who helped get the necessary two-thirds vote in the council of the Organization of American States to convert this into an inter-American operation were reported to have done so mostly to get the United States off the hook and save the inter-American system rather than in any spirit of sympathy with the original unilateral intervention.

The omens are not good. The US forces have the appearance of being aligned with those of Brig Gen Wessin y Wessin against the rebels despite assertion of American neutrality.

Wessin is not at all a popular figure, and American officials say emphatically that he must not become the new head of government. His forces and those of the United States are side by side and at peace with each other, although a US Army information officer insists that "tactically, logistically and administratively there is no relation between the two forces".

ON THE REBEL side, the key figure remains former President Juan Bosch, who was overthrown by Wessin in September 1963 and is in exile in Puerto Rico. He remains the hero of the thousands of rebels who are risking their lives by defying overwhelming odds in the continuing insurgency, although he has formally given up the right to the remainder of his term to Col. Francisco Caamaño.

Some of Bosch's best friends say that he was a poor president — weak as an administrator, naïve in his gentle handling of the Communists, and generally vacillating and temperamental.

They say that in the current situation he lacked personal courage.

One of Bosch's old friends and steadfast sympathizers points out that Bosch could have taken any one of a dozen planes in San Juan and flown to the Dominican Republic to lead the revolution that was trying to put him back into the presidency. Instead, he said, Bosch waited in vain for the air force to send a plane and tried to direct the revolution by telephone, radio and press conference.

BOSCH CLAIMS to have averted a bloody battle last Saturday between the rebels and the Americans. He told a reporter that Col. Caamaño had telephoned last Saturday afternoon and told him that the American marines were advancing but that the rebels would fight to the death.

Bosch said that he replied "Don't fight the Marines. If they kill you, you shall die. If you are captured, then you are to be prisoner. We are fighting for democracy against Wessin. Remember, we are not fighting the United States".

The previous head of government, Donald Reid Cabral, whom both the rebels and Wessin have turned against, was supported only by the military. When he tried to curtail the privileges of the military and invoked economic austerity for the civilian population, it was an easy matter to topple him.

W. TAPLEY BENNETT, the American Ambassador, is blamed widely for "over-reacting" when the revolution broke out for refusing a request by Caamaño and other rebel leaders on April 27 that he mediate with the Wessin forces, and for allegedly ordering the Marines to collaborate with the Wessin forces when they landed the next day. All those acts contributed to the present situation.

The appearance of an alliance between the American forces and Wessin became particularly embarrassing when the general began playing "The Star Spangled Banner" at the start of his daily radio broadcast. He was ordered to stop.

Skeptics here doubt the Central Intelligence Agency's report that Communists and Communist sympathizers said to be participating, only a few were actually known to be active. The others were merely reported to have entered the country recently.

References in the CIA report to non-Dominicans in the revolution turned out to have little basis. The only foreigners who could be identified were one Spanish loyalist, two former members of the French Foreign Legion and a Corsican.

The CIA's chief of Latin American operations is understood to have had little experience in the area. He is said to have made his first tour of Latin America last year, for an introductory "look-see", as he put it.

CIA operations in Latin America have been criticized also on the ground that its agents here mainly were transferred as a group from the Federal Bureau of Investigation — which used to have jurisdiction over the area — and that former FBI agents have little appreciation of political matters. Nonetheless, many critics are reluctant to say that there was no possibility of a Communist or Castro-style takeover of the rebellion.

THE WORST omen for the future is the pattern of the Johnson administration's overall record in respect to the Dominican Republic.

When the Bosch government was overthrown in 1963, Mr. Johnson waited only briefly before recognizing the junta that replaced it and resuming American economic aid, without which no government could survive. But when the Bosch forces tried in the last two weeks to overthrow the illegal government and re-establish their constitutional regime, the Johnson administration rushed in with troops.

Bosch and other rebel leaders say that they had already crushed the Wessin forces when the Americans arrived.

An American who was on the scene at the 1963 coup has written a detailed memorandum about what happened. He points out that Ambassador John Bartlow Martin was authorized to make it clear that the United States would never again allow a Castro regime to develop in the Caribbean. That guarantee has been backed by the full military might of the United States, the observer said.

"UNFORTUNATELY, it was not US policy to employ the same degree of force against the overthrow of constitutional government in the Caribbean by the extreme right", he writes.

"Had John Martin been given the authority to state that in equally forceful language, the tin soldiers with their gold-plated pistols and handful of rusty tanks would not have dared to venture out of San Isidro.

The irony is that the guarantee we have made is the most difficult to honor. If a Communist government were to come to power in the Dominican Republic it only could do so on the crest of a rather broad wave of public support. To put down a revolt which has the backing of a substantial percentage of a population is a considerable undertaking, yet this is what we have guaranteed in the Caribbean.

To put down a palace revolt involving a few-score brass hats with virtually no popular following other than the tutumpote (Bosch's word for "fat cats"), is a far less expensive guarantee to enforce. Yet the United States government was unwilling to make this kind of guarantee".

Such was the prediction in this private memorandum written in late 1963.

It has partly come true. The problem now is to keep it from coming true completely or, worse, making it come true eventually by inept efforts to stop it.

3. *Herald Tribune* 23 May 1965

## DILEMMA IN "CREDIBILITY GAP"

By David Wise

For the past two days, the Johnson administration has been grappling with what might best be described as a credibility problem of its own making. From the White House on down the highest officials of the government have been busily denying that the United States role in the Dominican Republic is anything other than one of strict neutrality.

These denials have come from Presidential Press Secretary George Ready, from Secretary of State Dean Rusk, from United Nations Ambassador Adlal Stevenson and from Ellsworth Bunker, US Ambassador to the Organization of American States.

The Administration is discovering, however, as other Administrations have in the past, that when the gap between a government's actions and its words become discernible, it is in trouble.

News reports from Santo Domingo, appearing in this newspaper and others, have told of US Marines assisting the junta forces of Gen. Antonio Imbert Barreras against the rebels of Col. Francisco Caamaño. News photos and television clips have reinforced this impression.

One film seen by perhaps millions of Americans on CES-TV showed an interview with a US Marine. As machine guns chattered in the background, the Marine described the rebels as the "enemy".

Were the Marines, then, assisting the junta? the reporter asked. "That's right", the Marine replied.

The problem is much larger than the opinion of one fighting man on the scene however. It goes to the roots of modern government trying to settle a complex political and military crisis with everybody watching.

The credibility problem began the very night that President Johnson made the decision to send in the Marines, the night of April 28.

The Chief Executive, determined to prevent another Cuba, called in Congressional leaders of both parties and informed them of his grave decision. Adm. William F. Raborn, sworn in less than seven hours earlier as the new director of the Central Intelligence Agency, warned the Congressmen of the danger of a Communist-Castro-style takeover in Santo Domingo.

The New York Herald Tribune was the first newspaper in the nation to report what had taken place at this meeting — and to report that the President was acting not only to save American lives, but in the hope of preventing a Communist uprising.

On the night of April 28, however, Mr. Johnson, in a two-minute televised statement to the nation, said simply that he had dispatched the Marines "in order to protect American lives". He made no mention of the alleged Communist threat looming in the background. The omission surprised some of the Congressmen.

The next day, the White House insisted that the Marines had landed for the reason given, to protect American lives. Not until Sunday May 2, four nights later, did the President make any direct mention of Communists.

That night he said on TV: "And what began as a popular democratic revolution, committed to democracy and social justice, very shortly moved and was taken over and really seized and placed into the hands of a band of Communist conspirators".

Could it be that the Communists had appeared in the revolt only after April 28 and before May 2? Not so. On May 4, the President spoke to a group of key Congressmen in the East Room of the White House. The official transcript includes this statement:

"In our first meeting that night (referring to April 28) from 3 o'clock when we got our cable, until 7 o'clock when we met with the Congressional leaders, our intelligence indicated that two of the prime leaders in the rebel forces were men with a long history of Communist association and insurrections. One had fought in the Spanish Civil War and both had been given detailed lengthy training in operations of this type. As reports came in, as they do every few minutes, it developed there were eight of those who were in the movement that had been trained by Communist forces".

In short, the Administration had first denied, then admitted, that one motive for landing Marines was the fear of a Communist takeover of the revolt. Soon, a new credibility problem arose.

The US encouraged Gen. Imbert to set up his new military junta as a counterforce to the rebels. Negotiations with Gen. Imbert to this end reportedly took place on the US aircraft carrier Boxer.

With the rebels pinned down in the southern Ciudad Nueva quarter, the Imbert forces last Saturday were free to move against one group of rebels north of the US-held corridor cutting across Santo Domingo.

But the news reports and films of US Marines assisting the junta endangered the US posture in Latin America and the world. They raised at length the spectre of an American Hungary, with American forces mowing down underdog rebels as the Russians did in Budapest in 1956.

So the insistence in the past two days that the US policy is one of "neutrality". But if, as the President said on May 2, "Communist conspirators" have seized the revolt, why is the US neutral?".

Facing that dilemma, the policymakers have said little in recent days about Communists in the rebel movement.

Like a series of Chinese boxes, each Administration explanation has in turn led to another. The result has been that officials already busy trying to settle the crisis in the Dominican Republic have had to take time out to deal with the credibility crisis at home.

4. *Washington Post and Times Herald*

26 May 1965

## GUZMAN BANK FRAUD TALE DENIED

### Accounting Firm Disputes Charge Spread by Foes

By Barnard L. Collier

Antonio Guzman Silvestre, whom American envoys and rebel leaders had agreed on for president of a Dominican coalition government, flatly denied today implications in Washington that he was involved in a massive bank embezzlement.

The implications were also completely rejected by the local manager of the New York accounting firm of Ernst & Ernst. An audit report by Ernst & Ernst was cited as the basis for the allegation against Guzman published by the Washington Daily News.

Presidential assistant McGeorge Bundy's efforts to work out a Dominican compromise through Guzman are reportedly being bitterly opposed in some official quarters in Washington. The presidential envoy was said to have been stunned Monday when the implied charges against Guzman were made public.

### Rumor Traced

American sources here suggested that supporters of the Dominican junta leader, Gen. Antonio Imbert Barrera, were responsible for the circulation of a falsified version of the Ernst & Ernst audit, from which the inference of wrongdoing on Guzman's part was drawn.

Published stories based on the purported findings of the audit said that the Dominican Banco Agricola, of which Guzman was a director, had overstated its assets by $75 million and that thousands of notes and $1 million worth of mortgage collateral were missing.

These allegations produced a last-minute snag on Monday in the talks between US negotiators and the "constitutionalist" rebels of Col. Francisco Caamaño.

Rebel sources said the snag was "only technical at first" but then grew into a US demand for an explanation of the allegations against Guzman.

### Pro and Con Battle

According to informed American sources, the real obstacle to a solution of the Dominican crisis is a "ferocious" battle within the Johnson Administration over the pros and cons of forming the proposed Guzman coalition.

The argument of the anti-Guzman or pro-Imbert people is said to be that any concessions to the rebels will be misinterpreted politically in the United

States as a back-down before a Communist-dominated group. The rebels at one time — though no longer — were so described by US officials.

The implications against Guzman were denied — indignantly — by Benjamin Berezowski, the Ernst & Ernst manager here who directed the six-month audit of the Banco Agricola. The audit was ordered in 1963 during the constitutional regime of now-exiled President Juan Bosch, in whose cabinet Guzman served as agriculture minister.

The Banco Agricola, designed to give loans to farmers on favourable terms, was, he added, "in no way connected with the Agriculture Ministry and Guzman's job as superior director in no way gave him influence or access to the Bank's funds without the knowledge of scores of highly respected officials and representatives of international organizations including the Inter-American Development Bank and the aid mission here".

Guzman himself insisted in a statement that the audit report showed "no dishonesty on my part or by any director of the bank".

He attributed the bank's financial weakness to "the economic prostitution committed during the tyranny of Trujillo" when, he said, the firm's capital was "increased fictionally" from $5 million to $100 million.

[In Washington, US officials said a copy of the audit had been received by the State Department recently, but Guzman had not been connected with the matter because the audit did not list the bank's directors by name, John Goshko of the Washington Post reported].

[The officials emphasised that they had no way of telling "at present" whether the implications of irregularities were true or whether Guzman could be tied personally to any scandal that might result, Goshko reported].

### 5. Latin Foreign Ministers Coming Here for Talks

By John M. Goshko

The foreign ministers of several Latin American countries are expected to come to Washington before the end of the week for discussion of the hemispheric problems raised by the Dominican Republic crisis.

Reports of the impending high-level meeting at the Organization of the American States highlighted a day on which the White House confirmed in effect a report published yesterday by the Washington Post that the FBI is conducting an investigation in the Dominican Republic.

The OAS delegations from Brazil and Ecuador announced that their respective foreign ministers, Vasco Leltao da Cunha and Gonzalo Escudero, will come to Washington on Thursday.

In addition, diplomatic sources said it appeared likely that the foreign ministers of Argentina, Bolivia, Paraguay would attend the OAS session. Also mentioned were the foreign ministers of Colombia and Venezuela, but the reports of their attendance were less firm.

Should a large number of foreign ministers show up, US officials said that Secretary of State Dean Rusk probably would take over as head of the US delegation.

Presidential adviser McGeorge Bundy was reported to be returning from Santo Domingo and there were indications that he also would take part in the meetings.

The current OAS deliberations were officially designated a foreign ministers' meeting shortly after the Dominican crisis broke out last month. Until now, however, each of the 20 members has been represented by its normal OAS ambassador acting in place of their respective ministers.

Although the Dominican situation will be the dominant topic, the indications are that the meeting will also consider the wave of unrest that has swept Latin America in the wake of the Santo Domingo revolution. Bolivia and Colombia have been especially hard hit, and there also have been stirrings of trouble in Uruguay, Ecuador and Guatemala.

The United States and some other members are expected to push for creation of a permanent OAS peace force and other machinery to deal with subversion in the Hemisphere.

However, most Latin diplomats seemed to feel yesterday [the files breaks off at this point ...]

6. *The Economist* 16 September 1967

**DOMINICAN REPUBLIC**

**As well as could be expected**

From a special correspondent

The uprising of April 1965 and its suppression by American military intervention are still the memories that obsess this disaster-weary nation. Santo Domingo is still divided into two enemy camps: the slums of the former rebel zone, where new peasant migrants have increased the population to nearly four times its 1950 level; and the quiet residential neighbourhoods surrounding the American embassy where the upper and middle classes live uneasily within a stone's throw of the chaos and despair of the poor.

Seven different governments have ruled since Rafael Trujillo was gunned down in 1961. (There were nearly twice that many if you count the regimes that lasted less than a week or established control over only part of the republic). In this period the American mission here has grown from a small consulate to the next largest American embassy in Latin America after Brazil; the 900 employees are double the number at the time of the 1965 revolution. Over the past five years more than $320 million in American aid funds has been spent, most of it in political and economic rescue operations. Long-range development schemes have been continually interrupted by political disorders. The American ambassador runs what amounts to a government in miniature with scores of American advisers coaching the armed services and taking part in the affairs of nearly all key government agencies.

President Joaquin Balaguer, who celebrated his first anniversary in power on July 1st, has shown remarkable political skill in using this vast American support. He has won wide respect for trimming costs in the government sugar mills so that sugar production, the country's principal dollar earner, is profitable for the first time in years. Moreover, President Balaguer and his principal Dominican advisers (most of whom were senior officials under Trujillo) have warmed the hearts of their American advisers by insisting that no more aid should be given as budgetary support; they have asked instead for plenty of capital funds as quickly as possible.

President Balaguer has also halted the terrorism that over the past two years has resulted in the death, disappearance or imprisonment of many of those who took the "constitutionalist" or "rebel" side in the 1965 uprising. Last spring Sr Casimiro Castro of the Partido Revolucionario Dominicano (PRD), the principal opposition party, was critically injured when a fire-bomb exploded in his car. In a televised speech, President Balaguer suggested that Sr Castro was carrying the bomb in order to plant it somewhere himself. When the entire

PRD group boycotted congress in protest, President Balaguer promised to take steps to end the terrorism at once. Since then, Santo Domingo has been quieter than at any time for the past four years.

A devout and ascetic Roman Catholic who has leaned heavily on the "communist" issue, President Balaguer has proved to be surprisingly shrewd and tough in handling the opposition. He has effectively split the "constitutionalist" movement, especially the PRD, by appointing several of its leaders to government or diplomatic posts. He has pressed his advantage home by changing the tax laws so that the revenues of the PRD-controlled municipality of Santo Domingo have been halved. For three months the city has been unable to pay its 4000 employees — who compose most of the party's rank and file.

Hunger and unemployment are as serious in Santo Domingo as in any Latin American city. Roughly half the adult males in the capital are out of work with the proportion reaching 90 per cent in some of the poorer *barrios*. Because a high premium is placed on government jobs, politics is more a do-or-die affair here than in most places. This is why Santo Domingo's slum-dwellers, who defeated crack Dominican tank and infantry units two years ago, are now talking about a renewal of the 1965 revolution.

Unemployment is also the driving force behind the formation of the Balaguer Veterans' Front, a ragged force claiming 10.000 adherents under the leadership of an old Trujillista general. The front has launched a campaign of "voluntary" street cleaning in the hope of profiting should the PRD lose control of the city at the municipal elections next June.

If President Balaguer's manoeuvres against the PRD do not backfire into a renewal of political violence, he may be able to claim to have given his people their first period of constructive calm since Trujillo's death. The 70-man American military mission has been taking great pains to dampen any sign of conspiracy among the rightist generals and colonels. But earlier this month the president dismissed the commanders of the air force and police and once again there were rumours of right-wing plotting. The hard-line right is campaigning vociferously for the return of its leader, General Elias Wessin, who was deported forcibly by American troops in late 1965 and later was named military advisor to the Dominican delegation to the United Nations, with residence in Miami. The pro-Wessin campaign has tried to broaden its appeal by calling also for the return of the "constitutionalist" leader Colonel Francisco Caamaño, who is still in exile as military attaché in London. It is just possible that the right and the left will be driven together by the continuing unemployment. But, given some luck, President Balaguer has a better chance than any recent Dominican leader to plan and to build.

7. *The Scotsman* (from *The Washington Post and Los Angeles Times News Service*) 8 December 1967

## MYSTERY OF THE MISSING DOMINICAN ATTACHE

When the name of an army colonel from a banana republic turns up on the missing persons' list it is rarely a matter of international concern. But when the colonel is Francisco Caamaño Deñó, who commanded the rebel forces in the Dominican Republic's 1965 civil war, it is something else. And Caamaño is missing in circumstances that can only be described as mysterious.

Caamaño, military attaché at the Dominican Embassy in London, was last seen on October 24 in The Hague. He is said to have stepped out of a friend's apartment to get a breath of fresh air, and there the mystery begins. Was he kidnapped or killed? Did he slip away to some Communist country to plot against his government? Is this disappearance a calculated political gambit?

### U.S. SIGNIFICANCE

All these possibilities have potentially grave consequences, not only for the tiny nation in the Caribbean — but for the US. For it was in Dominica, in the spring of 1965, that US Marines were put ashore as the first step towards ending the civil war. The action was not applauded unanimously in Latin America and the US has invested heavily in efforts to avoid a repetition.

Of the possible explanations for Caamaño's absence, homicide and abduction are regarded as the least credible. Caamaño's presence in The Hague, it is believed, points to something different.

Caamaño (34) was one of the rebel chiefs who, after the war, were persuaded to go abroad. Among the others were Capt. Hector Lachapelle Diaz and Capt. Manuel Montes Arache. It was from Lachapelle's home that Caamaño disappeared, and Montes Arache was present at the time.

### DOMINATING

In the past week, from the time the disappearance became public, Santo Domingo newspapers have carried little else in the way of political developments. The story has dominated the front page of virtually every newspaper.

The betting in informed circles is that the story will be on the front page for a long time, and that much more than a single army colonel will be involved before it is ended.

8. *New York Post* 23 February 1968

## A DOMINICAN TAKING CHE'S ROLE?

By Robert Berrellez

SANTO DOMINGO (AP) — Is Fidel Castro preparing a move against the Dominican Republic with a force led by Colonel Francisco Caamaño, the missing leader of the 1965 revolution?

This is a recurring question among Dominicans of all levels in this often-troubled Caribbean republic, Cuba's eastern neighbour. Even among some of his closest collaborators here there's almost a conviction Caamaño is in Cuba and will return with a guerrilla force.

Official anxiety over Col. Caamaño's whereabouts has reached such a peak that the Dominican armed forces reinforced vigilance and defensive measures in the northwest area adjoining Haiti.

The chunky, moustached chieftain of Constitutionalist forces in the 1965 fighting disappeared last Oct. 24. He had been Dominican military attaché in London since early 1966.

Listed as Deserter
Under the Dominican military code, an officer absent without authorization for more than 10 days is classified as a deserter. Caamaño's pay has been stopped but no other action has been taken.

It has been learned authoritatively that Caamaño will be tried in absentia as an army deserter probably within two weeks. A military tribunal could discharge him dishonourably from service and sentence him to a long prison term.

President Joaquin Balaguer said "We are almost certain he is in Cuba preparing acts against the country".

Caamaño disappeared just 15 days after the death of Ernesto (Che) Guevara in a Bolivian guerrilla clash. This has caused Dominicans to believe that Caamaño, after thorough Marxist brainwashing in Europe, was persuaded to take over Che's role as leader of Castroite penetrations into other Latin American countries.

There is a deep fear among many leftist moderates who backed the Constitutionalist cause that if Caamaño turns up in Cuba the Dominican army and police will take repressive measures against them. One said: "It's even possible the army may invent a so-called Caamaño invasion just to get at us".

9. *Washington Post* 12 May 1968

## EX DOMINICAN RED DESCRIBES CASTRO ROLE AND FUND-RAISING

By Carlos Martinez

MIAMI — After three years of training in guerrilla tactics, urban agitation, and military intelligence, Luis Genao Espaillat was ready to go home to the Dominican Republic.

This was the final briefing, and it was long after midnight when the bearded man in olive green walked with Genao to the door.

"Remember, Luis" said Fidel Castro, "the Dominican Republic is a primary objective to us".

It was late in 1962 when the Dominican Communist leader met in Havana with Castro for the last time. In September, 1965, Genao broke with the Castroist 14th of June Movement in the Dominican Republic.

### Tells of Plotting

Genao has now described how he plotted with Castro for a Communist takeover in the Dominican Republic. He also told of meeting with Mao Tse-tung, Ho Chi Minh and Nikita Khrushchev to seek financial and technical aid for Communist revolutionaries in Santo Domingo.

Genao, soft-spoken 33 year-old bachelor, was interviewed during a brief stay in Miami.

He was among the Communist leaders who fought in the civil war in the Dominican Republic in April, 1965. His name was high on a list of 77 Dominican Communists compiled by US intelligence sources and issued during the revolt as part of the justification for US intervention.

The visit to Miami marked the first time US officials have permitted Genao to enter the country. Since leaving the hospital seven months ago after being wounded in an assassination attempt, Genao has lived in virtual seclusion in a small apartment in Santo Domingo.

"I know they will try it again because I know too much", Genao said.

Before defecting Genao was a leading organizer of the central committee of the 14th of June movement.

From 1959 to 1962, he was the group's permanent delegate to Cuba, and met with Castro to map strategy "from 30 to 40 times — as often as the circumstances required".

Genao said Castro has been supporting the 14th of June group financially for the last eight years. He also has provided instruction in Cuba for "several hundred" movement members who travelled to Havana on phony passports, Genao said.

"Castro is still subsiding the 14th of June on a monthly basis. He's generous with his money — contributions are in dollars, in bills of small Deñóminations — but he demands itemized descriptions of how the money will be used", Genao noted.

## Money Comes From Paris

A delegate from the movement travels to Havana once a month to meet with Maj. Manuel (Barba Roja) Pineiro Losada, 35, head of the Dirección General de Inteligencia [Cuban Intelligence Service, part of Ministry of Interior], in charge of planning and financing subversion in Latin America.

Genao said sometimes Pineiro hands out the money himself. Other times the cash is made available in Paris by the intelligence officer at the Cuban embassy there.

"The actual delivery of the money never takes place inside the embassy", said Genao. "It's always done at some small café or at the intelligence officer's private apartment".

Even the 14th of June's powerful radio transmitter-receiver, which Genao helped smuggle into the Dominican Republic, has been provided by Castro. The Cuba government periodically provides the codes used in the broadcasts.

## Deported to Lisbon

Genao was among the leaders of an abortive guerrilla uprising in the Dominican Republic in 1963 that he and Castro had planned in Havana. He and several dozen guerrillas were captured and in 1964 Genao was deported to Lisbon.

It was there, Genao said, that he was given his "most delicate" assignment by the 14th of June — orders to visit Communist China, North Vietnam, North Korea, Albania and the Soviet Union to enlist aid for the Dominican revolutionaries.

Most generous of the leaders he spoke to, Genao said, was Mao Tse-tung. Mao quickly agreed to provide the 14th of June with a monthly allowance, which still exists, varying between $10000 and $20000, Genao said.

Mao also agreed to provide guerrilla training, but refused a request for training of doctors and engineers belonging to the movement. Genao said Mao told him: "Comrade, the fundamental task is to seize power. After that, we will have time to worry about engineers and doctors".

Ho Chi Minh, Genao said, was "harder to deal with" than Mao.

"He said it would be of great importance to Latin American revolutionaries to receive theoretical and practical guerrilla training in Vietnam, but pledged no financial help. He maintained that the seizure of power could only be achieved through armed action, and said that anyone planning to do it otherwise was not a good Communist".

Genao said Ho kept his promise to train Dominican revolutionaries.

Genao said Khrushchev expressed interest in the Dominican movement but turned down a request of assistance.

"Nikita was very sympathetic, but said he was already providing financial assistance to the Dominican Communist Party, a more orthodox Communist organization".

### Returned with Disguise

After completing his mission, Genao flew to Paris in mid-1965. From there he returned to the Dominican Republic clandestinely with the help of Red Chinese agents.

Experts from the Chinese embassy in Paris changed Genao's features by mounting dentures over his natural teeth and coloring his hair. He said they taught him to talk and act like a wealthy Spaniard on a business trip. He made it easily through Dominican customs.

10. *Elite* (Caracas) 18 May 1968

**Caamaño TO REPLACE CHE GUEVARA**

[Article by Raimundo Valecillos; Caracas, *Elite*, Spanish, 18 May 1968, pp. 48–9, 73]

The big Venezuelan evening newspaper El Mundo has produced a sensational continental news scoop by revealing that Colonel Francisco Caamaño, the ex-leader of the Dominican revolution who mysteriously disappeared from Holland last year, now occupies the position formerly held by Che Guevara; he has been in Colombia and Venezuela directing guerrilla activities in both countries. In an abrupt political turn-about Caamaño has given up Social-Christian proclivities for Communism.

The mystery concerning the whereabouts of Colonel Francisco Alberto Caamaño Deño was solved during the past week due to publication by the evening newspaper El Mundo — belonging to Capril Publications — of a series of confidential reports which reveal the Dominican soldier's presence in the guerrilla movement in Venezuela and Colombia. This is the outcome of his rise to leadership of the insurrection aimed at subverting continental political order; an office Havana has given him as a substitute for Che Guevara.

The confidential reports published by El Mundo have caused a real sensation the world over, constituting a news "first" with the greatest journalistic impact of the year. The suspense caused by Colonel Caamaño's mysterious disappearance had given rise to the most controversial stories about his fate and activities, creating a question which overshadowed not only the personality of the man who directed the Santo Domingo revolt in April 1965 and the last conflict with OAS military forces, but also the strategic and political situation in all of Latin America.

Today it is already known that Havana has substituted Colonel Caamaño for Che Guevara to lead and coordinate the guerrilla movement on a continental scale. Thus ends a suspenseful mystery and a new chapter in the elements constituting the political unrest which has shaken our continent has just begun: the legend and subversive mystique of Che Guevara will now be maintained physically by the personality of the man who gained notoriety in Santo Domingo when he took command of a political movement which faced troops from six countries on our continent.

A short while after the death of Che Guevara in Bolivia, Colonel Caamaño suddenly disappeared from The Hague, in Holland, while preparing to visit his wife and children who were living — and still live — in Madrid, since the cold in the Dutch capital where Caamaño held the post of military attaché for the Dominican Republic affected them very much.

Colonel Lachapelle, another Dominican soldier who fought under Caamaño in the Dominican Republic during the April 1965 revolution, said that his former leader had left behind a suitcase of clothing which he was to have taken to Spain. Colonel Lachapelle — also military attaché in The Hague — explained that Caamaño had gone out to complete the details concerning his pending trip to Spain in order to see his family when he disappeared without a trace of explanation.

Afterward it was said that Caamaño had gone to the Soviet Union, and other sources placed him in the Dominican Republic, where he was supposed to have gone illegally to face an eventual ultra-rightist revolt led by General Elias Wessin y Wessin — his major opponent during the armed struggle of April 1965 — against the present government of President Joaquin Balaguer.

The most conflicting stories arose: some said that he had been kidnapped and assassinated in a repetition of the former cases of Ben Barka and General Humberto Delgado, who were kidnapped and murdered in France and Spain respectively some years before. Elsewhere it was asserted that his supposed flight to the Dominican Republic had taken place so that he could lead an armed uprising against the government of Dr. Joaquin Balaguer, in order to establish a "people's dictatorship". This is the only formula able to deal with the influence of national oligarchies in Latin America, according to a theory put forth a little later by ex-President Bosch in Spain. The suspense and intrigue which immediately surrounded Caamaño's disappearance suddenly increased when ex-President Juan Bosch declared that the Dominican soldier had "himself decided" to get away, due to the real spiritual crisis he suffered when bombarded with bribery attempts by US government agents. Ex-President Bosch also referred to complaints ascribed to Caamaño himself stating that he was the object of spying and endeavours to control him in the Dutch capital.

### "People's Dictatorship"

What relationship exists, objectively speaking, between the theory of a "people's dictatorship" issued by ex-President Juan Bosch in Spain — a little after the disappearance of Caamaño — and the proven presence of the Dominican soldier, as sensationally revealed by El Mundo, in the increasing guerrilla movement on this continent? When ex-President Bosch issued his theory he astonished Latin American politicians: Bosch had always been considered a liberal, even when weighed down by the evident bitterness that, from his Spanish exile, tinged his statements against the United States, which the ex-President blames for having frustrated his rise to the Dominican Presidency after the April 1965 revolution.

The theory of a "people's dictatorship" issued by Bosch a little after Caamaño's disappearance not only began to be linked with that event but also with the frequency with which the ex-President pointed out the young colonel was his "own child" from a political point of view. In Venezuela where Bosch is well-known, his emphatic espousal of "people's dictatorship" as a system of government for Latin America was received with wonderment, but this fact scarcely touched the name of Caamaño, who was always regarded as a nationalist soldier, and as an honest man who had grown tired of the vice and corruption in the Dominican garrisons inherited from the Trujillo era.

Nevertheless, in the Dominican Republic even the Dominican Revolutionary Party — a political organization led by Bosch — began to show signs of uneasiness: on one side wide sectors of the PRD (Partido Revolucionario Democratico) were surprised by the "people's dictatorship" theory formulated by their greatest leader; on the other, the disappearance of Caamaño began to be a source of anxiety to those within the ranks of the PRD. They feared a party linked with a soldier (Caamaño), considered to be the operative arm of Bosch's "people's dictatorship" plans, could be subjected to official repression.

Furthermore, the Dominican Republic's Social Christian Revolutionary Party — to which Caamaño's name had always been linked ideologically — made the public aware of its uneasiness over the evidence that Caamaño's disappearance was part of a political scheme plotted outside the sphere of national politics. The Dominican Social Christians demanded that Colonel Caamaño, from wherever he might be, clarify the motives and circumstances of his disappearance.

For his part President Joaquin Balaguer has always shown great caution in examining the circumstances relative to Caamaño's disappearance. Due to newsmen and public opinion, it was evident that President Balaguer did not want to compromise his position at all: he always said that he had no idea of the reasons which had provoked the colonel to disappear, nor of his true whereabouts or activities.

But soon some unusual military activity gradually became evident in the Dominican countryside so a rumour grew that Caamaño had gone over to Cuba. The northern coast of the Dominican Republic — close to Cuba — was subjected to special vigilance, and an unusual concentration of military goods was observed in that area. Very recently the "14 June Revolutionary Movement", one of the seven Communist "miniparties" in Santo Domingo, categorically confirmed that Colonel Caamaño was actually in Cuba preparing a "national liberation". This story, released by pro-Castro Dominican Communists, could be taken to be one of their frequently irrational declarations, but was still seen as an interested party's admission in contrast with official calm and the incredulity of the Social-Christians and Bosch's own party.

### From London to the Andes
It is now known that Colonel Caamaño travelled from Europe to Havana at the invitation of Fidel Castro, who planned to give him the post of directing

the revolutionary movement in Latin America. Before leaving for Havana, according to known facts, Caamaño spoke with Bosch in the Spanish sea resort of Benidorm, next to the Mediterranean Sea, where the Dominican ex-President is living out his term of exile. What was said? El Mundo articles revealed that Colonel Caamaño had told Bosch of his plans after accepting Fidel Castro's personal invitation to travel to Havana, offered through a mediator, the Cuban diplomatic representative in London.

Also attending Caamaño and Bosch's meeting in Benidorm were Colonel Manuel Ramon Montes Arache — now Dominican military attaché in Montreal — and the leaders of Bosch's party, Jottin Cury, and Secretary General José Francisco Peña Gómez. Finally, Caamaño, accompanied by Montes Arache, returned to The Hague, where his self-abduction took place as later announced by Bosch.

It was then that Bosch gave approval to Caamaño's plans to let events develop according to the theory of introducing a "people's dictatorship" for Latina America as formulated by the former writer and ex-President. To supply further background to the story of Caamaño's disappearance from The Hague, it is worth mentioning that Bosch simultaneously affirmed his belief that the establishment of Fidel Castro's regime was what produced, historically speaking, the mobilization of the Latin American nations and genuine attempts by the United States to contribute to their development. Juan Bosch added that Fidel Castro deserved all our respect and that he would prefer to "die a thousand times as a Communist — although he was not one — than as an American".

Once in Havana, Colonel Caamaño was subjected to an intense Marxist indoctrination at the same time as leading a selected group of guerrillas who were trained to continue the process of subversion in all of Latin America. Recently, according to El Mundo, he went in disguise to Colombia, whence he entered Venezuela through Apure State to organise the reactivation of the guerrillas in both countries in accordance with Fidel Castro's orders and to deal with recent dissension in the guerrilla commands.

El Mundo states that Caamaño's presence in Colombia had been detected by the Military Intelligence Service of that country, which informed President Lleras Restrepo. The latter in turn informed President Leoni by official means. Lastly, the Information Service of Venezuela's Armed Forces (SIFA: Servicio de Informacion del las Fuerzas Armadas) also detected the presence of Caamaño in Venezuela, having discovered documents in camps abandoned by the guerrillas after recent intensive encounters with regular troops.

During Caamaño's visit to Venezuelan territory a meeting was held near the Colombian-Venezuelan border in Apure State. Representatives were present from the armed forces of Colombian liberation and a Columbian guerrilla group, three from Santo Domingo's "14 June Revolutionary Movement", and three from Venezuela's FALN (Fuerzas Armadas de la Liberacion Nacional).

According to El Mundo's exclusive sources, Caamaño must until now have been carrying out coordination and orientation activities between the most important guerrilla groups and factions in Latin America, as well as directing the funds to finance the armed insurrection on a continental scale. The Dominican high military functionary is famous for his asceticism and disregard for material wealth. Fidel Castro's frequent failures in his efforts to finance revolution in Latin America have led him — upon the death of Che Guevara, another life-long ascetic — to pass equal responsibility to a man who, like Caamaño, is also endorsed by having faced the might of the US when it intervened in the Dominican Republic, which was disastrous for the nationalist spirit in Latin America.

Nevertheless, El Mundo's confidential sources identify Caamaño as the leader of an armed force which is slowly and conscientiously preparing for battle. Caamaño is not a literary man, according to the unanimous opinion of his friends and associates. Furthermore, the ex-leader of the "Constitutionalists" suffered something very similar to a terrible depression stemming from his experiences during the civil war and the American intervention in 1965. Ever since he has appeared to be obsessed with confronting the United States about what he considered to be an outrage against the sovereignty of his country.

This appears to be the key to explaining Caamaño's desertion to the Castro camp and his sudden embrace of Marxism, when only just before he had made clear his affiliation to Christian Democracy — he had been a potential candidate for the Dominican Social Christian Party in the coming 1970s elections. Furthermore, some who are closely following Caribbean political developments have commented that Bosch has encouraged Caamaño to take his current course of action since the ex-President still nurtures hopes of being the new Dominican Revolutionary Party candidate, supported by the Constitutionalist leader as the only person capable of holding together a crushing and overwhelmingly popular movement in the Dominican Republic and with an almost undisputable chance of winning elections. Once Caamaño has been eliminated, from a political standpoint, for having supported insurrection, the Leftist and nationalist factions of all shades in Santo Domingo would have no recourse other than to support Bosch from a lack of any other attractive personality with past experience of holding the voters.

# PHOTOGRAPHS

*Caamaño interrogates captured Marines.*

*US Ambassador John Martin, Hector Aristy, Caamaño and the Nuncio during negotiations.*

*8 Palace Gardens, SW7, Caamaño's first residence in London.*

*Dino's Restaurant (now 'Romano's'), Kensington Church Street.*

*Kensington Palace Hotel, scene of Caamaño's press conference, January 1966.*

*13 Orchard Rise, Richmond, Caamaño's second residence in London.*

# CHRONOLOGY

## 1961

30 May: assassination of Rafael Trujillo, dictator since 1930. Emergency council of state assumes authority.

October: return of Juan Bosch from many years in exile.

## 1962

20 December: Juan Bosch wins presidential elections.

## 1963

27 February: Juan Bosch sworn in as President.

25 September: conservative military coup, Congress dissolved, Bosch goes into exile. Reid Cabral nominated as President. Rule by military Triumvirate.

December: 14 June Movement guerrilla actions defeated.

## 1965

24 April: Constitutionalist army officers take power.

24–28 April: this period became known as the 'Civil War' to distinguish it from the later 'Patriotic War'.

25 April: mass demonstrations in Santo Domingo in support of the Constitutionalist action. Reid Cabral resigns as President.

27 April: crew of American ship *USS Boxer* begin evacuating US citizens at midday. US decision to invade taken, then rescinded. Meeting of American ambassador Tapley Bennett with provisional president Molina and Caamaño. Caamaño incensed by arrogant manner of US envoy.

27–28 April: 'La Batalla del Puente', a confrontation on the Duarte Bridge over the Rio Ozama between General Wessin's tanks, coming from San Isidro, and mass demonstrations throwing Molotov cocktails. Caamaño leads and organises military resistance, distributing arms to the civilian population. Wessin appeals for help to the American ambassador. President Johnson orders occupation. By mid-May there are 22,000 US troops in the country with an estimated further 20,000 in support roles at sea.

29 April: two US 82nd Division battalions occupy San Isidro. Santo Domingo divided into US-occupied and Constitutionalist zones, the latter centred in the Zona Colonial.

3 May: Colonel Francisco Caamaño, Constitutionalist leader, elected President by Congress.

7 May: establishment of Government of National Reconstruction, replacing military based in San Isidro.

14 May: in response to appeal from President Caamaño, UN Security Council agrees to send observers to Santo Domingo.

15 May: military offensive against Constitutional zones, pushing forces out of the northern suburbs and reducing area under their control to Zona Colonial.

16 May: US mission, led by White House special adviser, McGeorge Bundy, with mission to set up moderate government 'hostile to both right- and left-wing dictatorship'. McBundy meets with Caamaño and agrees to plan. Plan later rejected by General Imbert, leader of the 'Government of National Reconstruction'.

19 May: clashes around the Presidential Palace; death in combat of founder of Constitutionalist movement, Colonel Rafael Tomás Fernández Dominguez, returned from exile as military attaché in Paris a few days beforehand.

Late May: compromise proposal negotiated by McGeorge Bundy to nominate Antonio Guzmán Fernández interim president, with the aim of organising new elections; accepted by Constitutionalists, rejected by right-wing military.

15 June: offensive action by 'Inter-American' forces reduced area under control of Constitutionalist forces.

30 August: agreement, termed an 'Institutional Act', signed by both Constitutionalists and 'Government of National Reconciliation'. Both governments to dissolve themselves, end of armed confrontation.

3 September: Caamaño, in speech to thousands of supporters in Santo Domingo, resigns as President. García Godoy takes over as President.

25 September: Juan Bosch returns from exile in Puerto Rico.

19 December: attempted assassination of Caamaño and other Constitutionalist leaders in Hotel Matún, Santiago, by right-wing military.

**1966**

6 January: President Godoy assigns 34 army officers from right-wing and Constitutionalist forces to posts outside the country.

22 January: Colonel Caamaño and family leave Santo Domingo by air, via San Juan, Puerto Rico and New York, for London. Crowds of Dominicans greet him at both airports.

23 January: Colonel Caamaño, accompanied by his wife, cousin, uncle and two children, arrives in London.

26 January: press conference in Royal Garden Hotel, London.

4 March: speech to Oxford University Labour Club.

1 June: 1966 Presidential elections in Dominican Republic. Juan Balaguer elected, Bosch defeated by 760,000 to 495,000 votes.

## 1967

October 7: death of Che Guevara in Bolivia, news confirmed a few days later.

October 24: Caamaño dines with Constitutionalist exile Lachapelle and his wife in The Hague, Holland, leaves their house late in the evening, disappears, travels in disguise to Prague, and then by air to Cuba. Disappearance and lack of accurate information on his whereabouts leads to widespread international speculation (see Documents, p. 199).

## 1966–1974

Continued repression of Constitutionalist military and civilian personnel in the Dominican Republic. Balaguer authorised actions of paramilitary group 'La Banda', dedicated to repressing leftwing opponents. Over 3,000 killed. Caamaño, despite lack of support from Dominican opposition in general and disintegration of officer group at core of Constitutionalist movement, and against strong advice of Cubans, plans secret military operation inside the country.

## 1970

March: Juan Bosch returns to Dominican Republic. Now adopting more radical positions, he leaves PRD, now led by Francisco Peña Gómez, and founds Partido de la Liberación Dominicano (PLD).

## 1973

February: Caamaño, accompanied by seven comrades with whom he has trained in Cuba, lands on Caracoles beach, in Bay of Ozcoa, on southern coast west of Santo Domingo, captured, executed 16 February. Only two of his guerrilla group survive. News of his death, broadcast over state radio, occasions mass mourning in Santo Domingo.

## 1978

Election of Antonio Guzmán.

## 1982

Election of Salvador Jorge Blanco. Suicide of Guzmán.

**1986**

Re-election of Balaguer. Remains President till 1996.

**1996**

Election of Leonel Fernández, leader of the centre-left Partido de la Liberación Dominicano (PLD); official rehabilitation of Caamaño as President of the Dominican Republic and as 'Heroe Nacional'.

**2000–4**

Presidency of right-wing Hipólito Mejía.

**2004**

Re-election of Leonel Fernández as President.

Erection by the official historical body CPEP (Comisión Permanente de Efemerides Patria) of statue in memory of Colonel Caamaño on recently-named Avenida Francisco Caamaño (formerly Avenida del Puerto), near Duarte Bridge over Ozama river, scene of heroic confrontation 28 April 1966 between right-wing tanks and popular movement, led by Caamaño.

**2008**

Re-election for third term of President Fernández.

# BIOGRAPHICAL NOTES

**Acevedo, Maria Paula:** wife of Francisco Caamaño, accompanied him to London January 1966, with their two children, later returned to Santo Domingo.

**Aristy Pereyra, Héctor:** Constitutionalist military leader 1965, accompanied Caamaño in negotiations with American ambassador Martin, April 1965; minister of the presidency in Caamaño government, exiled as military attaché, January 1966.

**Balaguer, Joaquín:** lawyer, appointed President under Trujillo 1960, elected President 1966, held post, with some interruptions, until 1994.

**Bell, Ian Wright:** British ambassador, Santo Domingo, 1965–9.

**Bennett, William Tapley Jr:** US ambassador, Santo Domingo, 1965.

**Bosch, Juan:** born 1899, writer and historian, in exile 1937–61, returned October 1961, elected President 27 February 1963, ousted 25 September 1963 and exiled to Puerto Rico; leader of Partido Revolucionario Dominicano (PRD). Returned to Santo Domingo, September 1965, ran unsuccessfully for President June 1966. Went into exile again, met with Caamaño and other Dominican political exiles in Benidorm, Spain, summer 1967.

**Bunker, Ellsworth:** long-serving senior American diplomat, envoy to Organisation of American Unity meetings on Dominican crisis in 1965, chair of tripartite OAU mission to the Dominican Republic June 1965; later ambassador to South Vietnam.

**Caamaño Grullón, Claudio:** cousin of Francisco, army major, and the only Constitutionalist officer to remain with him till the 1973 expedition. Since 1993 president of the Francisco Caamaño Foundation. Author of *Caamaño, Guerra Civil 1965*, Mediabyte, 2007.

**Caamaño Deñó, Francisco A.:** born 1932, son of Lieutenant General Fausto Caamaño Medina, senior military officer in Trujillo Administration, at one time minister of war and of the navy. Career officer in Dominican army and police, starting 1949, trained in USA and Panama, commander of 'Anti-Riot' brigade, led police operation in 'Palma Sola' action 1963; 1964 began working with opposition military group led by Colonel Fernández Domínguez. Leader of April 1965 Constitutionalist revolt, elected President May 5 1965; resigns as President 3 September 1965; assigned as military attaché to London January 1966, travels in disguise to Cuba October 1967, killed after capture in guerrilla action at Nizaíto, San Jose de Ocoa, in south-western mountains of the Dominican Republic, 16 February 1973.

**Caamaño, Rafaela:** cousin of Franciso Caamaño, accompanied him and his wife to London, later returned to Santo Domingo, proprietor of *Manikin* restaurant.

**Deño Suero, Alejandro:** uncle of Francisco, career army officer, accompanied him to London 1966, remaining there for a time, before spending rest of his life in Spain.

**Fernández Domínguez, Colonel Rafael Tomás:** founder of Constitutionalist movement within Dominican armed forces; exiled 1964 as military attaché to France; returned Santo Domingo May 1965, killed in combat a few days later. Upon his return to the country, Caamaño, by then President, told Fernández that it was he who should be President of the country.

**García Godoy, Héctor:** compromise President, elected 3 September 1965, in office till 1 July 1966. Former ambassador, member of the Juan Bosch government and director of tobacco company. A moderate. Organised exile of 34 army officers, from the left and right, in January 1966. Had been ambassador in London and told Caamaño he was sending him there as it was the place he himself most liked to be.

**Guerra, Captain Pedro Julio:** Dominican military officer, deputy military attaché London 1966–7, accompanied Francisco Caamaño during his time in Britain, including visit to Oxford University in March 1966, later went to live in the USA.

**Hermann, Hamlet:** engineer, biographer and former comrade of President Caamaño, former senior official of UASD (Autonomous University of Santo Domingo) and, 1996–8, minister of transport in President Leonel Fernández's first Administration.

**Imbert Barrera, General Antonio:** President of right-wing 'Government of National Reconstruction' set up on 7 May 1965. One of only two surviving members of core group involved in assassination of Trujillo, 1961.

**Johnson, Lyndon B.:** President of the USA, 1963–8, ordered invasion of Dominican Republic April 1965. Johnson took it upon himself, without evidence and against the advice of some of his officials, to argue that the April 1965 uprising was controlled by Cuba. Intelligence and diplomacy were distorted to confirm this — false — assumption.

**Lachapelle Díaz, Héctor:** Constitutionalist military leader, exiled as military attaché January 1966.

**Lockheart, Stephen Alexander:** British ambassador, Santo Domingo, 1962–5.

**Mann, Thomas:** under secretary of state for Latin American Affairs, US government, till March 1965, urged President Johnson to invade the Dominican Republic.

**Martin, John Bartlow:** former American ambassador to Santo Domingo, diplomatic adviser to right-wing military in crisis April–May 1965.

**Molina Ureña, José Rafael:** president of the Chamber of Deputies during 1963 Bosch Presidency; short-lived provisional President of the Dominican Republic, 25–27 April 1965.

**Montes Arache, Colonel Ramón:** commander of the frogmen commandos, member of Constitutionalist military leadership, April 1965, exiled as military attaché in January 1966 with Caamaño and Lachapelle, one of the three main Constitutional leaders in April 1965.

**Palmer, Bruce, Lieutenant-General:** US officer, commander of US occupation forces in the Dominican Republic from April 1965, vice-commander of the Inter-American Peace Force May 1965–January 1966.

**Peña Gómez, José Francisco:** PRD leader, replaced Bosch in 1966, elected President of the Dominican Republic 1994.

**Phillips, David Atlee:** CIA station chief, Santo Domingo, 1965. Phillips was a veteran of the 1954 CIA coup in Guatemala.

**Reid Cabral, Donald:** military-installed President, December 1963–April 1965.

**Rusk, Dean:** US Secretary of State.

**Rikhye, Major-General Indar Jit:** Military advisor to UN, May 1965–October 1966.

**Tavárez Justo, Manuel:** leader of pro-Cuban 14 June Movement ('*catorcistas*'), killed in combat 1963.

**Trujillo, Rafael Leonidas:** dictator of the Dominican Republic 1930–61; assassinated 30 May 1961, officially entitled 'Benefactor of the Country and Reconstructor of its Financial Independence'. Born 1891, San Cristóbal, commander of national police during American marines' invasion 1916, appointed commander-in-chief of army 1928.

**Trujillo Martínez, Rafael (Ramfis):** eldest son of dictator, appointed colonel at the age of three, at 19 sent to American military academy, famous socialite and polo-player, went into exile after death of his father.

**Wessin y Wessin, General Elías:** commander of the air force training centre, San Isidro base, Santo Domingo. Main military opponent of Constitutionalist forces 1965. Later marginalised by García Godoy presidency, forced to leave to be military attaché in Miami, January 1966.

INSTITUTE FOR THE STUDY OF THE
# AMERICAS
UNIVERSITY OF LONDON · SCHOOL OF ADVANCED STUDY

The Institute for the Study of the Americas (ISA) promotes, coordinates and provides a focus for research and postgraduate teaching on the Americas – Canada, the USA, Latin America and the Caribbean – in the University of London.

The Institute was officially established in August 2004 as a result of a merger between the Institute of Latin American Studies and the Institute of United States Studies, both of which were formed in 1965.

The Institute publishes in the disciplines of history, politics, economics, sociology, anthropology, geography and environment, development, culture and literature, and on the countries and regions of Latin America, the United States, Canada and the Caribbean.

ISA runs an active programme of events – conferences, seminars, lectures and workshops – in order to facilitate national research on the Americas in the humanities and social sciences. It also offers a range of taught master's and research degrees, allowing wide-ranging multi-disciplinary, multi-country study or a focus on disciplines such as politics or globalisation and development for specific countries or regions.

Full details about the Institute's publications, events, postgraduate courses and other activities are available on the web at www.americas.sas.ac.uk.

**Institute for the Study of the Americas**
**School of Advanced Study, University of London**
**Senate House, Malet Street, London WC1E 7HU**

**Tel 020 7862 8870, Fax 020 7862 8886, Email americas@sas.ac.uk**
**Web www.americas.sas.ac.uk**

Breinigsville, PA USA
25 January 2011
254115BV00001B/1/P

9 781900 039963